Sports Spectators

SPORTS
SPECTATORS

ALLEN GUTTMANN

New York **Columbia University Press** *1986*

Library of Congress Cataloging-in-Publication Data

Guttmann, Allen.
Sports spectators.

Bibliography: p.
Includes index.
1. Sports spectators—History.   2. Violence in
sports—History.   I. Title.
GV715.G88   1986   363.3'2   86-8268
ISBN 0-231-06400-4

Columbia University Press
New York   Guildford, Surrey
Copyright © 1986 Columbia University Press

Printed in the United States of America

Book design by Laiying Chong.

TO JOHN WILLIAM WARD
In Memoriam

Contents

Acknowledgments

Acknowledging help, unlike asking for it, is a pleasure. Portions of this present study have been revised from work previously published in the *Journal of Popular Culture*, the *Journal of Sport History*, *Sports Violence* (edited by Jeffrey M. Goldstein and published by Springer Verlag), and *The Yale Review*. I am grateful for their permission to revise and republish.

I am also grateful for permission to quote from *The Comedy of Eros*, translated by Norman R. Shapiro (Middletown, Conn.: Wesleyan University Press); Horace, *Satires and Epistles*, translated by S. P. Boyle (Chicago: University of Chicago Press, 1959); Juvenal, *Satires*, translated by Rolfe Humphries (Bloomington: Indiana University Press, 1958); Ulrich von Lichtenstein, *Frauendienst*, translated by J. W. Thomas (Chapel Hill: University of North Carolina Press, 1969); Ovid, *The Art of Love*, translated by Rolfe Humphries (Bloomington: Indiana University Press, 1957); "Neither Out Far Nor In Deep," from *The Poetry of Robert Frost*, edited by Edward Connery Lathem. Copyright 1936 by Robert Frost. Copyright © 1964 by Lesley Frost Ballantine. Copyright © 1969 by Holt, Rinehart and Winston. Reprinted by permission of Henry Holt and Company.

For various kinds of humane and scholarly assistance, I am indebted to Doris Bargen, Leslie Bialler, Richard Cashman, Wolfgang Decker, Hideo Higuchi, John M. Hoberman, Peter Marshall, Gunter A. Pilz, Steven Riess, Egon Steinkamp, and Wray Vamplew.

The initial stages of my research were financed in part by the Guggenheim Foundation and by the Deutsche Forschungsgemeinschaft. Sabbatical leave from Amherst College enabled me to complete the work.

Sports Spectators

INTRODUCTION

IT MAY STILL BE common but it is no longer true to say that we know very little about sports. The obvious importance of sports in modern society has attracted historians, sociologists, anthropologists, psychologists, and a host of other specialists eager to investigate the past and present activities of *Homo ludens*. The trickle of scholarship has become a torrent and the compulsive researcher can easily drown in the flood of monographs, dissertations, essays, and conference papers. Since much of this recent scholarship is well done, there is reason to express some satisfaction with the present state of sports studies.

Inevitably, some aspects of sport have been studied intensively and some scarcely at all. Every season brings a new lineup of baseball histories and biographies, some of them admirable, but they seldom tell us very much about the fans who pushed through the turnstiles and took their seats in the grandstands and the bleachers. There are other difficulties. In general, the meager scholarship devoted to sports spectators is concerned, almost exclusively, with twentieth-century behavior. Reliable information about sports spectators of the past is in very short supply. One reason for the paucity of data is that our ancestors were like us; they cared more for the runners and the wrestlers and the ballplayers than for those who cheered them on. Jean Froissart's multivolume history of the Hundred Years' War describes many a tournament and *pas d'armes*, like the famous one fought by Jean Boucicaut at St. Inglevert in 1389, without saying anything at all about the spectators. When they *are* mentioned in ancient, medieval, Renaissance, or early modern documents, they are, of course, mentioned in ways historically appropriate to the age. The historical documents frequently omit the information one most wants because such information was of no interest to contemporary chroniclers. Tertullian, one of the most articulate of early Christian polemicists, was obsessed by the religious faith but not by the age, sex, race, or social class of the idolatrous Romans who thronged the Colosseum and the Circus Maximus. Ulrich von Liechtenstein had a great deal to say about the damsels and ladies whose favor he sought and before whom he jousted, but it is unlikely that even the most clever historian with the most sophisticated computer program can tease from his poetic text any quantified data about rates of participation in thirteenth-century sports.

One's frustration is often increased by the fact that those few modern scholars who *do* write about spectators tend to focus exclusively on the problem of sports-related violence and the measures taken to control it. Has spectator violence become more prevalent? How can it be eliminated or at least minimized? Important as these questions are, they are not the *only* ones worthy of sustained attention. It is also important to ask just who the spectators were and how they behaved when they *weren't* rioting. It is important to ask about the political functions of spectatorship, about the social role of the spectators, about their gender and social class, about the relationship between the "active" participation of the athlete and the "passive" participation of the fan.

Answers are often hard to come by. One needs a panoply of methods. Useful information can be found in the anecdotes of Suetonius and in the projective tests administered by twentieth-century psychologists, in the measurements of the ruins of Greek and Roman stadia and in the photographs taken at Victorian cricket matches, in the *Nibelungenlied* and in the Miller High Lite Survey of modern American spectators. Since even the best methods are employed by imperfect researchers, there are limits to what can be accomplished. I have, for instance, attempted to study the spectators of preliterate cultures and of the great civilizations of Asia, but the inadequacy of the scholarship available in languages I can cope with persuaded me finally to limit myself, except for occasional comparisons, to Western civilization, a domain vast enough to preserve me from any accusations of excessive modesty.

The nature of my task dictates that I rely more heavily upon the methods of the historian, anthropologist, or archeologist in the early chapters of my study and on those of the economist, sociologist, and psychologist in the later chapters. Accordingly, Part I is a history of sports spectatorship from antiquity to modern times. Since a discussion of the spectators for each and every sport played from the Homeric age to the Super Bowl would be humanly impossible and, even if accomplished with divine aid, tediously repetitive, I have selected those sports which seem most representative of their historical moments and most illustrative of my argument.

Chapter 1 is devoted to Greek spectators, especially those who journeyed to Olympia and Delphi to observe the athletic contests celebrated at those sacred sites, and to Roman and Byzantine spectators, especially those who thronged the arenas and hippodromes where gladiatorial games and chariot races took place. The decision to do a single chapter entitled "The Middle Ages and the Renaissance" raised the problem of periodization. Since the sports of the sixteenth century were by and large versions of the sports played five hundred years earlier, I chose to follow the more or less continuous development of three important sports: the tournament, the archery contest, and the game of folk-football. Geographically, my focus, like that of the medievalists and Renaissance scholars upon whom I have relied, is upon English, French, German, and Italian spectators. Chapter 3 is mostly about England, where modern sports (and modern spectatorship) emerged in the nearly two hundred years between the Restoration and the coronation of Queen Victoria. The emphasis is on animal sports (bear baiting, bull baiting, cock fighting), "pedestrianism" and horse races, combat sports (sword fighting, stick fighting, boxing), and cricket. Chapter 4 concentrates upon England and the United States from the mid-nineteenth to the mid-twentieth centuries when modern sports spectatorship was institutionalized in the forms now familiar the world over. The spectrum of representative sports widens beyond those discussed in Chapter 3 to include rowing, tennis and golf, baseball, and the various modern forms of football.

Part II results from a different approach. Although I continue to place sports spectatorship in its historical context, I have shifted my emphases from historical narrative to economic, sociological, and psychological analysis. Since the formal characteristics of modern sports and the modalities of modern spectatorship have become nearly ubiquitous, I have felt free to draw evidence and examples from societies as far apart spatially as Switzerland and Brazil and as distant culturally as India and the Soviet Union. My linguistic limitations have, however, led me to stress American, British, French, German, and Italian spectators. Chapter 5 concerns the dramatic transformation of spectatorship that occurred when the print media were supplemented by radio and then overshadowed by television. Chapter 6 deals with the radical critique of modern spectatorship from the perspective of Neo-Marxism. Since this critique stresses the alleged apathy induced in the masses by direct or mediated spectatorship, Chapter 7, which discusses behavioral excesses, follows logically; it is an analysis of sports-related violence, i.e., "spectator hooliganism." Chapter 8 is a concluding set of speculations on the ideal and the actual motivations of spectatorship. At one point I wrote a more formal conclusion in which I offered summary remarks about spectatorship from antiquity to the present, but the generalizations seemed either too insipidly general ("male spectators have always outnumbered female") or too intricately qualified ("the upper classes have always watched more often than the middle and lower classes except that certain sports, like medieval folk-football and Regency pugilism, have been most popular with the poor and other sports, like Renaissance archery and mid-twentieth-century golf, have drawn disproportionately middle-class crowds"). To avoid the opposed extremes of vapidity and gnarledness, I have, therefore, offered my conclusions *en passant* and at a less than global level of abstraction.

If this disavowal of generalization seems excessively nominalistic, I can assure the reader that certain repeated questions run through the length of my text. Who were and who are the sports spectators? What has been their social status and their gender? Have they normally been participants as well as fans? To which sports have they been most attracted? What kinds of behavior have characterized the spectator's role? How violent (or peaceful) have the spectators been? Has spectator violence increased or decreased?

Repeated mention of the word *violence* reminds one that analysts have an obligation to define their central concepts. A few words are necessary about *sports, spectators, fans, class,* and *violence.* I have argued on more than one occasion that it is useful to define *sports* as autotelic physical contests, i.e., nonutilitarian competitions carried out for their own sake. I must, however, concede that this definition is a Weberian "ideal type," an abstract model important as a limit which empirical reality can approach but never reach. No matter how clear one's definition, one wanders into shadowy areas. The boys and girls who are pictured in Minoan frescoes were engaged in cultic activities; the degree to which their acrobatic engagement with the bull might have been autotelic is and will forever remain unclear. The gladiatorial games of Roman times were true sports in the strictest sense only for those, probably a minority, who volunteered, who were attracted by the risk involved, by the sheer love of mortal combat. The others, the majority, fought not "playfully" but in earnest, not of their own free will but under coercion. The openly paid professional athlete of the twentieth century certainly performs for economic reasons, but the question of motivation is not settled simply by the signing of a paycheck. Do John McEnroe and Martina Navratilova still play for the love of the game as well as for pecuniary rewards? It is likely that motives are and always have been mixed. Having insisted on the usefulness of a strict definition of sport, I shall nonetheless discuss numerous borderline activities that may or may not be sport in strictest sense.

I shall also be latitudinarian about human participation. Since animals can scarcely be said to participate in sports as a form of play, contests with no human contestants ought, strictly speaking, to be ruled out of any study of sports spectators. Nonetheless, there are important similarities of spectator behavior at a chariot race, which is a true sport in my definition of the concept, and a cock fight, which is not. I have, therefore, discussed spectators of "blood sports." (I do not, however, deal with spectators for what may have been the most popular of all eighteenth-century spectacles—public executions.) I do occasionally compare sports spectators with the audiences for dance, music, and drama, but such audiences are clearly *not* sports spectators, not even when they watch the dancers dance Martha Graham's *Rodeo* or listen to the orchestra play Arthur Honnegger's *Rugby*. Watching films like *Champion* or *Personal Best* is certainly *like* watching a boxing match or a track meet, but I have excluded moviegoing from my consideration of sports spectatorship, because films are aesthetic constructs with implicit and even explicit ethical dimensions that are not an inherent part of an actual sports contest.

The term *spectator* is less problematical. The sports spectator is anyone who views a sports event, either *in situ* or through visual media such as film or television. In their social roles, the fans who follow sports in the newspapers and magazines or on the radio are certainly similar to those who sit in the ballpark or flip on the TV, but a conceptual line has to be drawn *somewhere* between those who experience a sports event "fully" and those whose experience is partial. I draw my admittedly arbitrary line between those who can see an action taking place and those who cannot. The term *fan* refers here to the emotionally committed "consumer" of sports events. The terms overlap but are obviously not identical. In practice most fans are spectators and most spectators are fans, but it is logically possible to be one and not the other. Some fans have never actually attended a sports event or watched one on television; some spectators stare absent-mindedly at televised sports without a flicker of interest, some allow themselves to be dragged to games that they then observe without any of the emotional involvement characteristic of the fan.

Since all complex societies are stratified and hierarchical, the concept of *class* is at once necessary and problematical. I agree with Marx that economics are the crucial determinant of class identification and with Weber that there are sources and forms of social status which are not economic (which led Weber to distinguish between *Klasse* and *Stand*). Whether it makes sense to universalize the concept of class and to speak of an Athenian or Roman or medieval upper class, middle class, and lower class, I am not competent to decide. In practice, I have chosen, for my discussions of antiquity, the Middle Ages, and the Renaissance to refer whenever possible to historically specific groups—e.g., the senators, knights, and plebeians of ancient Rome, the knights, clerics, and peasants of medieval Europe—but for early modern and modern societies I have referred to social class. To avoid simplistic notions of some historically invariant system of exactly three clearly defined classes, I have tried to speak in the plural—i.e., of the upper, middle, and lower *classes*. I have, however, employed the convenient hyphenated adjectives, "upper-class," etc. I have also, occasionally, referred to the elite, which I am tempted to define as the top dogs, and the masses, which I take to be everyone else. These locutions are not meant to imply a moral hierarchy.

Although spectator *violence* is only one important aspect of my study, the concept of violence is probably the most difficult to be clear about. Following ordinary linguistic usage, which is imprecise but nonetheless a first approximation, we can say that violence is physical damage done to persons or property. In this sense we can speak of a violent storm or of the violent collision of two football players but not of violent words, which are violent only in a metaphorical sense (just as "sweet talk" is poetically but not physiologically sweet). Within the world of sports it is arbitrary but convenient to restrict the definition to physical damage done to one's opponent. The injuries that one brings upon oneself, ranging from the tennis player's blistered thumb to the automobile racer's explosive immolation, can be excluded along with damaged objects such as worn-out golf balls and tattered archery targets, but the battering inflicted by a boxer or a baseball player's spiking of a second baseman trying to tag him out are both examples of sports violence.

It is immediately obvious that the boxer's punches are an example of *legitimate* sports violence while the base runner's spiking is not. The boxer's punches are legitimate because they are theoretically, practically, and morally separable from those of a street-corner thug; they are within the rules of the game. The base runner's spikes, however, are not supposed to be used to wound his opponent; such use is foul play and ludically *illegitimate*. That the players and fans sometimes find spiking acceptable indicates only that the official rules are not infallible guides to the actual moral consensus. Despite the difficulty in knowing exactly what is legitimate sports violence and what is not, it is essential that the theoretical differences remain clear. One may deplore the violence of a game of rugby or a bullfight, but it is morally distinguishable from the less intense but also less legitimate violence of the runner in a 1500-meter race who jabs his rival in the ribs. In discussing sports violence, it is always necessary to be clear about the cultural context as well as the degree of the damage done. There existed within the context of Roman sports an apparently paradoxical situation: in the Colosseum, a gladiator's lethal sword thrust was an instance of legitimate violence; meanwhile, at the Capitoline Games, a runner's tripping his opponent was not.

In addition to the distinction between legitimate and illegitimate violence, one must be attentive to the distinction between *expressive* and *instrumental* violence. The first is a form of rage, essentially spontaneous and uncontrolled if not uncontrollable; the second is a form of what Weber called *zweckrationalitaet*, i.e., behavior calculated to achieve a goal. Within sports, instrumental violence occurs, for example, when a hockey player repeatedly and intentionally shoves an opponent against the wall of the rink in order to keep him from the puck. Expressive violence occurs when the repeatedly shoved player loses his temper and punches his tormenter (and ends up in the penalty box).

In differentiating sports violence into legitimate and illegitimate, expressive and instrumental, forms, I have thus far omitted mention of the violence committed by the spectators. Clearly the "soccer hooliganism" of British fans is sports-related behavior, but knifing supporters of rival teams and throwing beer cans at the umpire are not, strictly speaking, examples of sports violence. We must distinguish, as many writers do not, between the narrow category of sports violence, which can be either legitimate or illegitimate, and the much broader category of sports-related *spectator violence*, which is illegitimate except perhaps from the perspective of a deviant subculture. (I shall speak henceforth of "spectator violence" and "spectator hooliganism" and drop the implied adjective "sports-related.") Since spectator vandalism and riots are not *sports* violence per se, we need not restrict the concept of spectator violence to physical damage done to an opponent whom one meets within the rules of the game. Damage done to the stadium or to automobiles parked adjacent to the ballpark and injuries suffered by fans drunkenly mauling each other or innocent bystanders are all familiar aspects of spectator violence. On the whole, spectator violence can be classified as expressive rather than instrumental, but one must reckon with the possibility that some hardened types go to the stadium lusting for a "rumble" or primed for a bit of "aggro." Then, in a paradoxical sense, expressive violence itself can be thought of as instrumental—as a means to achieve a sense of manhood or to avenge oneself upon a hostile world. Psychological distinctions rarely have the clarity of sociological categories.

My tentative effort to answer some questions about sports spectatorship has been aided by the work of an array of scholars whose names appear in my text or in the notes. Two scholars have been especially helpful. In his seminal study, *Ueber den Prozess der Zivilisation* (1939), translated as *The Civilizing Process* (1978), Norbert Elias has offered a model for the historical study of manners. His argument is that the specialization of labor and the rise of the modern state have together made modern men and women dependent upon one another in ways that prohibit (or at least tend to lessen) the unpredictable

emotional outbreaks characteristic of medieval and Renaissance society. Combined with the increased efficiency of the modern state,
which forces upon all of us a certain degree of rational behavior, the
"lengthening chains of interdependence" have diminished the level
of interpersonal expressive violence. Modern men and women have
internalized codes of restraint and respect for others which normally
prevent them from sleeping with their boots on or bludgeoning those
who annoy them. (Unfortunately, this welcome transformation has
not eliminated the enthusiasm of political leaders for what might be
termed Clauswitzian instrumentalism.)

Eric Dunning and his associates have applied this model of the
"civilizing process" to the study of sports.[1] In collaboration with Kenneth Sheard, Dunning has demonstrated that the transformation of
medieval folk-football into the modern games of soccer and rugby has
meant, until very recently at any rate, a diminution in the level of
expressive violence within the game. Working with a group of sociologists at the University of Leicester, Dunning has published a series
of important books and articles attempting to explain "soccer hooliganism" as a phenomenon associated with those least touched by the
"civilizing process." While I am a disciple neither of Elias nor of
Dunning, I do feel intellectually indebted to both for their insights
into spectator violence. I shall use their model to ask, at several points
in my text, whether spectator violence is waxing or waning.

Readers who compare this study with my earlier work, especially
with *From Ritual to Record* (1978), will notice a shift in emphasis
from cultural to social history, from a concern with conceptualizations
of sport to the observation of demographic variables and behavior.
While the shift in emphasis is obviously related to a difference in
topic, I wish also to acknowledge that I have modified my intellectual
stance somewhat in response to the work of Richard Gruneau, Stephen Hardy, Alan Ingham, and other practitioners of materialistically
inclined sports studies.

The preceding paragraphs have been rife with cautionary remarks
meant to alert the reader. It is difficult to discuss modern spectators
and doubly difficult to write of spectators who are spatially, temporally,
and culturally distant. Nonetheless, if one gathers information from
a variety of sources and interprets it carefully, one can say a great
deal. *Diligentia vincit* (almost) *omnia*.

I
From Antiquity to
Modern Times

ONE
GREEK AND ROMAN SPECTATORS

I BEFORE THE GREEKS

OF EGYPTIAN, Minoan, and Etruscan sports spectators we know little and are unlikely to learn very much more. In a frieze which shows Egyptian wrestlers and stick fighters, the spectators address Ramses II in hieroglyphics which praise him as like the god of war.[1] This evidence is one of our best sources for Egyptian sports spectators. We know still less about the Minoans. As for the spectators in the famed "Grand Stand" or "Temple" fresco which archeologist Sir Arthur Evans discovered in the Palace of Minos on the island of Crete, we cannot even be sure what the rows of men and women are looking at. If they do observe "ceremonial sports in honor of the Goddess," we can only guess which sports and argue about whether or not they really *are* sports rather than aspects of cult.[2]

Etruscan graves, especially the *Tomba delle Bighe* and the *Tomba delle Olimpiadi*, depict what are unquestionably male and female sports spectators apparently entranced by boxers, discus-throwers, runners, jumpers, and charioteers, but that is about all we can safely say. On the basis of the visual evidence, scholars have ventured the opinion that the female spectators were shocked by a chariot accident and that the athletes were slaves who competed "for the pleasure of the gods and perhaps also for [upper-class] men seated in the stands according to a strictly hierarchical order."[3]

On the basis of a fragment from Theopompus, other scholars have asserted that "uncovered" Etruscan women competed among themselves before the eyes of male spectators.[4] Since the evidence relevant to prehellenic sport is minimal and liable to misinterpretation, it is best to begin with the Greeks.

II GREEK SPECTATORS

In light of the philhellenism which characterizes most modern scholarship, one must beware the temptation simply to announce that the
Greeks were participants in sports while the Romans were merely
spectators, but there is evidence to indicate that this was indeed the
case. Physical excellence was part of the Greek ethos. Homer tells in
Book VIII of the *Odyssey* how Odysseus, washed ashore among the
Phaiakians, was insulted by the allegation, "You are no athlete."
Odysseus, resentful of the insult, demonstrates his prowess. There are
reasons to think that participation in the athletic festivals of the Homeric age may have been limited to the aristocracy while "the people
functioned solely as spectators," but such exclusivity certainly vanished by the classical period, when it was assumed that every citizen
had a moral obligation to be athletically active.[5] Xenophon relates in
his *Memorabilia* that Socrates met a physically undeveloped youth
and promptly rebuked him for his disgraceful failure to make the most
of his body.

We cannot know from such anecdotes, nor from the Olympic and
Pythian odes of Pindar, nor from the vases commemorating victories
at the Panathenaic Games, nor from the athletic statues of Polykleitos
and Myron, how many Greeks actually lived up to their cultural ideals
of physical excellence, but the archeological evidence corroborates the
written record and the visual arts. In Book X of his *Description of
Greece*, Pausanias assured his second-century A.D. readers that every
polis worthy of the name had its gymnasium along with the agora and
the theater. At least 126 Greek cities had gymnasia. Hellenistic Per-
gamon had at least five. Athens had nine public gymnasia and many
private ones.

In Book XXIII of the *Iliad*, Homer describes the funeral games held
by the Greeks in honor of Achilles' friend Patroklos, whom the Trojan
Hektor slew. In the course of his beautifully crafted description, Homer scarcely mentions the spectators, except to say that they were
numerous and that they laughed, applauded, and "thundered approval." Homer does not refer to any special arrangement for the
spectators, but facilities were constructed for them at the sites of the
sacred athletic festivals, which were celebrated regularly on a biennial
or quadrennial basis. The first Olympic contests probably took place

in the eighth century B.C. on leveled ground near the altars of Zeus and Hera; earth removed in the process was formed into an embankment for the spectators. It was not until the sixth century that the first stadium was constructed at Olympia. Except for a few officials, the spectators sat or stood upon the ground, as they did in most stadia of the classical era. The stone seats familiar to modern visitors of ancient sites are from Hellenistic and Roman times.[6]

Olympia was, and still is, fearfully hot in the summer. It was, during the sacred games, overrun with visitors from the entire Greek world. The Leonidaion was constructed in the fourth century to house wealthy or politically important visitors to the games, but most of the spectators had to make do with tents or with nights under the stars. As late as the first century A.D., after there had been considerable effort to provide some minimal comforts, the Roman philosopher Epictetus used attendance at the games as a metaphor for stress:

> But some unpleasant and hard things happen in life. . . . And do they not happen at Olympia? Do you not swelter? Are you not cramped and crowded? Do you not bathe badly? Are you not drenched whenever it rains? Do you not have your fill of tumult and shouting . . . ? But I fancy you bear and endure it all by balancing it off against the memorable character of the spectacle.[7]

Although early stadia were built "in close connection to a sacred site," classic and Hellenistic cities tended to build their stadia adjacent to the gymnasia, which strongly suggests a close connection between active and passive participation in sports.[8] There is no reason to doubt that those who watched the athletes perform emulated what they saw. Lucian's *Anacharsis* is a fictional dialogue, written in the first century A.D. and difficult to interpret, but it seems clear from "Solon's" remarks to his Skythian interlocutor that the Athenian youth did not "fritter their time away" when they attended athletic encounters; they were inspired by the sight of "manly perfection" to train themselves for similar feats which might then, in turn, inspire others.[9]

We cannot conclude that all the throng of spectators consisted of men who were themselves active athletes, but we can be sure that Greek women were generally excluded both from watching and from participating. Except in militaristic Sparta and in Plato's ideal republic, modeled largely upon Sparta, athletics were usually for male citizens, whose physical perfection interested the Greeks more than women's beauty did.[10] Women, slaves, and foreigners were all excluded from participation in the sacred athletic festivals at Olympia, Delphi, Korinth, and Nemea. Slaves and foreigners were allowed to watch; women weren't. Except for the priestess of Demeter, married women were definitely forbidden to attend the Olympic games even as spectators, and most authorities believe the prohibition was extended to girls as well. Johann Heinrich Krause, the best informed nineteenth-century historian of Greek sports, wrote that he knew of "no evidence for the presence of even a single maiden at the games."[11] Apart from the Olympic games, there were also games sacred to Hera. They were unusual because girls competed and women watched them. Male spectators were barred from the sacred site, but men may have served as officials.[12]

There is evidence to indicate that professional athletes—i.e., men whose only occupation was training for and competing in athletic events—came to dominate Greek athletic festivals, at least numerically. In time, Greek culture accepted even gladiatorial games fought by slaves, which certainly violated classical ideas about social roles, but this was a late development explained by Roman influence. Sadly acknowledging the existence of gladiators in the centers of Greek culture, the French historian Louis Robert has explained that "Greek society was ill with a sickness spread from Rome. It was an instance of the romanization of the Greek world."[13]

Did the romanization of Greece include the development of the unruly mob of spectators, whom the Roman poet Juvenal dismissed in his Tenth Satire with a reference to *panem et circenses*? For that matter, were Greek spectators an unruly lot even in the classic and Hellenistic periods? We know that the Olympic games were occasions for oratory and poetry, that Herodotus read his history of the Persian wars from the rear portico of the temple of Zeus and that Thucydides heard him and was presumably inspired to go and do likewise, but we have no warrant to assume that the atmosphere was quietly literary. Olympia and Delphi, with their temples and altars and victors' statues, were sacred sites, but we must not imagine that the Greek spectators behaved with the hushed awe of the modern visitor. On the contrary, there is every reason to concur with the Italian historian Roberto

Patrucco that they behaved with the uninhibited "human passion" of modern sports spectators.[14] M. I. Finley and H. W. Pleket agree that Greek crowds were "as partisan, as volatile, and as excitable as at any other period of time."[15] Upon the fragment of a sixth-century B.C. vase by Sophilos we can see the excited spectators responding with outstretched waving arms to the chariot races held in honor of the slain Patroklos (Book XXIII of the *Iliad*). The tiny figures are quite obviously screaming their heads off.[16]

There is other evidence for what Epictetus called "tumult and shouting." The *Hellanodikai* who were in charge of the management of the Olympic games had to employ assistants who kept athletes and spectators under control. The names of these assistants, *mastigophoroi* and *rabdouchoi* ("whip-bearers" and "truncheon-bearers"), implies disorderly conduct and the necessity for externally imposed restraint. At the Pythian Games at Delphi, rowdy drunkenness was such a problem that the spectators were forbidden to carry wine into the stadium.[17]

Drawing upon Pausanias, Philostratus, Pindar, Isokrates, and a wide range of other ancient authorities, Krause wrote vividly of the spectators at Olympia:

> With what an indescribable enthusiasm those present dedicated themselves to the spectacle, with what a lively sense of participation did they share the athletes' fates and enact the outcome of the contests, how their spirits were excited by what they saw! They were impelled unconsciously to move their hands, to raise their voices, to jump from their seats, now with the greatest joy, now with the deepest pain.[18]

Sharing vicariously the athletes' fates, the spectators were intensely partisan. Each *polis* honored its winners with material rewards as well as with statues and victors' odes.[19] An anecdote told by the historian Polybius beautifully dramatizes the emotional conflict between sympathy for the underdog and commitment to "the home team." As Aristonicus of Alexandria challenged the mighty Greek boxer Clitomachus, the crowd

> at once took the part of the former and cheered him on, delighted to see that some one . . . ventured to pit himself against Clitomachus. And when, as the fight continued, he appeared to be his adversary's

match, and once or twice landed a telling blow, there was great clapping of hands, and the crowd became delirious with excitement, cheering on Aristonicus. At this time . . . Clitomachus, after withdrawing
a few moments to recover his breath, turned to the crowd and asked
them what they meant by cheering on Aristonicus and backing him
up. . . . Did they think he himself was not fighting fairly, or were they
not aware that Clitomachus was now fighting for the glory of Greece
and Aristonicus for that of King Ptolomy? Would they prefer to see an
Egyptian [i.e., a Greek from Egypt] conquer the Greeks and win the
Olympian crown . . . ?

This speech by Clitomachus won the spectators over. The demoralized
Aristonicus was beaten.[20]

Whatever decorum was maintained at Olympia seems to have vanished completely during the chariot races in Alexandria, where Dio
Chrysostom condemned the outrageous behavior of the crowd:

When they enter the stadium, it is as though they had found a cache
of drugs; they forget themselves completely, and shamelessly say and
do the first thing that occurs to them. . . . At the games you are under
the influence of some maniacal drug; it is as if you could not watch
the proceedings in a civilized fashion. . . . When you enter the stadium, who could describe the yells and uproar, the frenzy, the switches
of color and expression in your faces, and all the curses you give vent
to?[21]

Dio's passion matches that of Tertullian or the modern moralist appalled by mob behavior.

One must ask if modern historians have been justified in routinely
citing Epictetus, Dio, and other authors of the first or second century
A.D. as evidence for the habits of spectators who lived five or six
hundred years earlier. After all, it may be that the tumultuous Greek
spectators of Hellenistic and Roman times were quite unlike their fifth-
century B.C. ancestors. It seems reasonable, however, to conclude in
the absence of any evidence to the contrary that there was continuity
rather than discontinuity in the patterns of Greek spectatorship. If
Greek sports spectatorship was similar to Greek political behavior, the
atmosphere at Olympia was anything but "Olympian."

III THE ROMAN ARENA

Roman sports were different from those of the Greeks. In the first place, Roman citizens tended to perform physical exercises rather than to do sports. Sport as activity done for its own sake attracted them less than exercises performed for some ulterior purpose, usually military. In general, there was hostility to Greek athletics. [22] The poet Horace reacted typically when, in his Second Satire, he scornfully contrasts Greek sports to rough Roman drill. In Book X of his *Metamorphoses,* the poet Ovid describes the excited spectators cheering Hippomenes on as he chases after fleet Atalanta, but the imagined spectators, like the legend, are Greek. Augustus founded several athletic festivals modeled after the Olympics. They were hopefully referred to as *isolympia,* i.e., "equal to the Olympics," but they never became popular. Of the athletic events that were a basic aspect of Hellenic civilization, the Romans were attracted mostly by wrestling, boxing, and the brutal *pankration,* which combined wrestling and boxing in a fierce and occasionally mortal combat. The sports for which the Romans are rightly remembered are gladiatorial games and chariot races, both spectator sports. Popular ball games like *harpastum* and *trigonaria* seem to have been either noncompetitive pastimes or else contests which attracted few, if any, spectators. [23]

Like the ball games of the Mayans and Aztecs, which ended in ritual sacrifice, gladiatorial combats originated as an aspect of Roman religion (and thus were not true sports in the very strictest sense because they were not, at least in their origins, autotelic). The Greeks of the *Iliad* were content that the funeral games in honor of the fallen Patroklos terminated merely in symbolic death—that is, in athletic defeat—but the Romans, who may have adopted this particular custom from the Etruscans, celebrated funeral games in which the dead were honored by additional deaths. The first games, held by Marcus and Decius Brutus in honor of their father in 246 B.C., consisted of three duels (six gladiators) and were held in the cattle market. One can assume that the number of spectators was fairly small. In the centuries that followed, Livy, Polybius, Suetonius, Tacitus, Dio Cassius, and other Roman historians recorded an apparently irreversible tendency toward the spectacular in that the number of gladiators continually increased and the facilities available to the spectators grew ever grander. By 183 B.C. there were sixty duels; in 65 B.C., Julius Caesar celebrated his election to the aedileship with combats between 320 pairs, which were staged in a wooden amphitheater constructed especially for the show. By this time, gladiatorial games functioned as much more than funeral observances and had become a complex fusion of religious, political, and—presumably—ludic elements.[24]

The Senate, worried about the manipulation of the populace by means of these magnificent spectacles, attempted to limit the number of gladiators at any single set of *ludi* to sixty pairs, but the effort was futile and, in imperial times, emperors (except for the stingy Tiberius) seem to have competed among themselves to see who could stage the most grandiose and overpowering show. The emperor Trajan is said to have celebrated his victory over the Dacians, at the end of the first century A.D., with combats among 10,000 gladiators, a spectacle which failed numerically to equal the naval battle staged by Claudius in 52 A.D. with 19,000 combatants.[25]

Since temporary stadia built of wood sometimes collapsed, killing large numbers of spectators, they were replaced by monumental stone structures the most famous of which is the "Colosseum," more accurately referred to as the Flavian amphitheater because it was erected by the Flavian Emperor Vespasian and his son Titus. This gigantic structure, finished in 80 A.D., seated 50,000. Such stadia provided comforts unknown to Greek spectators. When we read that the arena at Pompeii lured the audience with promises of *vela et sparsiones* (awnings and perfumed sprays), we are apt to think both of the contrasting primitive accommodations at Olympia and of the similarly luxurious boxes available at our modern domed stadia.[26]

While Greek sources provide meager information about sports spectators, Latin history and poetry are rich in references. There can be no question about the division of roles into performer and spectator. This was certainly the case for the gladiatorial games. That many gladiators were professionals is undeniable. Although the legal status of professional gladiators was quite low, they unquestionably enjoyed popularity enough for a number of adventurous free citizens to volunteer for the *munera* (gladiatorial games). The exact number of those who were free men is and will remain uncertain, but incomplete inscriptions referring to the *familiae* of gladiators at Venusia show eighteen slaves and ten free men.[27] That the spectators preferred free men to slaves or condemned criminals is clear from the remarks of Echion, a character in the *Satyricon* of Petronius, who speaks excitedly of an imminent show with new fights "and . . . not a slave in the batch."[28] Michael Grant's explanation for this preference is simple: "Free fighters were more sought after than slaves, presumably because they showed greater enthusiasm."[29] Georges Ville takes the analysis a step further and writes that "the public preferred a free gladiator to a slave and a knight or a senator to an ordinary citizen."[30] The plebeian spectator must have thrilled to see the high and mighty on their own, exposed for once to risks and hazards comparable to those encountered by ordinary mortals.

The Latin poets were almost always condemnatory when they mentioned the occasional member of an aristocratic family who signed a gladiator's contract and the gossipy historian Suetonius tells us that the Senate tried to keep the knightly class out of the arena, but an Italian scholar who has recently studied 82 Latin documents concerning the gladiators at Pompeii has concluded that knights and even senators continued to take up arms.[31] Indeed, emperors like Caligula and Nero sought to humiliate knights and senators by forcing them into the arena. The extreme was reached by Emperor Commodus, who dressed in a lion skin, shouldered a Herculean club, descended into the arena, and scandalized Roman moralists with his boasts of having personally fought 1,000 gladiatorial duels (against opponents armed with dummy weapons—there were limits even to his vainglory).

As the inscriptions from Venusia indicate, the volunteers were probably a minority. Most of their "colleagues" were condemned criminals, prisoners of war, or slaves purchased from owners eager to profit from a marketable skill or simply anxious to rid themselves of a particularly unruly piece of property. Horace refers in his *Epistles* to those who get themselves hopelessly in debt

> and so
> End up in the driver's seat of some vegetable cart
> Or in a gladiatorial show.[32]

There was, for persons of this sort, a technical term. They were the *auctorati,* those who sold themselves; they were legally derogated as *infamus* but were not deprived of citizenship.[33]

In other words, there was a tendency in Roman times to reverse the Greek division into free men who participated in sports and slaves who watched. The citizen now became the observer while the slave or prisoner performed. The citizen who took on the slave's role, either from necessity or from the desire to live dangerously, degraded himself. Although gladiators were often popular heroes, in no Roman city were they honored with the kind of statue sculpted to commemorate the feats of victorious Greek athletes.[34]

Nonetheless, the readiness of *some* of the aristocracy to enter the arena indicates that many Romans were rather ambivalent about the official degradation of their gladiators. There were rumors that Commodus had been genetically primed for the gladiatorial role because he had been fathered not by Marcus Aurelius but rather by the renowned gladiator Martianus. Such rumors simultaneously slandered Commodus and suggested that his mother Faustina preferred a gladiator to her philosophical husband. If Faustina did make such a choice, she was certainly not alone. Gladiators were often idolized by female spectators. In Juvenal's satires, a senator's wife is said to have thought gladiators

> look better than any Adonis;
> This is what she preferred to children, country, and sister,
> This to her husband.[35]

And an inscription on a wall in Pompeii says that the gladiator Celadus was *"suspirum et decus puellarum,"* which might be translated as "the hero and heart-throb of all the girls."[36] In the Palaestra, where Celadus and his fellows lived, the excavators of Pompeii found the bejeweled skeleton of a woman whose weakness for athletic virility seems to have led her foolishly to brave the dangers of erupting Vesuvius.[37]

The word "Pompeii" summons up visions of volcanic catastrophe, but the wealthy town was also the scene of a disaster which the inhabitants brought upon themselves. The historian Tacitus reports that tumults erupted there during the *munera,* after which the town was for a decade deprived of the right to stage gladiatorial games.[38] This episode of spectator violence was, however, very unusual. There was, in fact, an "almost total absence of documented riots."[39] One explanation for this nonviolent spectatorship is the tightly regulated seating arrangements at Roman stadia. At the gladiatorial games, both communal organization and social hierarchy took spatial forms. In the amphitheaters of Arles, Lyon, Nimes, and probably in those of Rome as well, different "tribes" were seated in different *cunei* (wedges) of the stadium.[40] Augustus had definite ideas about social rank and seating. He arranged for the Senate to decree

> that at every public performance, wherever held, the front row of stalls must be reserved for senators. At Rome, Augustus would not admit the ambassadors of independent or allied kingdoms to seats in the orchestra, on learning that some were mere freedmen. Other rules of his included the separation of soldiers from civilians; the assignment of special seats to married commoners, to boys not yet come of age, and, close by, to their tutors. . . . Also, whereas men and women had hitherto always sat together, Augustus confined women to the back rows . . . at gladiatorial shows.[41]

Augustus himself was seated, or reclined, on the *pulvinar* (couch).[42]

The Vestal Virgins had separate places and aristocratic women were seated near them. A modern historian with a gaudy prose style has described the latter as arriving "in a litter . . . carried by eight trotting Syrian slaves whose muscles throbbed under their red liveries." The pampered beauties were preceded "by African runners in white tunics."[43] Whether unaccompanied slaves were admitted to the gladiatorial games in the days of the late Republic is unclear. In the prologue to *Poenulus*, the dramatist Plautus assumes their presence. It is certain that Augustus admitted them to the upper seats.[44]

While most spectators paid for their seats, the poorest of the poor, the *plebs frumentaria* (i.e., those supplied with "welfare" grain), had free tickets.[45] Neither penury nor servile status was a bar to enthusiastic fandom. A funerary inscription for the slave Crescens informs survivors that he was a Blue and a Thracian, i.e., a partisan of one of the two main charioteer teams and of the Thracian style of fighting.[46] The slave Davus, owned by the poet Horace, appears in the Second Satire, where he marvels "at the posters of athletes straining their muscles in combat."[47] A common archeological find at Roman sites is an inex-

pensive clay lamp with gladiatorial motifs. Richer folk had terra sig-
illata or statuettes. In the *Satyricon*, Trimalchio has *his* favorite
gladiator pictured on silverware. Horace tells us in his Second Satire
that Maecenas, the great patron of the arts, was not above a gossipy
curiosity about individual gladiators. Not even Christians were wholly
immune from the appeals of fandom. St. Augustine's ardent young
disciple Alypius suffered a dramatic setback when he ventured into
the amphitheater and was overcome:

> For so soon as he saw that blood, he therewith drunk down savageness;
> nor turned away, but fixed his eye, drinking in frenzy, unawares, and
> was delighted with that guilty fight, and intoxicated with the bloody
> pastime. Nor was he now the man he came [in as], but one of the
> throng he [joined].[48]

The spectators at the gladiatorial games shared this reaction to
blood. While many must have admired the fine points of the highly
trained gladiators, others seemed to have had eyes only for the outcome of the struggle. They cried out not for the skillful use of weapons
but for the victory of their favorite (on whom they often wagered
considerable sums of money). Noting this tendency of the *munera*
and the *venationes* (combats between animals or between men and
animals) to become increasingly sensationalistic and perverse, Ludwig
Friedlaender commented:

> soon bloodthirsty combats and magnificent scenery failed to excite the
> dulled nerves of the mob, aristocratic or vulgar; only things absolutely
> exotic, unnatural, nonsensical, tickled their jaded senses.[49]

The truth of this moralistic comment can be seen when we consider
that modern boxers and wrestlers are divided into weight categories in
order to establish roughly equal conditions for the match. The assumption behind this concern for equality is that the mauling of a
flyweight by a heavyweight is no demonstration of fine skills. The
gladiatorial games dispensed with such scruples. Gladiators fought in
different styles and with different equipment; a *retiarius* armed with a
net and trident was frequently matched against a *myrmillo*, whose
sword, shield, and helmet marked him stylistically if not ethnically as
a Gaul.

Another form of inequality was achieved in imperial times by the use of female gladiators.[50] In the *Satyricon* of Petronius, one of Trimalchio's guests complains of a poor gladiatorial show and looks forward to a better one, including "a girl who fights from a chariot."[51] The emperor Domitian courted the masses by pitting women against dwarves.[52] It was, wrote Juvenal, difficult *not* to write satire when "a limp eunuch gets wived, and women, breasts Amazon-naked, / Face wild boars at the games."[53] Sadistic Caligula pitted "feeble old fighters against decrepit criminals" and Christians were, as popular mythology still remembers, condemned to fight, either armed or weaponless, against gladiators and against wild animals.[54] When they went to their deaths, the statues of the pagan gods were veiled—as they were when ordinary criminals were torn to bits.

Understandably, Christians were the most vocal and, finally, the most effective foes of the gladiatorial games. There was certainly very little opposition from pagan moralists. In 55 B.C., when Pompey consecrated the Temple of Venus Genetrix by the slaughter of a number of elephants, the dying animals "excited pity by their agonized trumpetings" and "the spectators rose and cursed Pompey for his cruelty," but this was an unusual if not a unique moment of compassion.[55] The poet Juvenal wrote satirically about the mob and its need for bread and circuses and degenerate mismatches, but he and most other educated Roman spectators seemed to have taken the deaths of men and beasts for granted. Suetonius was indignant when Caligula, jealous of a handsome spectator, ordered the youth dragged from his seat and matched against a professional gladiator, but the historian's indignation was not aroused by the atrocity of the games per se, only by Caligula's cruel jealousy.[56] The philosopher-statesman Cicero praised the *munera* because they provided the spectators with an image of fortitude.[57] Ovid urged women to "go and look at the games, where the sands are sprinkled with crimson."[58] The motive here is the chance to display female physical charms ("What are good looks, unseen?"), but the poet clearly assumes that the bloodshed in the arena is no obstacle to dalliance in the stands.

The philosopher-dramatist Seneca was among the handful of pagan moralists who expressed the kind of horror that many twentieth-century critics feel at sports far less violent than the *munera*. For Seneca, the gladiatorial combats were cruel and inhuman. His comment on the spectators was certainly not the last word on the subject, but it is difficult to imagine a more succinct verdict: *"Mane leonibus et ursis homines, meridie spectatoribus suis obiciuntur"* ("In the morning they throw men to the lions and the bears; at noon, they throw them to the spectators").[59]

Among the Christian moralists, Tertullian was the most influential. His tract, *De Spectaculis*, set the pattern for generations of patristic invective and protest. His objections were partly to the violence in the amphitheater, but he was also appalled by the frenzy of the spectators:

> Look at the populace coming to the show—mad already! disorderly, blind, excited already about its bets! The praetor is too slow for them; all the time their eyes are on his urn, in it, as if rolling with the lots he shakes up in it. The signal is given. They are all in suspense, anxious suspense. One frenzy, one voice![60]

Salvian, a fifth-century bishop, showed the same outrage:

> there is almost no crime or vice that does not accompany the games. In these the greatest pleasure is to have men die, or, what is worse and more cruel than death, to have them torn to pieces, to have the bellies of wild beasts gorged with human flesh; to have men eaten, to the great joy of the bystanders and the delight of onlookers, so that the victims seem devoured almost as much by the eyes of the audience as by the teeth of the beasts.[61]

It was not only the violence and sadism that horrified Christian moralists; they were also shocked by the idolatry of the games.

Greek spectators were presumably, except for an occasional philosophical skeptic, worshippers of the gods of Mount Olympus, but the Roman Empire included citizens who honored Jupiter, Mithra, Isis, and Christ—among others. While Christians, like Augustine's disciple Alypius, were sometimes susceptible to the sadistic appeals of the *munera*, they were repelled by the paganism associated with the games. Georges Ville has asserted that the games held under Constantine and other Christian emperors were, despite the presence of pagan priests and images, "unrelated to the cult of the gods or the cult of the dead," but Ville's reluctance to take pagan ritual seriously may be the bias of modern secularism.[62] It is certain that Tertullian and probable that the post-Constantine church fathers were scandalized by the procession of priests carrying images of the Roman gods. Following Tertullian closely, Novatian expressed Christian horror and fear for the spectator's immortal soul when he exclaimed, *"Idolatria . . . ludorum omnium mater est"* ("Idolatry is the mother of all these games").[63] In the tracts of Tertullian and others, protests against violence are mixed together with horror at idolatry because, as indicated earlier, gladiatorial violence was, in Roman eyes, not only legitimate but also sacred. After a slave dressed as the god Mercury jabbed a fallen gladiator with hot irons to make certain that death was not feigned, another slave in the garb of Dis Pater dragged the corpse away, after which the dead man's blood was offered to Jupiter Latiaris by the priest who served him. That gladiators entering the arena saluted the emperor and declared themselves ready to die was but another indication that the games continued to benefit from a religious legitimation. After all, the emperor was an officially recognized deity. From a Christian perspective, the assertion that the emperor was divine was, of course, the ultimate blasphemy and the worst of idolatries, but Tertullian's rage did not lessen the fact that Roman spectators who were *not* Jews or Christians felt no conflict between piety and bloodshed.

It was largely the result of Christian opposition that Emperor Honorius finally closed the gladiatorial schools in 399 A.D. In the following century, the combats—which had become popular in the Greek as well as in the Latin half of the late Roman world—gradually died out. The *venationes*, pitting men against animals, lasted longer than the combats of men against men, but they assumed a milder, less violent form: "Gone were the heavy armour and shields of the . . . *venator*, to be replaced by a variety of devices designed to protect the combatants, both human and animal. . . . These scenes [carved on consular diptyches] suggest the tricks and turns of a modern circus act rather than the deadly combat of the Colosseum."[64] Although the evidence is lacking, we can conjecture that these milder gladiatorial games, held during the reigns of Christian emperors, were less obtrusively pagan than the spectacles which offended Tertullian and Novitian.

IV ROMAN CIRCUS AND BYZANTINE HIPPODROME

Quantified evidence of the relative popularity of the arena and the circus can be seen in the religious calendar. In the middle of the fourth century A.D., the 177 days of *ludi* were divided into 10 days of gladiatorial games and 66 days of chariot races. (The other 101 days featured theatrical performances.)[65] One must remember that the material cost of mounting gladiatorial games was enormous; such costs must have played an important role in the decision to provide one kind of entertainment rather than another. Commenting on the relative rarity of gladiatorial games in Greece itself (during Roman rule), Louis Robert observes that the economic factor was more important than moral considerations.[66] If we cannot rely upon the religious calendar for proof that chariot races were more popular than the *munera*, we must turn to architectural evidence. The Circus Maximus in Rome held a quarter of a million spectators, five times as many as the Colosseum. And the Circus Maximus was only one of five Roman hippodromes.[67]

The comments of Ammianus Marcellinus attest to the extraordinary popularity of the chariot races:

> Now let me describe the mass of the people, unemployed and with too much time on their hands. . . . For them the Circus Maximus is temple, home, community center and the fulfilment of all their hopes. All over the city you can see them quarrelling fiercely about the races. . . . They declare that the country will be ruined if at the next meeting their own particular champion does not come first of the starting-gate and keep his horses in line as he brings them round the post. Before dawn on a race day they all rush headlong for a place on the terraces at such a speed that they could almost beat the chariots themselves.[68]

The reference to the Circus Maximus as a temple should no doubt be taken ironically. Although the chariot races, like the gladiatorial games, probably had their origins in Roman cult and never completely lost their pagan religious associations, they eventually became secular enough to attract all but the most orthodox Jews and Christians.

In the days of the Empire, the races were contested by charioteers divided into four teams invariably referred to by their colors: the Reds,

Whites, Blues, and Greens. The first two teams were eventually absorbed by the second two, so that historians commonly speak simply of the Blues and the Greens. Since the chariots were usually *quadrigae*, that is, drawn by four horses, turns about the ends of the *spina* (thorn) which ran down the middle of the course required considerable equestrian skill.

Many of the charioteers were slaves who eventually purchased their freedom with their prize money.[69] Those who were free men were officially of low status, like the gladiators, but were actually lionized by the sports-mad public. The satirical poet Martial complained comically about the ubiquitous portraits of one charioteer: *"Aureus ut Scorpi nasus ubique micet"* ("The golden nose of Scorpus twinkled everywhere").[70] Porphyrius, who flourished early in the sixth century, was commemorated by monuments in Constantinople's hippodrome in which his stone figure towers over the four horses and the cheering, waving spectators.[71] He was also honored by at least 32 epigrams in the *Greek Anthology*.[72] That ancient partisanship was at least as emotional as modern is shown by the example of a certain Felix Rufus, who flung himself despairingly upon the burning funeral pyre of his favorite charioteer.[73] Nero displayed his excessive commitment to the races when his wife Poppaea scolded him for a late return from the Circus Maximus; he promptly kicked her to death.[74]

At the chariot races as at the gladiatorial games, sections of seats were allotted to specific groups. Claudius provided special stone seats for senators at the Circus Maximus in Rome; Nero provided them for knights.[75] As long as they did not usurp the seats of the senators and knights, plebeians of the early Empire seem to have sat wherever they wished.[76] With the emperor in his box, "surrounded by representatives of all ranks and classes seated in due order, the circus was indeed a microcosm of the Roman state."[77] In Rome, it is probable that the "circus factions" sat in their own sections. In Constantinople, it is certain that the partisans, wearing their distinctive blue and green jackets, sat in two sections on the northwest side of the hippodrome, directly opposite the emperor ensconced in his grand *kathisma* (the imperial box). The factions also had reserved sections in Antioch, Aphrodisias, Miletus, and other Byzantine cities.[78]

We can be certain that men and women sat together. Indeed, the games were often used as an opportunity for sexual adventure. While some of the crowd cared only for horses, others succumbed to Cupid's darts. Plutarch tells in his *Life of Sulla* how the dictator's wife first attracted his attention by sitting behind him at the games and plucking a thread from his toga. In the *Ars Amatoria*, Ovid offered lively advice to young men who hoped to seduce female spectators.[79] In the *Amores*, he described the erotic possibilities as a lovers' rendezvous: "You watch the races, and I watch you—what a wonderful system! / Each of us feasting our eyes on the delights that we prize."[80] Although Ovid's young woman is shown to have a keener interest in the races than her companion does, many writers disparaged the motivation of female spectators. Juvenal was, as usual, acerbic. He castigated "the tarts who display their wares at the Circus."[81] (Prostitutes who found customers at the races were able to take them to brothels conveniently located in the arcades of the Circus Maximus.[82]) The sixth-century historian Procopius was also skeptical about women's motives; he noted that female fans sometimes joined the Blues and the Greens in street riots "although they never even went to the games."[83]

Quite apart from the question of female motivation, how well informed were the spectators about the fine points of charioteering? One bit of evidence comes from a condescending letter by Pliny the Younger, who condemned the ignorance of the fans who judged charioteering performance crassly:

> I can find nothing new or different in [the races]: once seen is enough, so it surprises me all the more that so many thousands of adult men should have such a childish passion for watching galloping horses and drivers standing in chariots, over and over again. If they were attracted by the speed of the horses or the drivers' skill, one could account for it, but in fact it is the racing colors they really support and care about, and if the colors were to be exchanged in mid-course during a race, they would transfer their favor and enthusiasm and rapidly desert the famous drivers and horses whose names they shout as they recognize them from afar. Such is the popularity and importance of a worthless shirt.[84]

The "childish passion" scorned by Pliny and other critics of the circus factions has sometimes been construed as a sign of political apathy, but this is a false conclusion. The sports spectators of Rome, Alexandria, Antioch, and Constantinople were politically involved but scarcely in the forms presently institutionalized within modern political democracies. None of the cities of the Empire had political parties of the sort familiar to modern Europeans and Americans. In the absence of such parties, Roman sports became a mechanism for the expression and also for the manipulation of popular opinion.[85] They were a "safety-valve for dissatisfaction and a substitute for democratic assemblies."[86] In an age that lacked modern means of mass communications, the hippodrome was the place for whatever interaction occurred between the emperor and the populace.

Sports spectators, like theater spectators, were expected to greet emperors with shouts of acclamation. The emperors often used the circus to present heirs to the throne; on a more mundane level, criminals were often punished there and cowardly soldiers humiliated. Although the emperors and their consorts sat, surrounded by officials, in the imperial box, visible symbols of power and glory, they were apparently accessible to petitioners. They were also exposed to signs of discontent. Since the emperors were usually known to be partisans of the Blues or the Greens and to have their favorites among the charioteers, spectators were able indirectly to voice their displeasure by loudly supporting the rivals of whomever the emperor favored.[87] (This partisanship was sometimes dangerous. When the spectators jeered Caracalla's favorite charioteer, for political or for some other reason, the emperor sent soldiers to assault the offenders.[88])

The second-century A.D. historian Dio Cassius reported a day at the races when political protest took the form of an eerie silence after the sixth race, then clapping in unison and cries for peace. Dio attributed to the gods the amazing coordination of this antiwar protest; modern historians are undecided about whether or not to ascribe the timing to claques, which were highly developed as the cheerleaders of Roman antiquity.[89] Dio records another day when the races at the Circus Maximus were interrupted by a maiden who rushed forward, accompanied by a group of children, to accuse the official Cleander of hoarding grain. The excited crowd took to the streets, threatened the emperor's villa, and succeeded in "persuading" Commodus to dismiss Cleander.[90]

The protests of sports spectators were not always limited to shouts of disapproval and demands for the redress of grievances. The public was often violent, and to a degree still unknown in the modern world.

Although chariot races were nonviolent in the sense that the drivers were prohibited by the rules from doing each other very much physical damage, they occasioned an incredible amount of sports-related mayhem.

In Constantinople, the circus factions rioted at a level that makes modern mobs seem almost nonviolent. They set the city's wooden hippodrome on fire in 491, 498, 507, and 532 A.D., after which Justinian prudently invested in a marble stadium.[91] In the fifth and sixth centuries, spectator violence in the Byzantine Empire increased to the point where troops were repeatedly called upon to restore order. After a victory by Porphyrius in 507 in the circus at Antioch, the jubilant Greens ran wild and, in the course of the riot, burned the local synagogue, a quite typical instance of anti-Semitism.[92] The worst of these many riots took place in Constantinople in January 532 when supporters of both the Blues and the Greens joined forces. Prisoners about to be executed on the 13th were rescued by the mob, which subsequently ignored Justinian's attempt to appease them with the promise of additional games. On the 14th the emperor acceded to demands that he dismiss John of Cappodocia and other unpopular officials. By the 18th of January, the unpacified mob proclaimed a new emperor to whom a number of senators paid homage. Fortunately for Justinian, his most skillful general, Belisarius, arrived in time to save the day—at the cost of an estimated 30,000 lives.[93] In comparison with this bloodbath, the worst modern outbreaks of British and Latin American soccer fans seem relatively innocuous.

In his masterful book, *Circus Factions*, Alan Cameron has shown that the unruly charioteer fans of Rome and Constantinople were neither organized into political parties nor representatives of theological positions. (Previous historians had held both views.) Whether the hardcore adherents of the Blues and the Greens were "simply supporters' clubs" and essentially nonpolitical can, however, be debated, despite Cameron's evidence, because there is a distinction to be drawn between political behavior and political behavior institutionalized into parties. Cameron concludes that the "circus factions deserve no prominent mention in any history of popular expression." In his view, politics merely provided a pretext for behavior which he compares with that of twentieth-century "soccer hooligans." In the civil war of 609–610, for instance, "the political conflict became a convenient facade for the colors to fight each other openly and with impunity."[94] Although Cameron's authority is generally acknowledged, his insistence that the violence committed by supporters of the Greens and the Blues was essentially nonpolitical must be tested carefully against Traugott Bollinger's contention that the spectacles were often "gatherings of a political character."[95] Cameron seems to concede that there may have been "differences in behavior and even social class" among the faction members, but he holds that "partisans of both colors really moved in much the same world: young men with time on their hands—the *jeunesse dorée* rather than a representative cross section of the whole population."[96]

All modern evidence of an analogous nature indicates that Cameron is right to doubt that the factions were a representative cross section, but, if there *were* differences in social class, then differences in behavior were inevitable and it is quite impossible to believe that such class-based differences were wholly unpolitical. In modern Bordeaux, for instance, there are four rugby clubs appealing to four different social groups. In this and a myriad of other instances, various crass and subtle behavioral differences—including political distinctions—are detectable.[97] Cameron's failure, despite his awesome erudition, to detect similar patterns in ancient Rome or Constantinople may well be due to antiquity's lack of interest in such matters and to a consequent scarcity of documentary evidence. Clearly, it is now too late to seek by the chi-square test or other quantitative means whatever statistically significant correlations there may have been between faction membership, social class, and political behavior. Cameron's witty demolition of his predecessor's arguments about upper-class Blues and lower-class Greens is persuasive, but his own conjecture that both factions were comprised of the *jeunesse dorée* seems premature. If they *were*, then the spectator violence of ancient Antioch and Constantinople differed markedly from that of modern Detroit, Manchester, Hamburg, and Lyons, where sports-related violence is associated with the socially deprived rather than with the privileged. Curiously, Cameron actually refers to recent sociological work on the class basis of British soccer hooliganism, but he does not pursue the possibility that ancient disorders might have been instigated, as modern disorders are, not by the idle rich but rather by an alienated underclass.[98] Perhaps a Scotch verdict is called for: Not Proven.

It is probably best to adopt the same verdict in relation to the theory of a "civilizing process" as it applies to antiquity. The model offered by Elias does seem compatible with the fact that Byzantine riots were worse than earlier ones. The Byzantine state, like the Greek Orthodox Church, was centralized, bureaucratic, and absolutist, but the state's control of its own citizens was probably weaker than that of the Republic or the Principate. It is also probable that the division of labor was less minute and the "chains of interdependence" shorter and more fragile than in the days of Trajan and Hadrian. Finally, it is certainly plausible to argue that the Greek Orthodox Church did not encourage the kind of internalized self-restraint to which Elias refers. We may have in Byzantine sports evidence for the very opposite of a "civilizing process," for what Edward Gibbon might have denominated a "barbarizing process." On balance, however, hesitation is called for in the hope that Cameron or some other classical scholar with a sociological bent will test the model as it applies to ancient sports.

One can, however, rather emphatically reject one popular modern theory about spectator violence. While the level of the legitimate and illegitimate violence among athletes is unquestionably a factor to be considered in the instigation of violence among the spectators, it cannot possibly be the determining factor. While gladiatorial games were unquestionably the most violent sport of the Roman world, and quite probably the most violent sport of *any* time or place, their spectators were *less* violent than those who attended Roman and Byzantine chariot races.

TWO
THE MIDDLE AGES
AND THE RENAISSANCE

I TOURNAMENT INTO PAGEANT

A LTHOUGH MEDIEVAL SPECTATORS were often unruly and sometimes riotous, the evidence indicates that their disorders never approached the level of tumult and rampage exhibited by Byzantine chariot fans. The reason for this lower level of violence may well be the much smaller scale of medieval sports. The grandest tournaments were diminutive affairs compared with the races in the Circus Maximus or in the hippodrome of Constantinople. The two thousand persons attending the tournament at Sandricourt near Pontoise in 1493 were a mere one percent of those who regularly cheered for the Blues and the Greens.[1] A second reason may be that the social gap between the participant's role and the spectator's was considerably narrower than in Imperial Rome.

Since the sports of the Middle Ages tended to be specific to classes or to what Klemens Wildt prefers to call *Lebenskreise* (groups sharing a way of life), it is reasonable to look at sports spectators in three categories—in relation to the sports of the nobility, the bourgeoisie, and the peasantry. The clergy, commonly considered one of the three "orders" of medieval society, did not form a distinct category of sports spectators. Since each of the three groups occasionally imitated the contests of the others, it is somewhat of an exaggeration to say that "sport forms did not cross class lines," but there was nonetheless a clear distinction among the orders which assigned folk games like medieval soccer to the peasantry, crossbow contests to the middle-class burghers, and tournaments to the knights and squires.[2] It is typical of the state of historical scholarship in general that we know relatively little about the first category, more about the second, and most about the third, with which I shall begin.

For the medieval knight, the line between tournament and battle field, between mock and real warfare, was thin and often transgressed. "Games resembled war and war resembled games. . . . The union of warfare and games was so close that it is frequently difficult to decide if a given activity ought to be classified under one rubric or the other."[3] This was Jean Jusserand's opinion, put forth in 1901. The most detailed of recent studies of knighthood concludes similarly that "tournaments began as mimic wars in the twelfth century; wars take on the appearance of mimic tournaments in the pages of Froissart in the fourteenth century."[4] The warlike features of the tournament were especially pronounced in the twelfth century, when the typical tournament was a mêlée composed of parties of knights fighting simultaneously, capturing each other, seeking not only glory but also ransoms. Small wonder that a contemporary said of a twelfth-century tournament, "the fracas was such that God's thunder couldn't have been heard."[5] A lapidary modern statement is that the early tournament was "unregulated, it was not a spectacle, and there was little in the way of romantic chivalry attached to it."[6] Combats of this unregulated sort were apt to be deadly. Appalled by the violence of the early tournament, Innocent II condemned the sport at the Council of Clermont in 1130, but this and subsequent bans were ineffective. At Neuss in 1240, scores of knights were killed.[7] In 1471, a tournament was held in St. Peter's Square.[8]

The typical site for the early tournament was a meadow or a field. "The contests seem to have been held in open country, featured perhaps with little woods, a bridge and a stream."[9] There was one anticipation of the later *lices closes*—the *recet* or place of refuge, where knights were safe from pursuit.[10] Since the tournament was not intended primarily as a spectacle, there was little provision for spectators. Those who did come to watch were likely to be knights who might suddenly, with no prior notice, decide to join the mêlée. This was indeed the frequently employed ruse of Phillip, Count of Flanders, who waited unobtrusively on the sidelines until there was an opportunity to swoop down upon some exhausted, unwary combattant and bear him off for ransom. (On at least one occasion the tables were turned and the famed twelfth-century knight-errant William Marshal delayed his entry into the tournament until he saw a chance to capture Count Phillip.[11])

In the course of time, from the twelfth to the sixteenth century, as the "civilizing process" transformed the bellicose fragments of feudal society into something more organized and less violent, tournaments became more pageant and less contest. Eventually, they were "little more than a spectacle."[12] In the words of Jusserand, "The tumultuous battles of old, with horses galloping across fields and through villages, was gradually transformed into an elegant sport, into a spectacle where crowds of glittering aristocrats gathered, where 'the grand beauty of France' was on display in all its grace."[13] The joust between two knights became the typical form of encounter rather than the wild free-for-all clash of groups. Weapons were "rebated" to prevent serious injury. By the sixteenth century, opponents were usually separated by "tilts," that is, by wooden barriers eliminating the risk of head-on collisions. Since knights passed left arm to left arm, with lances held in the right hand, their weapons struck their opponents' shields at an angle which made it less likely for a sixteenth-century knight to be dangerously unhorsed. Jousts were decided not by the mere shock of lance against armor but by an extremely complicated system of points.[14]

As the tournament gradually lost its function as a preparation for war, the question of participation became vexed. When peasants mounted on donkeys or plowhorses staged rustic tournaments, members of the nobility watched with condescension and were amused at the clumsy imitation which no observer was liable to mistake for the real thing. The anonymous author of the fourteenth-century poem, *The Tournament of Tottenham*, can be presumed to have written from the English nobleman's point of view when he ridiculed the farmers' jousts:

> All the wives of Tottenham came to see that fight,
> To fetch home their husbands, that were troth plight.

All in all, there was "mickle mirth."[15] On the other hand, when urban patricians emulated their titled "betters," the nobility became distinctly uneasy about possible confusion of original and copy. A bourgeois tournament at Magdeburg in 1280 greatly annoyed the *Ritterstand*. After all, "tournaments served the nobility as a wall of separation between themselves and the bourgeoisie."[16] When some of the patriciate attempted actually to breach the wall by participating in a knightly tournament at Nuremberg in 1434, they were attacked and beaten.[17] When the knight Heinrich von Ramstein tried to enter a tournament at Schaffhausen in 1436, he too was chastized with a beating. He had lost his eligibility by marrying a middle-class woman.[18]

Although it may be difficult for twentieth-century scholars to accept a trend apparently contrary to that of our own day, the spectator's role *increased* as the sport became tamer, more civilized, and less spontaneous. The importance of the tournament as a carefully organized spectacle can be seen in the increasingly lengthy "lead time" between the announcement and the occurrence of a tournament. The impromptu joust never disappeared, but the grander tournaments, like modern championships, required months of preparation. For the famous combat at Smithfield in 1467, the challenge was issued two years before the principals finally engaged one another—a time as long as that which elapsed between Pierre de Coubertin's formation of the International Olympic Committee and the staging of the first modern Olympics.

The growing importance of the spectators changed the nature of the site as well as the length of time needed for preparations. Venues became increasingly festive. By the sixteenth century, the lists "were surrounded by gaily coloured tents and stands were crowded with spectators."[19] When a tournament was held in an urban environment, which was usually the case in the fifteenth and sixteenth centuries, spectators crowded toward the windows and even upon the roofs of adjacent buildings, as can be seen in an early sixteenth-century miniature by Simon Beining.[20] If the site was outside the city, children and young adults clambered into the treetops for a free view of the spectacle.

Stands and pavilions constructed for the benefit of the onlookers seem to have been no safer than the temporary stands of antiquity. John Stow's *Survey of London* records the collapse of tournament stands in 1331. The ladies fell from above and injured "knights and such as were underneath." King Edward III then did what his Roman and Byzantine predecessors did in similar circumstances; he ordered the construction of stone facilities "for himself, the Queen [Philippa], and other states to stand on, and there to beholde the [joustings], and other shewes at their pleasure."[21] There is little indication that later carpentry was better able to support the burden of the closely packed spectators. Ralph Holinshed's famous chronicles report on a similar accident at Westminster in 1581 in which "manie of the beholders, men as well as women, were sore hurt, some maimed, and some killed, by falling of the scaffolds overcharged."[22]

In the later Middle Ages, the question of who watched whom became very complex. As was inevitable in a highly hierarchical society, the spectators were socially segregated. At the tournament at Smithfield in 1467, there was a separate building for the mayor and other dignitaries of London. The stands for knights and squires and others of the nobility rose in three tiers, topped by the king's box.[23] Like sculpted Byzantine representations of chariot races, in which disproportionately large stone charioteers and emperors loom over diminutive carved spectators, medieval illustrations often use size to indicate social status. In a typical fifteenth-century manuscript, which shows the Earl of Warwick jousting at Calais, one sees the backs of the tiny spectators in the foreground and the faces of the much larger courtiers in the background.[24]

At the tournament in Smithfield, there were galleries for ladies, but it is difficult to say exactly when women began to be a part of tournament festivities. The long biography of William Marshal, perhaps the most famous English knight of the century, written shortly after his death, describes his involvement in a dozen tournaments but mentions female spectators at only one of them.[25] If women were present, they were clearly not the focus of the biographer's concern. Generalizing about the twelfth-century tournament as it appears in the romances of Chrétien de Troyes and Ulrich von Zatzikhoven, one early authority asserted that the spectators were seldom mentioned.[26] In fact, spectators—including women—appear in several of Chrétien's romances as well as in Wolfram von Eschenbach's *Parzival*, which contains lengthy comments on King Arthur and other royalty hastening with many hundreds of accompanying damsels to see the joust between Gawan and the Gramoflanz.[27] Writing of a tournament held in 1389, the poet Eustache Des Champs asks his knightly protagonist to "look sweetly at the angels of paradise" sitting in the stands.[28]

This theme occupied artists in pigment and thread as well as artists in words. The lady, sitting in her pavilion, lapdog beside her upon

an embroidered cushion, became the center of the artist's as well as
the combattant's attention. Thus is she pictured in the sixteenth-century tapestry *La Dame à la Licorne.*[29] In the poetic and prose romance,
from Chrétien de Troyes in the twelfth century to Sir Thomas Malory
in the fifteenth, in painting and in tapestry, we encounter the cult of
courtly love whose conventions called upon the knight to serve his
lady. What better way visually to demonstrate one's dedication than
to carry on the fight before her very eyes?

How realistically the poets wrote and the painters painted is hard
to say. One nineteenth-century authority assured his readers that the
tournament of the twelfth and thirteenth centuries was preserved "in
its most ideal form" in the poems of Wolfram and of Ulrich von
Liechstenstein, but we are left to conjecture on the historicity of the
ideal form.[30] There are certainly elements of fantasy in *Parzival* and
other medieval romances; they justify skepticism about historicity. On
the other hand, *Le Clef d'Amors*, a thirteenth-century adaptation of
Ovid's *Ars Amatoria*, is characterized by such mundane detail that
there is less reason to doubt its testimony about male and female
spectators. To a young man eager for seduction, the narrator remarks,
"All kinds of people come to view / This knightly sport, so why not
you?" The affable narrator assures the youth that the crowd includes
lovely women as well as tournament buffs:

> These tourneys, I repeat, provide
> A fitting field for you who would
> Learn the delights of womanhood.
> For many a fancy wench abounds
> Round and about the tilting grounds;
> Gaily they flock from far and near.

The presumably male narrator questions the female spectators' motives
as men have done since Roman times (and still do): the women are
"less intent to see, I fear, / Than to be seen and amply eyed."[31] Those
who expected to be "amply eyed" prepared themselves carefully for
their roles. Isabella and Joanna, the daughters of Edward III, made
their first recorded public appearance at a tournament in Dunstaple
in 1342. For their gorgeously embroidered robes, eighteen workers
had been employed for nine days. The workers, who used eleven

ounces of gold, were supervised by the king's armorer, John of Cologne.[32] Historians may remain skeptical about the code of courtly love as a guide to daily behavior, but they agree at least that tournaments were characterized by "strong erotic undercurrents" and were therefore a place for the spectators to conduct "affairs of the heart."[33]

The presence of upper-class women at tournaments plainly signals transformation in function. The perfection of military prowess became ancillary and the tournament became a theatrical production in which fitness to rule was associated with fineness of sensibility. It may seem odd to us, but one of the main themes of the late medieval and Renaissance tournament was the notion that good rulers make good lovers. Whatever the tournament became, it ceased to be the deadly mêlée experienced by William Marshal.

Telling of the entry of Queen Isabelle into Paris in 1389, Jean Froissart dwelled upon the elaborate pageantry. When 1200 burgesses accompany the queen from St. Denis into the city, when damsels chorus their praises, when an allegorical castle is constructed at Chatelet with a figure of St. Anne lying upon a bed, with twelve young maidens wandering among symbolic animals (a hart, a lion, an eagle, symbolizing vulnerability and two forms of protective strength), when an effigy of Saladin's castle appears, to be attacked and defended by real knights, it is clear that the demonstration of bellicose prowess with deadly weapons has been overshadowed by the dramatic spectacle in which it has been embedded.[34] At the famous *Pas de la Bergère* René d'Anjou staged at Tarascon in 1449, there was a thatched cottage occupied by a "shepherdess" and knights disguised as shepherds riding forth from pavilions disguised as cottages; the chivalric combat was "entirely absorbed into the fanciful disguisings originally designed as an adornment to it."[35] René's *Traictié de la Forme et Devis d'ung Tournoy* is a compulsively detailed etiquette book regulating exits and entrances, proper verbal formulae, and appropriate dress. Little is said of the clash of weapons.[36] A modern authority on medieval leisure comments that "King René, who adored sumptuous festivals, was essentially interested in ceremony and costume; he regulated the minutest detail; but he did not indicate how the jousts were to be carried out."[37]

At the *Pas de l'Arbre d'Or* held at Bruges in 1468 to celebrate the marriage of Margaret, sister of Edward IV of England, to Charles of

Burgundy, "the tournament had become a vehicle for fantastic, even prodigal, artistic expression."[38] A brief quotation from a long description illustrates this fact:

> There were two entrances to the lists, one painted with a golden tree from which was suspended a real golden hammer, the other built with two towers which were filled with trumpeters during the contests. Opposite the ladies' seats was planted a pine tree with gilded trunk—the Tree of Gold itself—and a so-called *perron* with three pillars which served as a stage for the Arbre d'Or Pursuivant, his dwarf, and the captive giant.[39]

The ceremony was, of course, as elaborate as the stage set. When the Duke of Buckingham staged a tournament at Westminster in 1501, the English showed themselves capable of emulating their Burgundian mentors in these matters. The pageant cars—like modern Rose Bowl floats—were a phantasmagoria of dwarves, giants, wild men, mountains, and allegorical animals (including a unicorn who, quite conventionally, laid his head upon a virgin's lap). The actual tilting, however, was "inept."[40] In the letters of the Lisle family, we read of a tournament at Brussels which took place "not without great banquetings, where some took more hurt with the cups than at the barriers with cutting of the sword."[41] The English tournament was, in the words of a modern authority, "a highlight of Elizabethan courtly life, but it was a spectacle and pageant, not a field for decisions of justice or a realistic preparation for war."[42] Nor was it much of a sports event either.

Perhaps the most interesting tournament to illustrate the transformation from sport to spectacle was held by Henry VIII at Westminster in 1511 to celebrate the birth of a son by Katharine of Aragon. Within the vast allegorical pageant, Henry himself appeared as "Ceur loyall" while his fellow challengers, Sir Thomas Knyvet, Sir William Courtenay, and Sir Edward Neville, appeared as "Vailliaunt desyre," "Bone voloyr," and "Joyous panser" ("Loyal Heart," "Valliant Desire," "Good Will," and "Happy Thought"). The most revealing insight into the relationship of pageantry to sport at this tournament is contained in the thirty-six vellum membranes of the Great Tournament Roll of Westminster. The Roll is a pictorial representation of the tournament.

The first membrane contains a heraldic device; the last contains another device and a poem. Membranes 24–27 show Henry VIII tilting before the pavilion in which the queen sits; the remaining thirty membranes picture the entry and exit processions.[43] If the modern Olympics were to have the same proportion of pageantry to athletics, we might expect a week of opening ceremonies followed by two days of sports and a week of closing ceremonies.

In such fanciful tournaments as the *Pas de la Bergère*, the *Pas de l'Arbre d'Or*, and Henry's extravaganza at Westminster, one can detect a new relationship between literature and the tournament. The medieval tournament left its mark, as we have seen, on *Parzival* and other romances; now the romances left their mark upon the Renaissance tournament. The literary myths of Tudor England exerted an especially powerful influence upon what had once been a fiercely martial sport. The bloody struggles of the mêlée were transformed into dramatic reenactments of the adventures of King Arthur and the knights of the Round Table, with ingeniously gorgeous stage-sets for the eager impersonation of Lancelot and Tristram, Gawain and Percival, Guinevere and Morgan le Fay.[44] The tournament, which anxious civil and ecclesiastical authorities once attempted to ban, became an instrument of centralized rule, a demonstration of royal prowess, and an allegory of English history. A parallel development took place on the continent, where English myth was often borrowed by kings and princes staging *les Tables Rondes*. Whether or not one accepts the contention of Norbert Elias that centralized state power was a key factor in the "civilizing process," one must grant that the princely tournament was a tame affair. When King René of Anjou played Arthur and his consort took the part of Guinevere, the tournament was a very civilized affair indeed. It is quite unlikely that either of them was in any danger. It was a moment, if not an age, of romance; and sport had completely disappeared into spectacle.

The men and women who sat in the pavilions were members of the ruling class. That others were anxious to watch is proven by chronicle and romance as well as by the visual arts. Although extremely stringent rules barred all but the nobility from actual participation in the lists, tournaments which also excluded commoners from the ranks of the spectators seem to have been rare. When Antoine, the Bastard of Burgundy, accepted the challenge of Anthony Woodville, Lord

Scales, the city of London seems to have been as excited as a modern metropolis hosting a world championship. When the long-expected tournament took place at Smithfield in the spring of 1467, a public holiday was proclaimed and commoners unable to crowd into the enclosure climbed trees to obtain a glimpse of the marvelous pageantry and the rather disappointing combats.[45] At the tournament held in 1501 to celebrate the birth of Prince Arthur, son of Henry VII, there was a charge for admission, but this hardly cut down on the attendance, and a contemporary chronicler reported of the standing-room-only throng that there "was no thynge to the yee but oonly visages and faces, without apperans of their bodies."[46]

That the Renaissance tournament had lost none of its appeal can be inferred from a print of 1570 which depicts the fateful joust in 1559 in which Henri II of France lost his life. In order to observe the tournament, held in the square in front of the "ancien hotel royal des Tournelles" in the Quartier Saint-Antoine of Paris, the spectators filled the stands, crowded into the windows of the buildings fronting the square, and even clambered up to perch like birds upon the rooftops.[47]

Literature also shows that medieval tournaments provided entertainment for the entire populace. In his comic poem, *Frauendienst*, Ulrich von Liechtenstein sends the rebuffed lover, to whom he gives his own name, off to fight a whole series of tournaments in honor of the aloof and disdainful lady. At the first of them, the whole town turns out:

> I tell the truth when I declare
> so many folks were gathered there
> there wasn't any open space
> in all Treviso, not a place
> where we could joust or that allowed
> our steeds to gallop through the crowd.
> We met upon a bridge at last
> but even there were people massed.[48]

The joust is delayed until the magistrate can clear at least some of the spectators away. Sir Thomas Malory's account of a tournament alleged to have occurred centuries earlier, in the interregnum following the death of Uther Pendragon, reveals Malory's fifteenth-century assumptions about the popularity of the sport. He tells how the young and unknown Arthur was sent home to bring the sword forgotten by Sir Kay. The house was absolutely deserted because *everyone* had gone to see the tournament (and Arthur innocently fetches the only sword he sees, the one that he pulls from a stone, thereby proving himself Britain's rightful king).[49]

With crowds of spectators came the problem of crowd control. Although no sports event of the entire Middle Ages seems to have approached the level of violence reached by the destructive Byzantine riots, there was reason enough for the gallant young man to worry about the comfort if not the safety of his female companions. As the narrator of *La Clef d'Amors* advised,

> Shield her from tread of trampling feet.
> Be on your guard, as well, to soften
> Those jostling jolts that, all too often,
> Come from the people sitting near.[50]

There were frequent outbreaks of a more serious nature. The chronicler Matthew Paris wrote in his *Historia Anglorum* of the ill will between the English and their opponents at a tournament in Rochester in 1151. There was *"ira et odium inter Anglos et alienegas."*[51] At a tournament held at Chalons in 1274, Edward I was illegally seized by the Comte de Chalons, whom he had challenged, and a brawl broke out in which several people were killed.[52] When a group of squires held a tournament at Boston Fair in 1288, the fact that one side dressed as monks and the other costumed itself as canons of the church failed to prevent a riot during which the fair was sacked and part of the town burned.[53]

To prevent such outbreaks, strict rules were promulgated. The *Statuta Armorum*, published by an English committee of the late thirteenth century, reveals a high degree of official worry about spectator violence. "And they who shall come to see the Tournament, shall not be armed with any Manner of Armour, and shall bear no Sword, or Dagger, or Staff, or Mace, or Stone."[54] Regulation was ineffective in England and on the continent. As late as 1376, a bloody tumult occurred in Basel when middle-class spectators, trampled by mounted noblemen, responded violently and killed several knights.[55]

II CONTESTS FOR ARCHERS AND MUSKETEERS

Although the tournament lingered on into the seventeenth century, and was feebly revived in the nineteenth century (in America as well as in England), the most typical sports event of the latter Middle Ages and the early Renaissance was the archery contest. (Hunting had been and continued to be a popular sport, but it attracted few spectators.) Among the oldest and most widely practiced of human activities, archery gradually detached itself from considerations of utility (such as warfare and hunting for food) and had become a more or less autotelic sport by the early fourteenth century, when the earliest guilds of crossbowmen were founded. Modern research has established that late medieval crossbow guilds were not primarily military or police units. Although their members were a welcome cadre for urban defense in times of crisis, when all citizens were summoned to man the beleaguered city's walls, the guilds were organized as such because the burghers enjoyed the sport. Ironically, guild membership sometimes exempted one from the night watch.[56]

Although the shooting guilds were manifestations of bourgeois life, aristocratic archers sometimes competed among themselves in socially exclusive contests like the one at Prague in 1585, at which "not only the participants but also the spectators had to be members of the nobility."[57] Noblemen were usually welcome at bourgeois archery meets, but they were not the center of attraction. In addition to the fundamental social distinction between the nobility and the burghers, there were subtle hierarchical gradations within bourgeois archery. The crossbowmen, whose patron was frequently St. George, were of relatively high status; they were officials, merchants, sometimes even members of the nobility. The longbowmen, under the patronage of unlucky St. Sebastian, tended to come from the same social strata but to be somewhat less affluent; they were often from the villages rather than the larger towns. Last of all in the procession marched the *nouveaux-riches* with their firearms, with images of St. Barbara.[58] It is likely that each of the groups took at least a spectator's interest in the feats of the others.

As crossbow guilds spread in the fourteenth century from Artois, Brabant, Flanders, and Picardy to northern France and to all of German-speaking Europe, their annual meets, the *Schuetzenfeste,* became major festivals combining sports, drunkenness, pageantry, buffoonery, banquets, and dances. Since archery guilds were usually restricted in membership (that of Abbeville, for example, was limited to fifty regular and to twenty-five "associate" members) festivals were frequently occasions for many to watch while few performed.[59] With a complicated instrument like the crossbow, one can be fairly certain that not all of those who took part as spectators were familiar with the fine points of the sport, but the least perceptive of peasants must have understood enough to have appreciated the difference between a hit and a miss and to have rejoiced when one of the local favorites hit the wooden bird customarily used as a target in the archer's rites of spring. Guilds of archers or musketeers often represented their towns, and their wives and daughters were presumably involved emotionally in "Antwerp versus Brussels" or "Basel versus Konstanz." Some of the German guilds had female members, but they were usually restricted to the religious and social functions that accompanied the meets.[60] Since visual evidence shows numerous female spectators were among the throng that watched the archery contests, we can safely assume that there were some women and girls who were simply fascinated by the sport of archery and who flocked to every match.

While medieval tournaments tended to be special events to celebrate special occasions like royal marriages, archery matches occurred at regular intervals—like the Greek "periodic" festivals (from *periodos).* Typically, the archery guild had its grandest match on the day of its patron saint.[61] As was the case with tournaments, there was a tendency for the printed announcements of a competition to be broadcast ever more widely and for the great shooting festivals to be announced many months in advance. For a match in Augsburg in 1509, for instance, invitations were issued seven months before the day of the competition.[62] Shorter notice than for the famous Smithfield tournament of 1467 but long enough to allow for elaborate preparations.

Exactly as with tournaments, the element of pageantry, which by definition shifts an event's center of gravity from the actors to the

audience, became increasingly important. Just as the antics and con-
vivialities associated with a modern college football weekend can become more salient than the game itself, the rituals surrounding a
major shooting match often overshadowed the achievements of the
archers or musketeers. The most memorable occurrence at Stras-
bourg's famous match in the spring of 1576 was not the demonstration
of toxophilic skill but the bravado delivery of a kettle of porridge
brought by water to win a wager. The legendary pottage was whisked
downstream on a boat from Zurich to the host city in a mere nineteen
hours. In the literature and art commemorating the match, the kettle
of still-warm porridge looms larger than the performance of the bow-
men.[63]

By the early seventeenth century, elaborate processions were common and woodcuts and other means of graphic represention show in
loving detail who marched where and what they looked like. Just as
there are some who admire the floats of the Rose Bowl or Orange
Bowl parade without having much interest in the football game, there
must have been townspeople who gaped at the procession and then
left the archers to their own devices.

Reports about spectator violence at these bourgeois archery contests
are rare, but a certain amount of rowdy behavior was expected. The
holiday atmosphere in which the matches occurred was an invitation
to alcohol-abetted license. There was usually, at least in German-
speaking Europe, a *Pritschenkoenig* who apparently combined the now
separate roles of policeman and poet-laureate. The "king of the whip"
was supposed to keep order and also to provide festive verses.[64] On at
least one occasion, at Nuernberg in 1614, the crowds attending the
prize ceremony were so dense that the awards had to be handed out
over their heads to the archers who were unable to reach the platform
of honor. Good humor seems to have prevailed on this occasion but
to have vanished in Konstanz in 1458 when quarrels in connection
with a match led to a war against the nearby city of Zurich.[65]

III MEDIEVAL AND RENAISSANCE FOOTBALL

Since historians have traditionally emphasized the deeds of the high
and the mighty rather than the "uneventful" lives of the lowly, we
know more about the tournaments of the nobility and the *Scheutz-*

enfeste of the bourgeoisie than about the athletic pastimes of the peasantry. We know that some peasants ran, jumped, threw, and wrestled while others watched, cheered, hooted, and thumped their neighbors' backs. But a paucity of information makes detailed speculation about active and passive roles extremely difficult. The folk sport about which we are best informed is the medieval ballgame which eventually evolved into soccer, rugby, and American, Australian, and Canadian football.

In the course of centuries, this sport changed from wild mêlées almost as dangerous as the early medieval tournament to ruled and regulated contests, but the process was not completed until long after the waning of the Middle Ages. Indeed, the more or less final modern forms of football were not established until the late nineteenth century. The football games of the fourteenth and fifteenth centuries were tumultuous affairs usually played at Shrovetide or Easter and related more or less closely to the religious ceremonies celebrating the spring's rebirth. In the words of Michel Bouet, the participants in the game of *soule*, the French form of the sport, were engaged in "a veritable combat for possession of the ball," for which they fought "like dogs battling for a bone."[66] Writing of British folk games, Eric Dunning and Kenneth Sheard describe them as "savage brawls" engendering "excitement akin to that aroused in battle."[67] That the British version of folk football did not become appreciably more civilized with the arrival of the Renaissance is suggested by Sir Thomas Elyot's condemnation in *The Governour* (1537) of the "beastly fury, and extreme violence" of the game. Even James I, famed for his defense of the legitimacy of traditional English sports condemned by the Puritans, wished to discourage his subjects from indulging in the game of football because the game was "meeter for mameing than making able the [players] thereof."[68]

In its medieval heyday, the sport was seldom the occasion for violent outbursts of spectator violence because there were generally no spectators as such. When depicting sports events, medieval artists usually included the spectators, "and the larger-scale and the more primitive the sport, the harder it is to tell player from spectator."[69] When village competed against village, kicking, throwing, and carrying the ball across fields and through narrow streets, over streams and into the portal of the opposing village's parish church, everyone was involved—

male and female, adult and child, rich and poor, clergy and laity. In a situation of this sort, everyone is a participant. In the terms of modern sociology, there is "the absence . . . of a clearly defined and strictly maintained distinction between players' and spectators' roles."[70] A comic illustration of this annihilation of "role separation" appears in a contemporary account of "knappen" (a folk game similar to medieval football):

> Neyther maye there be anye looker on at this game, but all must be actours, for soe is the custome and courtesye of the playe, for if one cometh with a purpose onlye to see the game, . . . beinge in the middest of the troupe, [one] is made a player.[71]

This is one way to make certain that the fans do not disturb the game.

Gradually, British football—the variety which we know the most about—became somewhat tamer and more civilized. Simultaneously, it underwent the process of modernization which, among other things, specializes roles and separates the player from the spectator. The citizens of London seem to have reached this stage of differentiation in the twelfth century, at a time when rural versions of the game were still wildly unregulated affairs. At Carnival, the young men of the city went into the surrounding fields to play ball and their elders watched. In the words of William fitzStephen:

> The seniors and the fathers and the wealthy magnates of the city come on horseback to watch the contests of the younger generation, and in their turn recover their lost youth: the motions of their natural heat seem to be stirred in them at the mere sight of such strenuous activity and by their participation in the joys of unbridled youth.[72]

With the substitution of some Darwinian language about "primitive instincts" for "the motions of their natural heat," these words might have been written about folk-football as it was still played in the late nineteenth century in the rural parts of England and Scotland.[73]

The emergence of separate roles for players and spectators can be observed in Renaissance Italy as well, where fashionable young aristocrats took over the rough and tumble sport of folk football and transformed it into the highly formalized—and somewhat less violent—game of *calcio*. This sport was particularly popular in the sixteenth century, when Giovanni de' Bardi wrote his *Discorso sopra il Gioco del Calcio Fiorentino* (1580). Early commentators referred to *calcio* as a *battaglia*, but the sixteenth-century version was a highly regulated contest played by teams of twenty-seven on a rectangular field exactly twice as long as it was wide. (The Piazza di Santo Spirito was a favorite place to play.) Participation was strictly regulated. The contestants, wrote de' Bardi, should be "gentlemen, from eighteen years of age to forty-five, beautiful and vigorous, of gallant bearing, and of good report." He urged also that every gentleman player should wear "goodly raiment and seemly, well fitting and handsome." The reason he gave is precisely the one which one expects—the participants must make a good impression on the spectators. After all, "the fairest ladies of the City, and the principal gentlemen are there, to look upon the game; and he who appeareth badly clad maketh but an ill show and acquireth evil report thereby."[74] The emphasis upon the aesthetic is rather what one expects in the Italian Renaissance. Good looks and "goodly raiment" obviously contribute to the sports spectacle, to the show. It is an aspect of spectator sports which remains with us.

In the case of *calcio*, the strict bifurcation into players' and spectators' roles appears to have occurred simultaneously with "the civilizing process." Although Italian sports of the Renaissance were frequently accompanied by disorders, the strict rules of *calcio* acted to restrain the players just as the spread of norms of civility helped to tame the spectators. When internalized codes were inadequate to prevent outbursts of passion, officials stepped in, on the playing field and off. One aspect of external restraint was the Renaissance equivalent of the cops. A contemporary print showing the commencement of a game of football in the Piazza di Sante Croce in Florence depicts the church and its square, the surrounding buildings, the rectangular playing field and the stands (divided into a pavilion for honored guests and "bleachers" for the less favored), and, surrounding the low fence that marked off the playing field, a series of pikemen.[75]

Although England is most definitely the homeland of *modern* sports, there is evidence that many of its medieval and Renaissance games were imported from France and Italy. Some authorities feel that the more civilized forms of English football can be traced to the

Renaissance gentleman's penchant for Italian travel and his consequent discovery of the aristocratic Italian version of what was still, in
England, a brutally tumultuous folk game.[76] This is a plausible theory,
but one must not assume that all the sports of northern Italy were as
civilized as *calcio*.

While the dandies adorned in silken uniforms entertained the ladies
and the gentlemen of Florence with exhibitions of skill at *calcio*, there
were hardier types who preferred traditional folk pastimes like the *gioco
della pugna* that was played all through northern Italy. As the name
implies, this was a game played with the fist. In fact, it was often little
better than a pitched battle, a tournament fought with the weapons
provided by nature. An even rougher version of this *gioco* occurred
when the "players" hurled rocks at each other, a pastime honored by
Savonarola's condemnation. In Perugia, a thousand or more men and
women joined in the annual stonefight, which became so violent that
the authorities attempted to moderate the bloodshed in 1273 by threatening that those who killed their opponents would henceforth be tried
for murder.[77] Sixteenth-century Florentine *calcio* was an improvement
on this type of street warfare, but we must not assume that the patronage and participation of the aristocracy ensured perfect civility and
left the attendant pikemen nothing to do. It is important to remember
that the Renaissance of Raphael and Botticelli was also the Renaissance of Cesare Borgia and other accomplished assassins.

THREE
ENGLISHMEN AND OTHERS:
EARLY MODERN TIMES

I INTIMATIONS OF THE MODERN

MODERN SPORTS began in England. About this there is little
disagreement.[1] Although the roots of modern sports can be
traced back to the early seventeenth century, the Puritans did more
to hinder than to help the development of distinctly modern forms of
sport. The crowd that came to watch the execution of Charles I in
1649 was a far cry from those who had flocked a few years earlier to
see Robert Dover's "Olympick Games"—actually folk contests—in the
Cotswalds.[2] The Puritans were concerned about proper hygiene and
adequate exercise, but their condemnations of skittles and darts as
diversions from prayer testified to their lack of enthusiasm for sport as
such. The years of Cromwell's rule are sports history's blank pages.
Unquestionably, the end of Puritan rule and the restoration of the
monarchy in 1660 marked a shift in emphasis from piety to hedonism.
"Merrie England" had not disappeared completely during the Commonwealth and an anxious scrutiny of the state of one's soul did not
vanish at the moment when Charles II assumed the throne from
which his father had been driven, but theaters and racetracks reopened
and there was a general sense that men and women were free, after
years of repression, once again to enjoy traditional English sports and
pastimes.[3]

Charles himself was no mean sportsman. He was a passionate tennis
player who "did play very well and deserved to be commended," and
his patronage helped establish the racecourse at Newmarket as the
center of the English turf.[4] While Charles was certainly not personally
responsible for the revival of English sports, his enthusiasm, and that
of his court, can quite properly symbolize their recovered legitimacy.

The Restoration did not restore the political relationships of Tudor or Jacobean England. Similarly, the ludic restoration was something other than a replication of what had existed before the Commonwealth. Sports began in the seventeenth century more clearly to approach their modern form.[5]

In the seventeenth century, the English began to quantify their sports and to move toward the invention of the sports record.[6] On May 24, 1606, John Lepton of York won a bet by arriving at Greenwich "by nine of the clock, as spritely and lusty as at the first day [of a five-day ordeal]; to the wonder of all, till another do the like."[7] For Lepton and the Londoners who greeted him, the wager was certainly more important than the recorded time and distance, and there was only a hint—"till another do the like"—that Lepton's achievement was a challenge for others to emulate. It would be another two centuries before men began routinely to abstract the quantified performance as a mark to be equaled or surpassed not simply to win a wager but for the satisfaction inherent in the achievement. Nonetheless, the process of modernization had begun.

II ANIMAL SPORTS

Animal sports like bearbaiting are clearly traditional pastimes and, as such, appear anachronistic to those with modern conceptions of what is and what is not an appropriate form of recreation. In retrospect, they can be seen as survivals even in the seventeenth century, when England's political and economic elite began to frequent the race-course more often than the bearpit. Nonetheless, "blood sports" remained widely popular among the lower classes and drew some aristocratic spectators even in the early nineteenth century when the historian Joseph Strutt asserted that they attracted only "the lowest and most despicable part of the people."[8]

A twentieth-century scholar has asserted the contrary, namely, that these sports were "familiar to everyone, from the most sophisticated Londoner to the simplest inhabitant of a remote hamlet."[9] This was indeed the case. In Tudor days, royalty led the way to the pits. Elizabeth I and James I delighted in bearbaiting; she prohibited theaters from performing plays on Thursdays because they interfered with "the game of bear-baiting, and like pastimes, which are maintained for her Majesty's pleasure."[10]

Reactions to exhibitions of animal sports depended on gender, social status, and individual taste. Not unexpectedly, middle-class opinion was less than enthusiastic. Although Samuel Pepys was certainly no prude, he visited the bear garden on August 14, 1666, and proclaimed it "a very rude and nasty pleasure."[11] John Evelyn's distaste is also obvious: On June 16, 1670, he was "forc'd to accompanie some friends to the Bear-garden . . . Where was Cock *fighting*, *Dog-fighting*, Beare and *Bull baiting*, it being a famous day for all these butcherly Sports, or rather barbarous cruelties." All in all, it was a "rude and dirty passetime."[12] Although the middle classes were the first to turn away from "butcherly sports," there were plenty of middle-class Englishmen who relished them. We read, for instance, in the diary of James Woodforde (September 5, 1759), "I went to the Bear-baiting in Ansford."[13] There is no indication of disapproval. It is probably significant that Pepys and Evelyn were Londoners while Woodforde, writing nearly a century later, was a country parson. In England as on the continent, traditional sports survived in rural areas long after they had disappeared from urban centers.

There is ample evidence that Queen Elizabeth was not animal baiting's only female fan. A German visitor to Elizabethan England, Thomas Platter, observed a "berenhatz" which culminated when a bear, old and blind, was beaten with sticks; it was convenient, thought Platter, that the bear garden lay just across the Thames so that the men and women (*"weibspersonnen"*) of London hardly needed to travel for entertainment.[14] During Evelyn's 1670 visit to the bear garden in Southwark, "One of the Bulls tossed a Dog full into a ladys lap, as she sate in one of the boxes at a Considerable height from the *Arena*."[15] John Houghton remarked in 1694 that bull-baiting was "a sport the English much delight in; and not only the baser sort, but the greatest ladies."[16]

Spectators were not always content to be passively entertained. Thomas Isham's diary (November 4, 1672) indicates that the passions aroused by bullbaiting led from watching to doing: "Bomeford of Houghton had a bull, on which they set dogs. . . . After they had finished, the spectators wrestled with one another till five o'clock."[17]

Whatever the attractions of animal baiting, which must have been considerable for the sport to have survived in England for at least seven hundred years, baiting had one disadvantage which probably helped to bring about its belated demise. Baiting is intrinsically rather unattractive to the gambler in that the inequality of the animals pitted against one another makes calculation difficult. Cockfighting diminishes this difficulty. Unlike "throwing at cocks," a traditional Shrovetide "sport" in which boys threw sticks at the birds until they killed them, the cockfight centers on more or less evenly matched birds. To the excitement of deadly combat, cockfighting adds the thrill of representation. It may be that spectators felt personally involved in the fate of their favorite bulldogs and there is certainly iconographic evidence that John Bull frequently thought of himself as a bulldog, but the identification seems more strained than the French fondness for their symbolic cock. Who can doubt that Europeans, like the Balinese brilliantly studied by Clifford Geertz, have invested more than their cash in the cockfight?[18] The animals have symbolized their owners' and their backers' identity, sexual and otherwise. (As Geertz points out, the association of the cock with the phallus appears in many cultures.) In other words, English cockfights provide more than sadistic thrills; they allowed Englishmen (but not many Englishwomen) risky occasions for vicarious self-validation.

Cockfights were held in London from at least the twelfth century, when William fitzStephen's famous description of London told of "scholars from the different schools" bringing fighting cocks to their clerical masters on Shrove Tuesday; the entire morning "was set apart to watch their cocks do battle in the schools."[19] Centuries later, Sir Thomas Wyatt was said to have believed that the cocks taught courage and Henry VIII was fond enough of cocking to add a pit to Whitehall.[20] In seventeenth-century England, cockpits like the one in Shoe Lane continued to attract aristocrats, who were seated in front, as well as the plebeian spectators, who crowded into the back rows.[21] *The Loyal Protestant* for March 13, 1683, reported that Charles II "and most of the Court went to see the sport of cock-fighting; where they received great satisfaction."[22] Pepys went to the pit in Shoe Lane on December 21, 1667, and marveled at "the strange variety of people," which included a Member of Parliament along with "the poorest prentices, bakers, brewers, butchers, draymen, and what not." Pepys was astonished at the large bets placed by men who looked "as if they had no bread to put in their mouths."[23]

Throughout the eighteenth century, cockfights were, in the judgment of a modern historian, "one of the diversions which cut sharply across class lines."[24] One of the best descriptions of the atmosphere is from Zacharias Conrad von Uffenbach's visit to London in 1710, where he witnessed a cockfight at "Gras Inn":

> The people, gentle and simple (they sit with no distinction of place) act like madmen, and go on raising the odds to twenty guineas and more. . . . If a man has made a bet and is unable to pay, for a punishment he is made to sit in a basket fastened to the ceiling, and is drawn up in it amidst peals of laughter.[25]

When young James Boswell paid a visit to the Cockpit in 1762, he was struck by the "uproar and noise" and by the frenzied bettors. He was also upset by the cruelty which he perceived on the faces of the spectators and was "sorry for the poor cocks."[26] His empathy, if it was something more than the anxious young Boswell's projection of his own sexual uncertainties upon the hapless birds, was an anticipation of coming attitudes.

Although the visual arts rarely pictured female spectators at the eighteenth-century cockpit, the French traveler Béat Louis de Muralt reported that one saw mothers bringing their sons and wives encouraging their husbands to attend cockfights.[27]

As England moved from the eighteenth to the nineteenth century, attitudes toward animal sports gradually changed. As early as 1737, *The Gentleman's Magazine* condemned "the rude Exercises of Cock-Throwing, Bull-baiting, Prize-fighting, and the like Bear-garden Diversions, (not to mention the more genteel Entertainment of Cockfighting)." It was charged that "these Brutal Sports . . . inspire the Minds of Children and young People with a savage Disposition and Ferity of Temper highly pleased with Acts of Barbarity and Cruelty."[28] Many of England's greatest poets—from Alexander Pope and James Thomson through William Cowper and William Blake to the Romantics—expressed their dislike for animal sports. The poet John Hamilton Reynolds, a friend of John Keats, wrote of a cockfight,

"When it was all over, what remained in the mind, but the dirty dregs of brutality and vice?"[29]

The poets were powerfully seconded by Quaker and Methodist reformers and by philosophical rationalists like Jeremy Bentham. By the end of the eighteenth century, even provincial newspapers like the *Bury and Norwich Post* agreed that "all such trainings of the mind of a people to delight in scenes of cruelty are as dangerous in their tendency to the public peace and order, as they are corruptive of the young and uninstructed, whose most natural principles (benevolence and compassion) they extinguish, and pervert their hearts to the contrary."[30] In the words of a modern social historian, "The Victorian bourgeoisie which set the moral tone of cities like Manchester and Leeds were not likely to patronize the cockpit as the Preston gentry of the late eighteenth century had done."[31] The opposition to blood sports was, in Keith Thomas's phrase, a "combination of religious piety and bourgeois sensibility."[32]

Bourgeois sensibility was a complex phenomenon. The appeal to moral sentiment, voiced by poets, pietists, and philosophers, was interwoven with economic considerations. Animal sports ran counter to what historians now refer to as "the work ethic." Such sports encouraged the lower classes in drunkenness, gambling, and absenteeism; in short, they "produced lamentable mill hands."[33] In addition, less specific motives were also at work. Undoubtedly, the attack on the animal sports of the poor, like the condemnation of folk-football, derived in large part from middle-class fears of uninhibited and tumultuous behavior. Behind the drive against animal sports was the Malthusian conviction that the English lower classes were "sunk in bestiality, improvidence, intemperance and lack of sexual restraint."[34] William Howitt, who took delight in Methodist suppression of "dog-fighting, cock-fighting, bull-baiting, badger-baiting, boxing, and such blackguard amusements," had a typically Victorian sense of true happiness, which, he argued,

> does not consist in booths and garlands, drums and horns, or in capering around a May-pole. Happiness is a fireside thing. It is a thing of grave and earnest tone; and the deeper and truer it is, the more is it removed from the riot of mere merriment.[35]

The contrast in imagery between the public world and the private, between the bearpit and the fireside, could hardly have been more extreme.

Although an early bill to outlaw bullbaiting went down to defeat amid "Tory taunts," England's elite eventually joined the battle against "blood sports."[36] The Society for the Prevention of Cruelty to Animals was founded in 1824 and middle-class sentiment finally prevailed, at least in the form of legislation, when bullbaiting was prohibited in 1835 and cockfighting in 1849. Many aristocrats of both sexes found themselves, however, in an awkward situation. They disapproved of the people's pleasure in pitting a bear against a dog, but they themselves were passionate hunters whose pursuit of foxes ended with the hounds tearing their quarry to bits. Henry Alken's very popular book, *The National Sports of Great Britain* (1825), laments the fact that, in the past, "animal misery was a grand and favorite source of pleasure" for women as well as men, but Alken saw little harm in a foxhunt.[37] The essayist Sidney Smith scathingly satirized such selfish inconsistency:

> A man of ten thousand a year may worry a fox as much as he pleases, may encourage the breed of a mischievous animal on purpose to worry it; and a poor labourer is carried before a magistrate for paying sixpence to see an exhibition of courage between a dog and a bear! Any cruelty may be practised to gorge the stomachs of the rich, none to enliven the holidays of the poor.[38]

It may have been awkward for the upper classes to deprive the poor of such thrills while keeping them for themselves, but they managed to overcome what guilty consciences they may have had with threadbare arguments about the need to maintain equine stock and to rid the countryside of vermin, which, in a legal sense, foxes were.[39]

Perfectly aware of the class-determined double standard which deprived them but not their "betters" of gory spectacles, the poor protested. They continued to relish what Howitt had depreciated as "the riot of mere merriment," and they fought doggedly to preserve the traditional sports and popular recreations which had become an embarrassment to middle-class sensibility and a violation of the criminal code. The miners of Northumberland, for instance, "loved dogfighting, prizefighting, and cockfighting" and saw no reason to give them up simply because their "betters" had developed inexplicably tender sensibilities.[40]

Bullrunning is a splendid example of the people's pertinacity in the face of organized reformist opposition. The sport, which may have ancient roots in fertility ritual, consists of pursuing bulls through city streets. When the town of Stamford prohibited the custom in 1788 on the grounds that it had been "productive of Vice, Prophaneness, Immorality, Disorder, Riot, Drunkenness, and Mischief," the magistrates provided the historian with an almost complete list of what it was that the middle classes did not like about the lower classes (only idleness is missing from the list).[41] Even with the assistance of troops, which had to be called out, the magistrates found themselves unable to enforce the laws. When the attempt at suppression was revived in the 1830s, at the request of the Home Office, which had been petitioned by the Society for the Prevention of Cruelty to Animals, popular protest took the form of riots which the local constables, in sympathy with local custom, half-heartedly attempted to quell. By 1839, "preparations took on minor siege proportions: 20 metropolitan police and 43 dragoons arrived in Stamford to assist the 90 local constables."[42] The authorities failed to prevent the bullrunning. The custom died in 1840, allegedly because the financial burden grew too great to maintain it, more probably because increasingly dominant bourgeois opinion adamantly opposed it.

Cockfights, dogfights, and rattings were outlawed too, but these sports had a great advantage over bullrunning or bearbaiting. The animals in question are small and relatively inexpensive. Cocks and dogs can be kept in the city without great inconvenience (and rats certainly abounded in Victorian London). The pit can be moved indoors and thus kept secret from the eyes of the police (who may, since they too are recruited from the classes most devoted to animal sports, pretend not to know what is going on). Not all the wealthy citizens shunned the pits, even in the early nineteenth century. Henry Alken's text informs us that dogfights were abominations that drew "the lowest and most infamous rabble," but his illustration shows men in top hats and coats; *they*, Alken assures us, were the exceptions who attended the pit at Tottenham Court Road where fights were conducted "respectably" and were thus able to attract "a few individual choice spirits of our Aristocracy."[43] Twenty-five years later, just before London's Crystal Palace Exhibition of 1851 celebrated the moral and technological achievements of the Victorian era, Henry Mayhew investigated London's poor and paid a visit to a rat pit located in a pub. He found that the "front of the long bar was crowded with men of every grade of society, all smoking, drinking, and talking about dogs." When it came time to pit the dogs against the rats, the spectators clambered upon tables and chairs and hung over the pit. The scene was clearly not Mayhew's cup of tea: "These were all sewer and waterditch rats, and the smell that rose from them was like that from a hot drain."[44] The most famous illustration of this mid-century "sport" corroborates Mayhew's judgment about the gender of the devotees; the crowd is shown to be composed entirely of men. While Mayhew may have erred in asserting that the spectators came from "every grade of society," they are shown in top hots, coats, vests, and ties. Drawings cannot be taken as photographic evidence, and Victorian dress was more formal than our own, but it is nonetheless difficult to believe that the top-hatted spectators were all drawn from the lower classes.

Cockfights have survived into the twentieth century as a clandestine, mostly rural, mostly lower-class sport. Cockfights proved to be an ineradicably popular sport in the American South. As early as the late eighteenth century, strangers to the region began to find the sport almost as repugnant as the "peculiar institution" of slavery. In 1774, Philip Vickers Fithian, the northern-born Princeton-educated tutor of the children of the aristocratic Carter family, observed with a touch of disdain that his employers and their slaves were at an Easter Monday cockfight.[45] A few years later, the French traveler François Jean de Beauvoir, Marquis de Chastellux, came upon a cockfight in rural Virginia: "While the bettors urged the cocks on to battle, a child of fifteen, who was near me, leaped for joy and cried, 'Oh! it is a charming diversion!'" Chastellux, however, thought the diversion insipid.[46] New Englanders were especially appalled by Virginian cockfights. Elkanah Watson described one in Hampton County, in 1787. "The roads . . . were alive with carriages, horses, and pedestrians, black and white, hastening to the point of attraction." There were "genteel people, promiscuously mixed with the vulgar and debased," and Watson was shocked to see "men of character and intelligence giving their countenance to an amusement so frivolous and scandalous, so abhorrent to every feeling of humanity, and so injurious in its moral influence." It was, concluded Watson, a "barbarous sport."[47] In the course of the nineteenth century, cockfighting lost favor with respectable Americans, Southerners as well as Northerners, just as it did with middle-class Englishmen. As a boy, Andrew Jackson was an enthusiast for the sport and wrote himself a memorandum on how to feed a cock before the main; as a candidate for the presidency of the United States, he wrote another memorandum: "It is a positive falsehood that Genl. Jackson had been either at a cock fight or sports of a similar nature for the last thirteen years."[48] Not all of the general's supporters followed his example. The sport remains popular in the rural South even though it has become illegal in every state.

Similarly, cockfighting has survived illegally in the rural areas along the border between France and Belgium. Descriptions are rare, but cockfighting's appeal to the peasants of Flanders has been well portrayed by a Belgian novelist once renowned for his realistic explorations of Flemish character. In Maxence van der Meersch's *L'Empreinte du dieu* (1936), the middle-class protagonist, a successful writer, surprises the villain, a tavernkeeper and smuggler, at the traditional cockfight held annually in honor of the local saint. The barn is full of peasants and their wives, who are "more passionate, more vehement than the men, screaming out their bets with sharp, piercing voices, mingled together without minding in the least this dust, this filth, this brutality."[49] Have the English and the Americans been any different in their responses to clandestine cockfights?

III MEN, WOMEN, AND HORSES

By the early nineteenth century, urban elites had turned away from cockfighting, but upper-class Englishmen and Americans continued to sponsor "pedestrianism" (i.e., footraces) and horseraces, on both of which large sums of money were wagered. Pedestrianism had its origins in the traditional holidays that have always provided an opportunity for folk games, including such amusements as sack races, "wheelbarrow races," "three-legged races," and "egg-in-a-spoon" relay races, but such entertainments are designed to demonstrate awkwardness as well as skill and to promote a comical sense of our common humanity. The phenomenon of pedestrianism was actually a midpoint on the road from folk games, with all the villagers mingled in a raucous medly of activities, to modern track and field, with athletes on the grass and spectators in the stands.

At a time when horses carried weights to handicap the swiftest and thus provide a more equal competition, men, women, and children were matched in ways that now seem utterly bizarre. As the German historian Maria Kloeren remarked in her pioneer study of English sport, the eighteenth-century Englishman seemed quite uninterested in the notion of equality, which is fundamental to modern sports: "there was no effort to assure equal conditions as the basis for the comparison of achievements; on the contrary, bets were made under a rich diversity of conditions and with increasing extravagance."[50]

The Loyal Protestant reported on March 3, 1683, lively betting (and the king's presence) when a hardy citizen walked five times around St. James's Park in two hours.[51] James Peller Malcolm's eighteenth-century compendium of odd events includes mention of a poulterer who, in 1729, walked 202 times around Upper Moorfields "to the infinite improvement of his business, and great edification of hundreds of spectators."[52] In 1733, according to Charles Louis de Poellnitz, a man ran in the nude to win a wager and the ladies strolling in St. James's Park were forced to turn their heads or to hide behind their fans, but they seem to have thrown coins to the "flasher" with as good a will as their male escorts.[53] On May 11, 1749, an 18-month-old girl toddled the half-mile length of Pall Mall in 23 minutes, seven fewer than required by her backers (and this "to the great admiration of thousands"[54]). Men running and walking to win a bet continued to fascinate the public. In the early nineteenth century, thousands thronged the roadsides to applaud the heroic pedestrian feats of Captain Allerdyce Barclay. On the very eve of modern track-and-field competition, *The Sporting Magazine* for April 1822 reported that some 15,000 spectators had come to cheer 56-year-old George Wilson as he successfully walked 90 miles in 24 hours.

Women ran too. In 1667, Samuel Pepys watched girls who "did run for wages over the bowling-green."[55] Smock races for women were especially popular. (The races were *for* a smock, not in one, but "the female competitors were often encouraged to come lightly clad."[56]) When London's females raced in 1733 for a Holland smock, a cap, shoes, and stockings, "The race attracted an amazing number of persons, who filled the streets, the windows, and balconies."[57] In 1769, a country parson recorded in his diary that there were "Great doings again to-day at Cary in the Park. At one o'clock there was a shift run for by women. . . . I never saw the Park so full of people in my life."[58] In Frances Burney's popular epistolary novel, *Evelina* (1778), bored "gentlemen" wager one hundred pounds on a race between two eighty-year-old women. The French traveler J. B. LeBlanc saw "strong robust country girls" run for smocks and the *Weekly Journal* noted that a crowd turned out expecting to see two girls run naked on Barnet Common.[59] In the latter instance, however, the girls were dressed and the voyeurs were disappointed. Plainly, the spectators' motives were mixed. Some came principally to bet, some—of both sexes—to gawk at lightly clad runners, some simply to spend an idle hour where the action was.

Pedestrianism was never as popular in America as it was in England, but for a brief period in the 1830s and 1840s it seemed about to take hold. In 1835, when the famous sportsman John C. Stephens bet Samuel L. Gouverneur a man could run ten miles in an hour, the diarist Philip Hone noted that the "great footrace" had "occupied the mind of the fancy for several months past." Hone thought the crowd as large as any he had seen and the *New York Post* estimated its number at more than 15,000.[60] Twenty-four-year-old Henry Stannard won the race and the prize. Nine years later, a crowd estimated at 30,000 gathered to watch Stannard and sixteen other runners compete in a ten-mile race at Hoboken's Beacon Course for a prize of $1,000. John Barlow, an Englishman, won in 54 minutes and 21 seconds.[61]

It was the horse, however, not the pedestrian, which won the race for popularity. If horseracing was not always the "sport of kings," it was certainly a favorite pastime of the English aristocracy and the American elite. It is indeed difficult to imagine a social history of Restoration England which did not describe the races at Newmarket, where Charles II and his court gathered to admire thoroughbreds and to back their admiration with large wagers. The hoi polloi were intentionally excluded from the course at Newmarket, but that was the exception.

When Uffenbach went to Epsom in 1710, he marveled at the vast unruly crowd. "One is certainly astonished at the tumult and hubbub made by the English on these occasions." Expecting a rough day, many females wore male's clothing and came on horseback rather than in carriages. The mounted spectators galloped along the course and sometimes interfered with the race. "Great unpleasantness can . . . arise," noted Uffenbach, "if one crosses the path of anyone racing and hinders him; for then all his backers fall on one."[62]

In the American colonies, horseracing, invariably accompanied by gambling on the nags, was a passion of the upper-class Southerner. Aristocratic William Byrd of Westover disapproved of the "swearing and drinking" at the track and refused to allow unsupervised slaves to frequent the races, but Byrd was an exception (and even he found it impossible to stay away from the excitement).[63] When some "merry dispos'd gentlemen" of Hannover, Virginia, decided to celebrate St. Andrew's Day with a horserace, they invited spectators but added suspiciously that "all Persons resorting there are desir'd to behave themselves with Decency and Sobriety, the Subscribers being resolv'd to discountenance all Immorality with the utmost Rigour."[64] In 1774, Philip Vickers Fithian, who probably expected horrors, commented in his diary that the crowd assembled for a horse race at Richmond Court House was "remarkably numerous; beyond my expectations and exceeding polite in general."[65] A generation after Fithian's stint as tutor to the Carter family, the British actor John Bernard attended the races at Williamsburg, Virgina, and was equally impressed: ". . . better order and arrangement I had never seen at Newmarket."[66]

Backwoods venues, however, were rather different. The crowd was "a motley multitude of negroes, Dutchmen, Yankee peddlers, and backwoodsmen, among whom, with long whips in their hands to clear the ground, moved the proprietors and betters, riding or leading their horses." Bernard described the Negroes present through the prism of racism; they were said to have been especially uninhibited, "hallooing, jumping, and clapping their hands in a frenzy of delight, more especially if the horses had happened to jostle and one of the riders been thrown off with a broken leg."[67] Thomas Ashe, another British traveler, was horrified by the frontier antics accompanying the races he observed at Wheeling, Virginia. When two men fell to quarreling over a bet, they fought rough-and-tumble fashion until one gouged out the other's eye, at which point "the citizens . . . shouted with joy." Ashe's sarcastic comments indicate his disgust: "This spectacle ended, and the citizens refreshed with whiskey and biscuit, sold on the ground, the races were renewed."[68] Small wonder that such lower-class affairs were "laughed at and ridiculed" by the aristocrats of the Tidewater.[69] As might be expected, eighteenth-century racing crowds were mostly male, even at Newmarket and Williamsburg.

Toward the end of the eighteenth century the noble patrons of the English turf founded a whole series of yearly events, many of which are still considered highpoints of the sporting season: the St. Leger (1776), the Oaks (1779), and the Derby at Epsom (1780). While such race meetings were arranged by and for the aristocracy, the lower classes were usually welcome "if they kept their place."[70] Commonly, the carriages of the wealthy lined the course so that lords and ladies were able to watch comfortably seated inside or atop them, while somewhat less privileged spectators drove whatever vehicles they were able to command. The hardy representatives of the urban poor trudged extraordinary distances in order to stand on the edges of the course or watch from nearby treetops. The great races attracted some of the "most polyglot assemblies to be found in England."[71]

In the 1770s, grandstands for upper-class men and women became common, but before 1840 races were not gate-money events. Nineteenth-century entrepreneurs finally realized that fence enclosures and gate money were ways simultaneously to control the crowd and raise considerable sums, but it was not until 1875 that "Sandown Park opened its turnstiles as an enclosed course, entry to which required a fee from *all* race-goers."[72] Such instances of economic rationalization were part and parcel of the overall tendency to modernize the institution. They paralleled the introduction of more precise measurements of the horses' times (for which purpose the stopwatch was invented around 1730) and with the incipient bureaucratization of the entire sport by such organizations as the Jockey Club.

Most of the great races were held some distance from London; those who wished to attend had to find lodgings. The great country houses were filled with aristocratic guests while the less fortunate spectators scoured the area seeking to rent rooms. They paid exorbitant sums and deemed themselves lucky to sleep two or three in a bed. The flood of spectators flowing to and from the races was itself a spectacle watched from village doorways and windows.

Newmarket continued to be the exception. As late as the 1830s, when the races at Epsom were drawing crowds of 100,000, Newmarket's seven annual meetings rarely attracted more than 500, "mostly of the higher classes, the majority on horseback, with perhaps a few close carriages and barouches for invalids and ladies."[73] Even in the early nineteenth century, the course had only one small private grandstand expressly for members of the Jockey Club, which had been founded around 1750 (not, of course, by jockeys but by "the owners and breeders, all rich and many titled").[74] When the Great Eastern Railway began to run cheap excursions to Newmarket, the Club arranged for consecutive races to be run at different tracks miles apart so that only mounted spectators were able to see the finishes.[75]

Epsom and Ascot were different. Their popularity was comparable with that of the great sports encounters of our own day. The difference between then and now lies not in the magnitude of the event but in its character. The milieu of the great races more closely resembled the chaotic bustle of a medieval fair than the functionalist surroundings of a modern sports event. They certainly attracted more women than the smaller and less fashionable venues. Mary Russell Mitford's somewhat fictionalized description of a day at Ascot is a fine account of "that celebrated union of sport and fashion." Mary Coxe, a carpenter's daughter, goes off with her beau and joins "a dense and crowded population of all ranks and ages, from the duchess to the gypsy, from the old man of eighty to the child in its mother's arms."[76] Although the young people are not especially interested in the races themselves, they are quite naturally drawn to the attendant festivities, including the marriages of those who fell in love the year before. William Powell Frith's painting, *Derby Day at Epsom*, is a wonderfully detailed rendering of the colorful crowd as it appeared a few years after the visit of Mitford's love-struck couple to Ascot. It is a carnival atmosphere with its hawkers and vendors, gypsy fortunetellers, acrobats, minstrels, pickpockets, idle thugs, and lost children. That Frith portrayed the scene realistically is attested to by numerable reports including a lively piece of journalism from the pen of Charles Dickens. On Derby Day, wrote Dickens, it seemed that "all London turned out." The roads were jammed with barouches, phaetons, broughams, gigs, four-wheeled chaises, four-in-hands, Hansom cabs, cabs of lesser note, chaise-carts, donkey-carts, tilted vans made arborescent with green boughs and carrying no end of people, and a cask of beer—equestrians, pedestrians, horse-dealers, gentlemen, notabilities, and swindlers by tens of thousands.[77]

The rich brought hampers from Fortnum and Mason and the gypsies brought their crystal balls and tealeaves. There was nothing like it.

Newmarket had little or no problem of crowd control, mostly because it had no crowds; but the great meetings of the eighteenth and early nineteenth centuries were often disorderly, even by the standards of the day, which were more tolerant of rowdy behavior than ours are. When gentlemen sponsored a race, ordinary spectators "were tolerated if they kept their place." If they did not, "there might be a pitched battle."[78] The Ipswich Journal reported a riot in 1749 when races were not run as expected. The common people were "so enraged . . . that they pulled down the Starting-post, Booths, Benches, etc. and made a large Bonfire with them in the Middle of the . . . Fields."[79] On another occasion, when the artist-jockey George Morland failed on the favorite at Mount Pleasant near Margate, he was surrounded by a mob "who used their whips on him." The unlucky Morland rode a winner in another race and was attacked by another mob allegedly composed of sailors, smugglers, and fishermen.[80] As late as 1822, The Annals of Sporting wryly suggested that "people should go armed to Epsom and Ascot."[81] Although gate money for entry to the grounds and an additional charge for a grandstand seat eventually reduced the level of tumult, the excitement of the race, the carnival atmosphere, and the ready supply of ale usually guaranteed a number of fistfights. Indeed, one of the sidelights of a great race was a good fight by a pair of renowned pugilists. Local constables were helpless to prevent such spontaneous (but routinely recurrent) matches. If the prospect of a clandestinely arranged bareknuckles encounter generated a crowd of 20,000, it is also true, at least in Regency England, that almost any crowd of 20,000 was liable to generate an impromptu bout with delighted spectators eagerly betting on the outcome.

IV COMBAT SPORTS

Pugilism was, of course, an independent phenomenon which flourished on its own as well as in conjunction with the races, but major fights, like the Tom Spring–John Langlan bout of 1824, were often held at racetracks. (There is a fine print by James Clements of Spring, Langlan, and the crowd at the Worcester track.) When planning an illegal bout, it was better to use facilities already in place than to arouse suspicions by erecting temporary stands in the middle of a meadow. In the course of the eighteenth century, pugilism gradually displaced various other (human) combat sports. (The term "pugilism" seems more appropriate than "boxing," which suggests the somewhat more civilized combats governed by the Marquess of Queensberry and subsequent rules.)

Wrestling, once proudly practiced by Henry VIII and patronized by his royal successors, slowly declined in status. John Evelyn's diary (February 19, 1667) tells of "a Wrestling-match for 1000 pounds in St. *James's* Parke before his *Majestie*" and "a world of Lords and other Spectators."[82] In time, such contests continued to lure the "buxom nymphs" and "jolly clowns" of the countryside but not the more sophisticated urbanites.[83] In 1737, 10,000 people were said to have gathered at Botley in Berkshire to watch the wrestling matches; it is hard to imagine such enthusiasm in London.[84] It is also wise to be skeptical of this and all other estimates of crowd size in times before the introduction of turnstiles and printed tickets.

Fencing was a popular spectator sport in Elizabethan days, when masters staged public exhibitions of their pupils' prowess and skilled fencers competed before vociferous crowds, but the popular swordplay of the Restoration and the eighteenth century was of a rougher sort. It was certainly not the elegantly formal sport practiced on the continent. Italian and French masters thought of their thrusts and parries as part of a geometric pattern, almost as a mathematical demonstration. Their matches often resembled a dance more than a contest. While English aristocrats too were attracted to this sort of exercise, they did not perform for the indiscriminate public.

Meanwhile, London's lower classes flocked to witness swordfights which were often inelegantly bloody affairs. In June of 1663, Pepys

went to see the fencers at the Royal Theatre in Drury Lane and found
"a woeful rabble" whose noise made "my head ake all this evening."[85]
In 1705, Thomas Brown graphically described an exhibition at the
"Bear-garden":

> Seats fill'd and crowded by Two: Drums beat, Dogs yelp, Butchers and
> Footsoldiers clatter their Sticks: At last the two Heroes in their fine
> borrow'd Holland shirts, mount the Stage about Three; Cut large Col-
> lops out of one another to divert the Mob, and make Work for the
> Suregeons: Smoaking, Swearing, Drinking, Thrusting, Justling, El-
> bowing, Sweating, Kicking, Cuffing, Stinking, all the while the Com-
> pany stays.[86]

Undeniably, "the Mob" turned out to watch the commercially sponsored combats of London and other urban centers as the rural poor
flocked to the stickfights and wrestling matches that accompanied annual fairs, but Uffenbach's report from the bear garden at Hockely in
the Hole makes clear that the poor were not the only patrons of combat
sports. There were

> wretched galleries with raised seats, like those on which the spectators
> sit at a play. But the common people, who do not pay much, are below
> on the ground. They tried with violence to clamber up on to the
> galleries and scaffolding, and when some would have hindered them,
> they cast up such monstrous showers of stones, sticks, and filth, and
> this with no respect of persons, that we were not a little anxious. . . .
> They behaved like madmen and things looked very ugly.[87]

There was, and still is, a tendency for combat sports to bring together the very top and the very bottom of the social scale. *The Loyal
Protestant* for July 23, 1681, reported "a great Wrestling, and Cudgel-
playing before His Majesty at Windsor" and an Italian visitor, Count
Lorenzo Magalotti, noted that Charles II also attended public swordfights.[88] Combat sports continued to excite the interest of the nobility
as well as the common people. Referring to the stickfighter-fencer-
boxer James Figg, a contemporary remarked that "most of the young
Nobility and Gentry made it Part of their Education to march under
his warlike Banner," which certainly suggests matches watched as well
as lessons taken.[89] The popular poet John Byrom wrote of "our com-

mons and peers" who stared entranced while Figg fought within "half an inch distance" of them.[90] J. B. LeBlanc thought that only "la plus vile populace" patronized Figg's entertainments, but numerous British and continental aristocrats seem to have been occasional if not regular spectators late into the "Age of the Enlightenment."[91]

There is every indication that eighteenth-century spectators rejoiced in the inherent violence of combat sports. The German visitor Charles Louis von Poellnitz noted that spectators cheered when wounds were inflicted.[92] The same custom was noticed by the French traveler Antoine Prévost when, a few years later, he visited Figg's famous establishment, the boastfully named "Amphitheatre," opened in 1743. Prévost and a crowd seated in banks that reached to the vaulted roof witnessed cudgeling, fistfighting, wrestling, and—finally—a combat with sabres. When the redoubtable Figg sliced off part of his opponent's calf, the crowd shouted for more of the same, "bravo, bravo, ancora, ancora."[93]

Voltaire worried highmindedly in his Lettres Philosophiques about the "jeunes filles" of England who were exposed to matches between half-naked "gladiateurs."[94] Joseph Addison and Richard Steele revealed similar sensibilities when they sent their fictional Sir Roger de Coverley to a combat at Hockley in the Hole, where the sight of blood sends "a poor Nymph . . . into a flood of tears"; but Addison and Steele wrote primarily for a middle-class audience.[95] These enlightened authors, however, need not have worried about the effects of nudity or bloodshed on "nymphs" and "jeunes filles." Neither upperclass nor middle-class Englishmen brought their wives and daughters to Figg's Amphitheatre or to the other exhibitions of combat, and the women who were present were not likely to exhibit girlish sensitivity. There is in fact plenty of evidence that lower-class women were present at eighteenth-century combat sports and that they were a hardy lot. Uffenbach reported that an "Englishman sitting behind us, who had probably drunk a considerable amount, was making a vast uproar and throwing down whole handfuls of shillings. His wife, who was sitting with him, was also rather vociferous."[96] In one of the finest of Thomas Rowlandson's prints, The Prize Fight (1787), which probably portrays the 1786 bout between Richard Humphries and Samuel Martin, a few tubby females appear among the generally nondescript spectators.

The vociferous wife whom Uffenbach met assured him "that two years ago she had fought another female in this place without stays and in nothing but a shift. They had both fought stoutly and drawn blood, which was apparently no new sight in England."[97] Apparently not. César de Saussure reported a bout between an Englishwoman and an Irishwoman, probably the one publicized in *Mist's Journal* for November 20, 1725. The *Guide des Etrangers* (1729) refers to "Amazones intrépides."[98] Saussure says that "il est rare de voir deux femmes faire les gladiateurs" and Prevost remarks that crowds were large *because* women's matches were rare, but James Peller Malcolm's *Anecdotes of the Manners and Customs of London* notes instances of female pugilists at Hockley in the Hole and what can only be referred to as "mixed doubles" at Figg's Amphitheatre, where Robert Barker and Mary Webb fought James Stokes and Elizabeth Wilkinson.[99] The most vivid account of female pugilism may well be from the memoirs of the late-eighteenth-century rake, William Hickey. At Wetherby's near Drury Lane, he went slumming and found two women

> engaged in a scratching and boxing match, their faces entirely covered with blood, bosoms bare, and the clothes nearly torn from their bodies. For several minutes not a creature interfered between them, or seemed to care a straw what mishap they might do each other, and the contest went on with unabated fury.

Neither the men nor the women present, "promiscuously mounted upon chairs, tables, and benches," objected to the "unladylike" brawl. Hickey, who might best be characterized as a deviant middle-class rake, reveals considerable ambivalence about the thrillingly unsavory spectacle.[100]

As the variety of combats carried out at Hockley in the Hole and in Figg's Amphitheatre proves, there was no clear demarcation from the days of cudgel and sword to the era of the fist. Figg the swordsman and stickfighter became Figg the pugilist who then reappeared with his trusty cudgel. Nonetheless, there was a transition. Figg's successor John Broughton, the first popularly recognized champion of England, was clearly a pugilist, perhaps even a boxer.

In Broughton's day as now, there was a tendency for butchers and colliers to batter each other with their fists while the rich cheered them on. The Tex Rickards and Don Kings who promote twentieth-century matches have often risen from the same social stratum as the pugilists they pit against each other, but mid-eighteenth-century fights were, if not part of a traditional holiday or a commercial venture, likely to have been sponsored by the aristocracy. *The True Protestant Mercury* for January 12, 1681, reported a combat between a butcher and a footman in the service of the Duke of Albemarle.[101] Uffenbach reported in 1710 how some lords, to wile away the time before their boat left, casually offered a crown for which a pair of sailors stripped and fought.[102] The Duke of Cumberland was a renowned sponsor of fisticuffs. Under his patronage John Broughton fought the last of his battles in 1750. It was, indeed, a famous moment in the history of the sport when Broughton, battered and blinded by Jack Slack, was gibed by the Duke: "WHAT ARE YOU ABOUT BROUGHTON—YOU CAN'T FIGHT!—YOU'RE BEAT!" To this Broughton answered, "I can't see my man, your highness—I am blind, but not BEAT." He lost the fight and his noble patron lost several thousand pounds.[103] The Duke of Northumberland sponsored the famous black fighter, Bill Richmond, whom he brought to England.

When aristocrats did not arrange the fight, they "honored" it with their presence. For a bout at Brighton's racetrack in 1788, "The town of Brighthelmstone was literally drained of its company, and the race-stand was crowded to excess with nobility and gentry; among whom was his Royal Highness the Prince of Wales."[104] When a nobleman spoke disdainfully of the boxing crowd at the Duke of Clarence's estate, Moulsey Hurst, the duke (later to be William IV) is said to have reproved him: "Be pleased to recollect, my lord, that we are all Englishmen here."[105] William Windham, Member of Parliament and Secretary for War and Colonies, once missed a debate in Commons in order to attend a prizefight.

The tradition of aristocratic patronage continued into the early nineteenth century. Lord Byron, for instance, admired John Jackson and decorated his firescreen with Jackson's pugilistic poses. "Here," wrote the noted sports journalist Vincent Dowling of Jackson's rooms, "all the elite of the fashionable world were daily assembled."[106] After 1802, "the fancy" (a term applied to all the sporting fans) were often found at the Fives Court in Little St. Martin's Street. After a visit there, the poet John Clare faltered in his devotion to the muses and admitted enviously, "I left the place with one wish strongly uppermost, and

that was that I was but a Lord to patronise Jones the Sailorboy."[107]
Three-shilling tickets bought at the Castle Tavern admitted commoners to the floor, which held one thousand, while the scions of the
nobility watched from a small elevated dressing room with windows
on the court. Some of the finest sporting prints of the Regency testify
to the elite's allegiance to the ring. George Cruikshank, for instance,
did a famous print which appeared in the *Annals of Sporting and
Fancy Gazette*; it shows the spectators in top hats and cutaway jackets,
the very height of fashion, gathered at the Fives Court to back their
favorite boxers. A few of the dandies emulated Byron and risked their
physiognomies as well as their purses.

While the young nobleman was often an enthusiastic fan, he was
far outnumbered by the rest of "the fancy," a term which the poet
J. H. Reynolds thought appropriate for "those who deal in scientific
knocks" but also

> For bull-dog breeders, badger-baiters—all
> Who live in gin and jail, or not at all.[108]

Washington Irving seems to have had some of the same thoughts.
"What is the Fancy itself," he wrote, "but a chain of easy communication, extending down from the peer to the pick-pocket, through
the medium of which a man of rank may find he has shaken hands
at three removes, with the murderer on the gibbet."[109] What Irving
did *not* point out is that the chain of social communication rarely
included decent middle-class people like himself.

An account of the boxing crowd at the Royal Cockpit in Tufton
Street is especially graphic: jostling and pushing "to procure a front
seat," there were

> flue-fakers, dustmen, lamp-lighters, stage-coachmen, bakers, farmers,
> barristers, swells, butchers, dog-fanciers, grooms, donkey-boys, weav-
> ers, snobs, market-men, watermen, honourables, sprigs of the nobility,
> Members of Parliament, mail-guards.[110]

Undoubtedly there were fewer barristers than butchers, but we shall
never know exactly the social composition of the colorful throng.

Historians of sport can revel in the eyewitness information collected from the past and reported for his own time by the redoubtable Pierce Egan, who covered the ring for *Bell's Life in London* and other journals.[111] Typically, Egan's accounts begin with the groundswell of enthusiasm as word spreads. Tom Cribb has agreed to defend his title against Tom Molyneux! Since middle-class pressures had made prizefights illegal, a certain amount of discretion was necessary; but, given the refusal of noblemen and journeymen to accept the judgment of ordinary middle-class gentlemen, discretion was often little more than a hypocritical show of deference to the letter of the law. The essayist William Hazlitt vividly described the pugilistic grapevine.[112] On the day before the fight, the roads leading from London to Moulsey-Hurst or some other supposedly secret site in the vicinity of the metropolis were jammed with vehicles of every sort, "from the splendid barouche" to the "mud-cart," with horsemen, and with pedestrians.[113]

The spectators en route to the fights were themselves a popular spectacle. When John Langan and Tom Spring fought near Chichester, the townspeople gawked: in Egan's slang, "the *mugs* of the *yokels* exhibited *gape-seed* enough to have filled a corn-chandler's shop."[114] As was the case with the great horseraces, inns were filled and overfilled and thousands took accommodations for the night in private homes and even in barns. Before John Gully's famous bout with Henry Pearce, "The innkeepers' prices soared gloriously."[115] Among those who simply had to be there were Lord Byron and his boxing instructor John Jackson.[116]

When Ned Painter met Tom Oliver in 1820, the town of Norwich had "as much anxiety and interest upon the event as if it had been the election for a Member of Parliament." The fight "engrossed the whole of the conversation, even amongst the most polite and *tender* circles."[117] Egan's detailed reports make it clear that few of the polite and tender women joined the crowds, but many were known to sigh their amorous responses to the sight of brawny boxers glimpsed from drawing-room windows.

The fancy never knew when a quick change in venue might become necessary. On one occasion, the local constabulary was determined to block a fight between Edward Neal and Philip Sampson. The affair was moved across the county line and the crowd followed the fight, literally for once. "Their *mugs*," wrote Egan, were "covered with perspiration, and their hind parts splashed all over with dirt."[118]

Invariably, Egan implied that *all* classes attended the fights, an assertion which, if true, would leave us to wonder who it was that made pugilism illegal and called out the constables to stop it. Undeterred by such thoughts in his propaganda on behalf of the sport he loved, Egan claimed that the 30,000 or more who had gathered in 1824 for the Tom Spring–John Langan match were "a union of all ranks, from the *brilliant* of the highest class in the circle of CORINTHIANS, down to the *Dusty Bob* graduation in society; and even a *shade* or two below that. Lots of the UPPER HOUSE [of Parliament]; the LOWER house, and the *flash* house." Egan felt the need of a George Cruikshank to portray the scene. Since this bout was held at a racetrack, there was a grandstand admission to which cost ten shillings. Those without the cash, including a number of "*Swells*, were seen sitting down in the *mud* with as much *sang froid* as if they were lolling on a sofa, *tête-à-tête*, with some attractive, lovely, fair damsel." On the river which flowed by the track, ships were moored with agile spectators perched monkey-like on the masts and spars.[119]

Commitment was intensified by what can be called "representative sport." Local idols aroused partisan devotion while Irish boxers were often jeered at by the English fans. Egan, a broad-minded man, commented sympathetically, "Langan is not a black, but unfortunately he is an Irishman."[120] When Langan met Matthew Weeping from Manchester, "It was a kind of war between England and Ireland." Meanwhile, British Jews cheered for Barney Aaron, "The Star of the East," who fought at Colnbrook, seventeen miles from London: "The road," wrote Egan, "was rather *thin* of company; but the *Sheenies . . .* were numerous, and full of *frisk* and *fun*."[121] Egan thought the crowds of the 1780s and 1790s were prejudiced against Daniel Mendoza, and surely some were, yet a contemporary account from *Sporting Magazine* indicates that he was "decidedly the favourite" and "loudly cheered" when he fought Tom Owen in 1820—at the age of fifty-five.[122] Black boxers certainly aroused racist emotions which must have been especially strong when intensified by nationalism, as was the case when Tom Cribb fought Tom Molyneux, a former slave from Virginia. Egan's journalistic rival William Oxberry wrote in *Pancratia* (1811) that "the NATIVES felt somewhat alarmed that a man of colour should dare to look forward to the championship of England."[123] As Egan noted, the American

had to contend against a prejudiced multitude; the pugilistic honour
of the country was at stake, and the attempts of MOLYNEUX were viewed
with jealousy, envy, and disgust: the national laurels to be borne away
by a foreigner—the *mere* idea to an English breast was afflicting.

No wonder interest exceeded "everything in the annals of pugilism."[124]

Preventing such partisanship from spilling into the ring was a perennial problem. The main event was usually accompanied by un-
scheduled fisticuffs and more than one fight came to a premature end
when the spectators abandoned their assigned social roles and began
to attack the pugilists.

The return to London was often boisterous and adventuresome.
Men, women, and children who were unable to attend the match
were eager to hear of the results, or simply to watch the milling
thousands make their way back to the metropolis.

V CRICKET AND COMMUNITY

Prizefighters were patronized by some (not all) of the aristocracy and
admired by the rural and urban masses, who resented the loss of
traditional pastimes and reveled in occasions for emotional release;
but pugilism flourished at the social edges of Regency England, de-
spised by the reformist middle classes, for whom the unruly mob was
a threatening image of anarchy. While the pugilist's ring was shoved
off to the periphery of society's sense of itself, the cricket field was
situated at the center.

Although the game goes back at least to the sixteenth century, when
Guildford's borough records noted the reminiscences of one John
Denwick, who, as a schoolboy, "did runne and play . . . at Creckitt
and other plaies," the game first became an important social institution in the eighteenth century when rules were codified, customs
fixed, and myths established.[125] By the early nineteenth century, at a
time when the tumults of folk-football had not yet been rationalized
into modern soccer, London's Marylebone Cricket Club, which had
been established in 1787, was seen as the game's most important single
organization. In time, the MCC took over the administration of
county cricket too, a very popular pastime. In the Victorian era, the

"players" (who received payment) gradually ousted the "gentlemen" (who did not), but cricket continued to be thought of as *the* English game until the twentieth century, when soccer finally displaced it.

By the early nineteenth century, cricket might almost be said to have defined what it was to be English. What speaker of English doesn't understand the judgment conveyed by the curt remark, "That's not cricket"? No doubt, this assertion about the cultural centrality of cricket was more true for rural than for urban England, but rural England still thought of itself even in the nineteenth century as the *real* England. The country squire played a far more significant part on the social scene than his French or German contemporaries. In playing his role, or roles, he was likely to appear as a cricketeer, bowling for a team that included his butler, the village wheelwright, and a number of other rural worthies. This sponsorship and active participation on the part of the upper classes must have made a difference in spectator behavior. The crowds assembled to play and to watch folk football were often disrespectful of their "betters"; at Derby's traditional Shrovetide football match, "it was customary for unpopular or just well-dressed persons among the spectators to be 'dusted' with bags of soot or powder."[126] In comparison, cricket crowds were deferential.

Mary Russell Mitford was one of the first Englishwomen to write of sports from a spectator's point of view (or from any other, for that matter). *Our Village*, an evocation of English life in the early nineteenth century, contains one of the most famous of all accounts of cricket. "I doubt," she wrote, "if there be any scene in the world more animating or delightful than a cricket match." Of course, it should be a "real solid old-fashioned match between neighbouring parishes, not some newfangled contest in London or Liverpool by people who make a trade of that noble sport." The village spectators are

> retired cricketeers, the veterans of the green, the careful mothers, the girls, and all the boys of two parishes. . . . There was not a ten-years-old urchin, or a septuagenary woman in the parish, who did not feel an additional importance, a reflected consequence, in speaking of "our side." An election interests in the same way; but that feeling is less pure. Money is there, and hatred, and politics, and lies.[127]

Her account is pure pastoral. She describes a "middle landscape" set in some partly real, partly imaginary world between Nature, where wild beasts prey on one another, and the City, where man is a wolf to man. Her fictionalized description matches John Nyren's equally pastoral descriptions. In his books, whole counties turn out to watch but never interfere with play. His spectators are preternaturally patient. For him the game symbolizes rural virtues imperiled by an industrial age.

Of course, Mitford and Nyren romanticized. There were frequent disorders at eighteenth-century matches. In 1744, nobles and gentlemen complained of disorderly spectators at matches held at London's Artillery Ground. Access was thereupon limited to gentlefolk, benches were then provided for those willing to pay two pence or six pence and the number present at the games dropped from seven or eight thousand to a scant 200.[128] When Leicester met Coventry in 1787, there was "a pitched battle in the streets of Hinckley"; in 1792, Westminster boys broke windows on their way to a match and an irate citizen was taken to court for firing shots over their heads.[129]

By the mid-nineteenth century, however, cricket crowds were usually quite civilized. They were also quite patient, a necessary virtue when matches began to stretch into a second and a third day. It may be dangerous for anyone but an Englishman to speculate about cricket, whose arcane rules have frustrated generations of outlanders, but it seems possible that the length of Victorian and later matches symbolized the pace of life in a rural society not yet dominated by an industrial sense of time. What better way to evoke continuity than to go on and on?

And what better way to symbolize community than to have everyone assemble, not by external coercion but because it was, after all, the thing to do? Common to most of those who have described what the poet Edmund Blunden called "cricket country" is a conviction that *everyone* watched. A modern historian writes that "lords and statesmen, tradesmen and working men all played together without distinction of rank, or jostled one another happily amongst the spectators on the green edges of the grounds."[130] Contemporary evidence that everyone did indeed watch the village game can be found in an anonymous denunciation of 1743: "British Champion" complained about "crowds of idle spectators" in which lords and gentlemen mingled with butchers and cobblers."[131] And they all might have been at some useful work!

Eighteenth-century prints show the rural scene, with spectators scattered in small groups around the perimeter of the field. Although a few women played the game, it was socially sufficient if they were interested in their cricket-player fathers, brothers, husbands, and sons. If Mitford is at all representative, most women were. Male children, like novelist Hugh de Selincourt's fifteen-year-old Horace Cairie, waited eagerly for the day when they might be invited to take their place among the men.[132] For the game to serve as a *rite de passage*, which it did, implies its cultural importance. It was also said to be a point of honor that play be fair. Nyren's classic, *The Young Cricketeers' Tutor* (1833), tells proudly of spectators who don't interfere with play when the ball is hit into their midst. "Like true Englishmen, they would give an enemy fair play."[133]

Derived as it was from a basis in historical reality, the pastoral myth took hold. The myth turned out to be more durable than the reality. Long after turnstiles, differential admission costs, ticket-takers, and grandstands created socially segregated seating, lyrical accounts—like Selincourt's *The Cricket Match* (1924) or Siegfried Sassoon's *Memoirs of a Fox-Hunting Man* (1929)—continued to portray the game almost as Mitford had in *Our Village*.[134]

There comes a moment, however, when the rosy haze of communal myth can no longer soften the harsh contours of conflict. In the religiously·divided India of the 1930s, the cricket grounds in Bombay and Calcutta physically segregated Hindus from Muslims from Europeans.[135] In the racially divided British West Indies of the 1950s, the British sat in the grandstand and the natives sat across from them. The cricket match became not a ritual of community but "a social drama in which almost all the basic conflicts within society are played out symbolically."[136] Clearly, the game of cricket has no intrinsic characteristics that make it an appropriate symbol for community rather than mutual hostility. It once brought people more or less amiably together in a traditional society that assumed inequality and yet valued moments of ludic togetherness. It now dramatizes and intensifies animosity in urban-industrial societies wracked by class conflict and on the verge of violent protest. It may be that cricket, once the very symbol of bucolic community, has declined in popularity because there is no longer any bucolic community to symbolize.

VI "THE CIVILIZING PROCESS"

The years from the Restoration to the early nineteenth century were marked by a diminution in the level of expressive (as opposed to instrumental) violence among sports spectators. To some degree, the decrease in spectator violence can be seen within a single sport. For instance, the "fancy" described by Pierce Egan were boisterous and disorderly and sometimes scuffled with constables arriving to stop a fight, but they were not the "Smoaking, Swearing, Drinking, Thrusting, Justling, Elbowing, Sweating, Kicking, Cuffing, Stinking" mob described by Thomas Brown a century earlier.[137] To some degree, the decrease in violence occurred as spectators shifted from one sport to another. For instance, as most of the traditional animal sports were eliminated or driven underground, horse races grew in popular favor. There is no reason to assume that John Bull simply trudged obediently from the closed bear pit to the races at Epsom, but the racing crowds *did* grow and they *were* less disorderly than the crowds assembled for "blood sports."

The diminution was not linear and there never was a moment when sports spectators were not liable to become unruly, tumultuous, or even riotous, but there is good reason to believe that spectatorship participated in the "civilizing process" which led to the internalization of restraint and to the development of a stronger superego. Whether this "civilizing process" can be related directly to the rise of the modern state, which Norbert Elias believes to be the case, is less clear. Certainly, political authorities became increasingly leery of Saturnalian release that threatened to turn into a rampage. The legal prohibition of most animal sports was related to political conceptions of civil order as well as to distinctly religious convictions about cruelty to animals and what such cruelty did to the men and women who observed and enjoyed it.

Economic factors have also been very important. The need for stable, punctual, sober, disciplined workers became a prime consideration for entrepreneurs, especially manufacturers, who were themselves dedicated to the more ascetic varieties of the Protestant ethic. There is, however, a good deal more to commercialization than incipient Taylorization. The entrepreneurial instinct responded to the obvious fact that the popular desire for recreation can be commercially exploited. No cunning capitalist had to manipulate the masses in order to create a desire to watch sports spectacles. The trick was to corner a market already very much in existence. Figg's eighteenth-century establishment was an early step which had already been anticipated by the Jacobean petitioners who hoped (vainly) to erect an amphitheatre on the south bank of the Thames. By the time Victoria ascended the throne in 1837, racetracks and cricket grounds had their grandstands and spectators were increasingly accustomed to the notion that they were supposed to pay for their pleasures with coin of the realm. With considerable property to protect as well as an obvious concern for larger and larger audiences, the owners had a vested interest in order. Although Marxist scholars have held capitalism responsible for the violence which disfigures modern sports, it seems more likely that the capitalistic instinct worked in the opposite direction. The decline in violence was certainly the result of a complex of factors, but there is little reason to doubt that traditional tumultuous merriment brought in less of a return on invested capital than the controlled enthusiasm of the ticketholders.

In short, political, economic, and religious factors combined to transform spectatorship as they transformed other institutions. English and American spectators of the early nineteenth century were somewhat more civilized than their counterparts in the Restoration or the days of Queen Anne. What happened in the later nineteenth century, when hundreds of thousands of lower-class men won the right to cease their labors on Saturday afternoon, and watch their mates play the newly invented games of soccer and baseball, is another story.

FOUR
MODERN SPECTATORS

I THE NEW ROLE OF MODERN SPECTATOR

BY THE MIDDLE of the nineteenth century, European and American sports had assumed their characteristically modern form.[1] They had long since broken the cords that bound them to conventional religious ritual. Indeed, they had begun to develop their own secular rituals, elaborate ceremonies culminating in the grandiose spectacle of the modern Olympics. Although sports were still not open to all participants, all who *did* participate competed under the same rules, an aspect of equality not always characteristic of premodern sports. Athletic events like track and field or rowing and ballgames like football, baseball, and cricket were highly rationalized, specialized, professionalized to the point where some men devoted nearly all their time to them, nationally organized, thoroughly quantified, and marked by an unprecedented mania for the modern sports record, that is, for the exactly measured unsurpassed achievement, the mark to be bettered if improvement upon the achievement is humanly possible. The *exact* moment when this last characteristic appeared cannot be established, but this meaning for the word "record" occurs in the 1880s and the concept itself probably antedates the usage by no more than a few decades.

One facet of specialization was the separation of roles that put increasingly skillful players on the field and increasingly unpracticed spectators on the sidelines. Certainly this separation of roles was far from complete. Most of those who watched had themselves played and intended to play again. There were important exceptions to this generalization, like horse racing, but few nineteenth-century sports required extensive training or expensive equipment. Some sports were popular with the lower classes and some with the middle and upper classes, but in almost all cases, except for horse racing, participants and spectators tended to come from the same social strata. This tendency minimized the split between watching and doing.

Association football can serve as a good preliminary example of the process. When soccer began to attract players from mines and factories as well as colleges and offices, workers turned out to watch, and their numbers grew from tens of thousands in the 1880s to the 200,000 that overflowed the capacity of Wembley Stadium for the Cup Final of April 28, 1923. Exactly how many of those 200,000 played soccer on the previous or the subsequent Saturday will never be known, but the evidence indicates that turn-of-the-century soccer fans were active participants in formal or informal games. Nonetheless, despite the eagerness of the observers to emulate the observed, the spectator's role became increasingly well defined. Alternation between playing and watching did not mean in the nineteenth century as it had in the Middle Ages that either role was diffuse. Rules for spectator conduct, written as well as unwritten, evolved.

Such knowledge was transmitted through local, regional, national, and—finally—international sports organizations. England led the way. The Football Association was formed in 1863 and the Amateur Athletic Association in 1880. Similar organizations sprang up in the United States, Germany, and France, in roughly that order. By 1904, the Fédération Internationale de Football Association was founded and the International Amateur Athletic Federation followed, as if on schedule, nine years later. While the governance of spectators was certainly not the central motive in the formation of any of the national or international sports bureaucracies, membership in the Amateur Athletic Union or the Deutscher Schwimmverband or Fédération Française d'Escrime separated the consciously committed athlete from the less organizationally involved occasional player. Since the sports organizations usually controlled the venues, as for instance London's famed Marylebone Cricket Club controlled Lord's, they were in a position to publish and enforce rules and regulations concerning spectator behavior. Where sports were avowedly commercialized, as in England's Football League and American baseball, the owners of the teams and the organizers of the leagues promulgated rules and struggled to enforce them. Official law-enforcement agencies were generally reluctant to intervene when not called upon for help.

Another institution which helped to establish what one might refer to as the "culture of spectatorship" was the press. Although *The Sporting Magazine* was begun in 1792, sports journalism was firmly institutionalized in the early nineteenth century in a quantum leap of innovation not equaled until the twentieth century, when radio and television once again transformed sports spectatorship. The *London Morning Herald* offered an occasional sports page in 1817, *The Globe* a year later, and the venerable *Times* followed in 1829. *Sporting Life* appeared as a daily in 1821 and Pierce Egan, the first great sports reporter, launched *Life in London and Sporting Guide* in 1824. It was not, however, until the end of the nineteenth century that daily newspapers began to carry regular sports sections. Among the earliest was the *Muenchener Neuesten Nachrichten* (1886).[2]

The first periodicals devoted entirely to sport were English, but American imitators, which usually reprinted swatches taken from their English models, sprang up in the early nineteenth century. The first was John Skinner's *American Farmer* (1819), which helped popularize horse racing. Skinner's paper was followed a dozen years later by William T. Porter's famous *The Spirit of the Times* (1831).[3] Porter was so successful that he was able in 1856 plausibly to claim 40,000 subscribers despite the competition from the *New York Clipper*, founded by Frank Queen in 1853. By the 1880s, Richard Kyle Fox boasted that *The Police Gazette*, which he had taken over in 1877, had 150,000 subscribers, "and each issue circulated through several hands."[4]

As modern sports began their triumphant sweep of the European continent, periodicals were founded to herald them and the relations between them quickly became "une histoire d'amour."[5] The first French magazine devoted entirely to sports was *Le Sport*, founded as a biweekly in 1854 by Eugène Chapus. In setting editorial policy for his Viennese weekly, *Allgemeine Sportzeitung* (1878), Viktor Silberer departed from elitist journalistic tradition and demanded that his staff write so that even "the cook's assistant" ("*Mehlspeisekoechin*") could understand the articles.[6] In some ways continental journalists and publishers were ahead of their English-speaking colleagues. By 1894, French journalists had organized a *Syndicat de la Presse sportive et touristique*.[7] When publishers realized that weekly and monthly publications were not enough to slake the insatiable thirst for sports news, they founded dailies like *Le Vélo* (1891) and *Sport im Wort* (1899).

By the mid-twentieth century, Spain had two sports dailies and Italy had four. Baseball-crazed Japan had five major sports dailies. The most important of the French sports publications, *L'Equipe*, had a daily readership of 2,225,000.[8]

By the end of the nineteenth century, the process of specialization had led to a proliferation of hundreds of single-sport periodicals. Today, the number of specialized journals appealing to runners, bowlers, fencers, gymnasts, fly-casters, tennis-players, and female body-builders has become incalculable. Every modern society has its glass-and-steel airports and every terminal has its magazine stand crammed with the latest illustrated news from the world's tracks, fields, stadia, pools, slopes, courts, and halls.

Turn-of-the-century newspapers and magazines did more than report the sports news. They frequently staged bicycle races and other sports events which they then described to their eager readers. The famed Tour de France began as a journalistic promotion in 1903 when Georges Lefèvre of *L'Auto* sponsored the first race (and sold 14,178,474 copies of his periodical).[9] The annual Golden Gloves Tournament for aspiring young boxers has been sponsored by the *New York Daily News* (since 1927) and the *Chicago Tribune* (since 1928). Arch Ward, another *Chicago Tribune* innovator, invented the All-Star Baseball Game in 1933 and the College All-Star Football Game a year later. The European Cup in soccer, 1956, was the inspiration of Gabriel Hanot of *L'Equipe*.

As the journalists meted out praise for "sportsmanlike" behavior and blame for "riotous indecency," readers came to understand what was proper behavior and what was not. Since, in our own time, the press and the electronic media have been condemned for sensationalism which encourages "soccer hooliganism" and other forms of spectator mayhem, it is important to remember that the press once acted to form and shape nonviolent modes of response to the excitement of sports. Of course, papers appealing to the lower classes, like *The Police Gazette*, might have encouraged a boisterousness upsetting to the upper-class readers of *Outing*, but the overall effect of the print media was to civilize the fans.

In this effort, newspapers and magazines were aided by the flood of juvenile literature which washed over England and the United States in the nineteenth and early twentieth centuries. *Tom Brown's School-*

days (1856) and Owen Johnson's *Stover at Yale* (1912) are among the
countless books from which boys (and sometimes girls) learned to
abhor the dastardly conduct of cheats on the playing field and bullies
on the sidelines. Since it was the secondary schools and the universities that actively nurtured our distinctively modern conception of
sports, it was appropriate that most of these children's books are about
schoolboys and collegians. Continental authors of children's books
seem never to have had quite the same devotion to sports. Jean Fayard
was an exception. He sent his youthful hero to Oxford, where the
impressionable Frenchman finds out about rowing and soccer and
falls in love with a girl who plays golf and tennis and is rumored to
play field hockey as well.[10]

The authors of boys' books may have thought of themselves as
entertainers rather than moralists, but English schools and colleges
deliberately sought to instruct the Victorian middle and upper classes
in a code of gentlemanly participation and proper spectatorship.[11] At
the beginning of the nineteenth century, schools like Eton, Harrow,
and Winchester seem to have been in no shape to teach much of
anything. They were famed for the idleness and dissipation of their
mostly upper-class residents (the term "student" seems too honorific).
Reform, which came early in the century, is associated mainly with
the name of Thomas Arnold, who became headmaster of Rugby in
1828. Arnold sought, with considerable success, to discipline his unruly charges and to bring them somewhat closer to his conception of
the Christian life. Although the prefect system, which placed control
of the younger boys in the hands of the older ones, was the main
instrument employed by Arnold and other headmasters, sports were
generally prized as a way to inculcate morality in the spectators as
well as in the players. Upon becoming headmaster of Uppingham
School in 1853, Edward Thring took up his diary, "On the tenth of
September," he wrote, "I entered on my Headmastership with the
very appropriate initiation of a whole holiday and a cricket match in
which . . . I got 15 [runs] by some good swinging hits to the great
delight of my pupils."[12] In time, the means seem almost to have
become ends in themselves. Masters prided themselves less on the
boys' facility with Latin than on their ability at cricket. By the early
twentieth century, many of the *masters* found it a good deal easier to
score goals than to parse sentences.

Staunchly anglophile American aristocrats like Endicott Peabody emulated the British ruling class. As a boy, Peabody was sent to Cheltenham; as a young man, he attended Trinity College, Cambridge. When he founded Groton in 1884, his friend Theodore Roosevelt, another passionate believer in fair play and hard knocks, sent his sons to Peabody's fount, there to imbibe lessons in strenuous good sportsmanship. After some initial hesitation, British and American colleges and universities persuaded themselves to tag along after the preparatory schools. They too decided that sports built character and that Christian athletes were splendid role models.[13]

It must be emphasized that athletic prowess was defended on moral grounds. It was, and still is, argued that athletic self-discipline and self-sacrifice (for the team, for the school) improves the character and prepares one for a life of leadership. The ideal athlete, who was also *ipso facto* the idol of the school, played strenuously but fairly. The code called for a generous spirit in the victors and the proverbial stiff upper lip on the part of the defeated. The ethos of fair play involved more than strict adherence to the rules. It included the realization that sports are a form of cooperative competition in which each contestant needs all the others. As Robert Frost might have said, good opponents make good games. This sporting display of admiration for one's opponent's excellence became a distinctive characteristic of the Victorian and Edwardian middle and upper classes.

The ethos of fair play definitely included a code of spectatorship. While the well-played point was expected to evoke restrained indications of approval from the stands, the spectators' passions were to be governed by strict rules of conduct analogous to the rules of the game (and also analogous to the behavior of middle-class concert and theater audiences). The player's respect for his opponent had its correlate in the spectator's applause for the rival team when it performed well. As Walter Camp of Yale wrote in 1893, "It is not courtesy upon a ballfield to cheer an error of the opponents. If it is on your grounds, it is the worst kind of boorishness. Moreover, if there are remarkable plays made by your rivals you yourselves should cheer."[14] Not to acknowledge the excellence of the visiting team gave the home team an unfair psychological advantage which undermined the ideal of equality in the conditions of competition.

This historically unprecedented code of spectatorship was an anomaly. The history of sports spectatorship shows nothing quite like it prior to the Victorian era. It must also be acknowledged that the code was never perfectly institutionalized. Writing in the *Atlantic Monthly*, one early-twentieth-century observer of the collegiate scene was mournful: "Nothing could be more discourteous or unfair to visitors [than rooting], and yet it seems impossible to make students understand this."[15] Not everyone wants to see a good game. There are those, perhaps a perennial majority, who prefer winning at all costs and humiliating the opponent whenever possible. Nonetheless, if the nineteenth-century sports crowd did not always behave as it was supposed to, at least it knew how it was supposed to behave.

II SPECTATORS AT SCHOOL, CLUB, AND COLLEGE

If schoolboys and collegians were the first to be drilled in spectatorship, it was at least in part because interscholastic and intercollegiate competitions in track-and-field sports and rowing were the first to be institutionalized and therefore the first which demanded implicit and explicit codes of conduct for the spectators.

The transition from the occasional challenge of pedestrianism, usually for a wager, to the organized track-and-field match, at which gamblers are *personae non gratae*, occurred in the Victorian era. The London Athletic Club (1866), the New York Athletic Club (1868), and Le Stade français (1883) symbolize milestones on the road to modern athletics, but the Scots were the pioneers in that their Caledonian Games, celebrated in Canada and the United States as well as in the British Isles, included many events, like the hammer-throw, that are now standard at track-and-field meets. The New York Caledonian Club, moreover, was formed a full twelve years before the New York Athletic Club.[16]

Organized track-and-field competition was never as popular with nineteenth-century spectators as pedestrianism had been. At the London AC's championships of 1886, there were only about 2,000 people ready to pay a shilling for admission to the grounds at Stamford Bridge and fewer still laid down a second shilling for a grandstand seat. (Montague Shearman, an early historian of sports, estimated that some

5 percent of the spectators were women. French journalists reporting on an 1884 meet sponsored by Le Racing-Club commented on the admiring "jeunes filles en robes printanières" but offered no estimate of their number.[17]) The clubs did not always welcome spectators. The New York AC and its chief rival, the Manhattan AC, were distinctly upper-class and exclusive organizations. The latter's "athletic carnival" of 1891 was open to spectators by invitation only, which pleased the *New York Times*: "Everyone who entered the gates did so by invitation of the club and the crowd was therefore a fashionable one."[18] There was some reason to suspect the motives and to beware the behavior of nineteenth-century track-and-field spectators. When New York's Caledonians added a 220-yard race for women to its 1886 games, the *Times* reported that it "excited immense enthusiasm, and the ropes were broken down in several places by the eagerness of the crowd to get a good view."[19]

The future of track and field, however, lay primarily in the schools and colleges rather than in the athletic clubs. Westminster School met Charterhouse in 1861 and the first Oxford–Cambridge track-and-field contest took place three years later. The latter was "possibly the most important date in the history of modern athletics."[20] American colleges, long accustomed to looking across the Atlantic for guidance and inspiration, followed suit in the 1870s. Although the newspaper entrepreneur James Gordon Bennett sponsored an intercollegiate two-mile race in 1873 (as an offshoot of the Saratoga regatta), only three students competed. A year later, there was a meet with races over five distances, but the sport did not "take off" until the Intercollegiate Association of Amateur Athletics was formed in 1876.[21]

Accounts of spectator behavior at these intercollegiate track meets are tantalizingly unspecific. The crowd was enthusiastic; everybody had a wonderful time. Interscholastic and intercollegiate track and field seldom drew large crowds; there were few if any problems of tumult and violence. What disorder occurred was attributed to youthful exuberance. No one thought to castigate the sons of barristers and stockbrokers as "athletics hooligans."

For whatever reason, rowing brought out throngs who were apparently more enthralled by aquatic than by terrestrial muscular effort. For the most part, the multitude was welcome, which was a good thing, for rowing required a river or a lake from which it would have been difficult to bar access.

Rowing, like track and field, had its "prehistory" in the sense that professional watermen had traditionally challenged each other to races, either as a way to enliven an ordinary transit or as a special contest (usually to win a prize or a wager). Most historians cite Doggett's Coat and Badge Race (1715) as the beginning of the sport, but the date is obviously arbitrary. In any event, detailed accounts of boatmen's races on the Thames exist from 1791. By the early nineteenth century, crowds of as many as 50,000 were said to have watched more or less extempore boat races in American waters. When the "Whitehallers" challenged the oarsmen of the Fulton Meat Market in 1837, "It appeared as if the city had poured forth all its inhabitants to witness some great contest on which their existence depended."[22] In England, similar races held on the Tyne near Newcastle drew as many as 100,000 spectators in the 1840s.[23]

Such challenges turned out, however, to be a historical cul de sac. The modern sport of crew was created not by watermen and dockworkers but by English and American schoolboys and college students. Since neither Oxford nor Cambridge lay on or near a large body of water, both universities had to improvise ingenious races on what narrow streams flowed through their campuses (e.g., "bumping" from behind so that faster boats won the right to move ahead of slower ones). The first Oxford–Cambridge boat race, arranged by Charles Wordsworth, occurred in 1829, twenty-five years before the universities met in track-and-field competition. In order to have what a modern spectator might call a "real" race, the universities set aside the complicated rules of "bumping" and moved the contest to Henley on the Thames. About the race, which took place on June 10th, *Jackson's Oxford Journal* was enthusiastic: "Amongst the assembled multitude were to be seen the very flower of the kingdom, for such surely may be called the fine high-spirited young men of the universities of Oxford and Cambridge, of Eton and Westminster." *Bell's Life in London* told of a crowded town in which six guineas was too little to purchase a night in a room with a view of the river.[24] The event became a fixed part of the sporting year in 1836.

Eventually, the banks of the Thames were lined with crowds of spectators and the river itself was jammed with so many spectator-laden craft that the race itself was difficult to row. While nautical spectators in their "punts, canoes, and row boats" threatened to interfere with the rowers, equestrian fans galloped along the banks and endangered the lives of the more sedate enthusiasts.[25] By the 1880s, some elitists were lamenting the popularity of the races: "Cabmen, butcher boys, and omnibus drivers sport the colours of the Universities in all directions: the dark blue of Oxford and the light blue of Cambridge fill all the hosiers' shops, and are flaunted in all sorts of indescribable company."[26] The writer's father, Charles Dickens, might have described the company, and probably with less disdain.

The Harvard–Oxford race of August 27, 1869, attracted an estimated one million spectators on the banks of the Thames between Mortlake and Putney. American interest in the international contest can be gauged by the fact that the race received more press coverage than any sports event of the previous fifty years.[27] The *London Echo* sold an unprecedented 25,000 copies of its postrace "extra" in a mere forty-five minutes. On the 28th, the *New York Times* gave all but one of its front-page columns to the race. Nearly two weeks later, interest was still intense enough for the *New York Tribune* to allot four of its six front-page columns to a belated report on the race by its London correspondent. When the newly laid Atlantic cable faltered, publisher Whitelaw Reid took communications entrepreneur Cyrus W. Field to task; it was, after all, the "topic to which the attention of two continents had been directed for over a month."[28]

In their enthusiasm for the first intercollegiate sport, American students certainly did not lag far behind their British models. Yale had its first boat club in 1843, and Harvard followed a year later. The first intercollegiate regatta was held at New Hampshire's Lake Winnepesauke on August 3, 1852. Since the shores of the scenic lake were rather less densely populated than the banks of the Thames, most of the spectators came from urban centers, transported by the railway which had organized the regatta and provided the nonathletic spectators with a view from flatcars stationed on the tracks along shores of the lake. About 1,000 watched the first race.[29]

In the post-Civil War years, tens of thousands took advantage of improvements in transportation to follow the oarsmen to Lake Winnepesauke, to New London, Springfield, and Poughkeepsie. Although the railroads offered excursion rates, it was the middle and upper classes who had the time as well as the money to make the journey.

One of the best accounts of the American regattas appeared in *Outing* in 1908. Described in "Poughkeepsie's Great Day" were a dance held the night before the race, cars parked along the banks of the Hudson, scalpers with tickets to sell, picnics, strolling lovers, a handful of Negroes "with guitars slung over their shoulders," young men "with faces prematurely bored and broker-like," and a fat man in a pink shirt mixing lemonade in a washtub. There were as many girls in their summer dresses as boys in their collegiate colors. [30]

Representatives of the rural and urban poor were noticed at Poughkeepsie, New London, and other venues; but they frequently wore the colors of schools they had never seen, much less attended, and they seem to have taken their cues from the collegiate crowd. The celebratory rampage now characteristic of American intercollegiate sports was still to come, but there were early signs of unrestrained enthusiasm. There were riots in 1860 and 1870, after which the organization of the Rowing Association of American Colleges (1870) seems to have quieted the waters. At the Harvard–Yale race of 1885, "frantic undergraduates" jumped with joy, embraced, and rushed "knee-deep in water."[31] Since President William S. Clark of Massachusetts Agricultural College was known to have celebrated a victory in crew by shouting "We've won! We've won!" and driving his carriage across the campus, the students were hardly extreme. [32]

President Clark's explosive exuberance was the kind more likely to be sparked by football than by crew. In the last quarter of the nineteenth century, football became the "college game." The first intercollegiate game took place on May 15, 1874, when Harvard met McGill. Football, in its continually revised version, quickly became a prominent part of the American college scene. Indeed, the salience of the game on American campuses is unique. The "Big Game" became "the most vitally folkloristic event in our culture."[33] One can see this in a young man's 463-page account of how he, as a boy, came upon the Yale team "on the day of a great football conflict with Princeton," heard the cheers, saw the flags, "joined the hero worshippers," and, eventually, became one of the stalwart players. [34] One can see this, more succinctly, in young Stephen Crane's report to the *New York Journal* for November 8, 1896. Crane described the game "crisply, unmistakably," but the "ritualizing, celebrating" crowd is what most caught his eye. When Princeton scores, Harvard banners droop:

> The Harvard flags were dead; the Harvard throats were silent. Everyone in the crimson stands might have been undergoing a surgical operation. But the Princeton crowd, minute proportionately, made havoc of the ears of the people across the bay in Boston. They howled and roared and raged. The enthusiasm of the orange and black for their team . . . went to that acute stage which is almost the verge of tears.[35]

Subsequent accounts of collegiate crowds have rung variations on Crane's basic theme: the passionate identification of alma mater's fortunes with the outcome of a football game.

By the end of the nineteenth century, the college game threatened to become professionalized in the sense that universities began to pay coaches to train students who were not always students. As traditional rivalries like the Harvard–Yale game loomed larger and larger in the consciousness of undergraduates and alumni (and faculty and administration), violence became a problem; but it was the violence on the field that worried observers, not the violence of the spectators, whose whoops and cries and drunken revelry were grudgingly accepted as youthful (i.e., tolerable) exuberance. Since the crowds at intercollegiate football games consisted mostly of students and alumni, they were (and to some degree still are) drawn from the privileged classes. The undergraduates were expected to "let off a little steam" and to tear down an occasional goalpost. The police took little note of their behavior. The presence of upper-class and middle-class women was a good indicator that there was no great danger of bodily harm. Although male spectators have always outnumbered female at coeducational and men's colleges, detailed accounts of the fans seldom ignore the students' girlfriend, "standing on tiptoe, with sparkling eyes and flying tresses and fluttering ribbons, adding her applause to all that which is thundering in your ears."[36]

American football spread from the colleges to the high schools, but the high schools of the late nineteenth and early twentieth centuries graduated a tiny percentage of the population. The high-school football game which fills a stadium holding more than the total population of the home team's home town is a twentieth-century phenomenon because it was only in the twentieth century that more than a handful of any given age cohort was to be found in high school. Once it became standard for all or nearly all adolescents to complete twelve years of formal education, high-school football games began attracting a more racially-mixed and socially heterogenous audience, at which point the high schools began to experience serious outbreaks of spectator violence.

Intercollegiate baseball never successfully rivaled football, probably because it was already a popular lower-class sport before the Amherst–Williams game of 1859 (which was the earliest intercollegiate encounter). Besides, baseball is a "summer game" played at the wrong time of the collegiate calendar. Crowds at intercollegiate baseball games have never been as large as at football matches, and they seem never to have become as unruly.

Intercollegiate basketball has become a "contact sport" whose spectators shout and scream as loudly as football fans, but it started out innocuously enough in the gymnasium of the Springfield, Massachusetts, YMCA, where it was invented on December 21, 1891, by a Christian gentleman named James Naismith. Almost immediately, the game became popular in colleges across the nation, with women as well as men. As early as April 4, 1896, women's teams from Berkeley and Stanford faced off in the San Francisco Armory before an audience composed exclusively of females, all of whom paid a fifty-cents admission charge. The *Examiner* reported the next day that a curious man who looked in the window was "driven off by hisses."[37] In the 1930s, many of the best college teams were from New York City and Paul Gallico thought that the game was one "that above all others seems to appeal to the temperament of Jews."[38] The popularity of the game increased dramatically nationwide after the NCAA began sponsoring national invitational tournaments in 1939. While acknowledging that basketball lags behind its rivals in the television ratings, Neil D. Isaacs claims in his history of intercollegiate basketball that the game became the nation's "number one participant/spectator sport" in the 1930s, "and it has widened its lead ever since."[39] In the late 1940s gamblers cashed in on the popularity of the game, bribed a number of collegians to fix the point spread, and soured many of the spectators; but the game bounced back and, by the 1960s at the latest, began regularly to experience the kind of spectator mania now associated with the Boston Celtics, with North Carolina State or, say, high schools all over Indiana.[40]

III COUNTRY CLUB AND RACE TRACK

The tendency of the elite to segregate itself was seen most markedly in tennis and golf, the two sports most closely associated with the American country club. Although it is true that American sports have generally flourished within the educational system rather than in the private sports clubs characteristic of Europe, partial exception must be made for the country clubs which were organized toward the end of the nineteenth century. The first of them was the Brookline Country Club, founded in 1882 to allow Boston's self-styled "Society" to amuse itself without unwelcome intrusions.[41] The most spectacular of the clubs was probably Tuxedo Park, opened in 1885 by Pierre Lorillard III on 5,000 acres of his Orange County, New Jersey, estate.[42] Such clubs allowed the Anglophile American élite to indulge undisturbed in the sports of their British role models. The country club's limited and discriminatory membership included the "right sort" of people—i.e., people of the proper class, race, ethnic group, and religion. For the privileged, the country club seemed almost a continuation of college days. At these socially segregated institutions, upper-class men and women watched and played the games they had learned at Harvard, Yale, Princeton, and Amherst, or at Vassar, Smith, Mount Holyoke, and Wellesley.

Touched by the wand of wealth, the entire city of Newport, Rhode Island, seemed to turn into the grandest country club of them all. At Newport, the *nouveaux riches* of the Gilded Age erected their palatial homes, docked their splendid yachts, and snubbed the great British sportsman Sir Thomas Lipton because he had made his money in the tea trade.[43] At Newport, privacy became a fetish and the grandstand for the tennis courts was placed where it blocked the view of the "*hoi-polloi* of Freebury park."[44]

Despite Lipton's failure to come up to snuff in Newport, England was generally the model for the American leisure class. For those who took their sport seriously, the All-England Croquet and Lawn-Tennis

Club at Wimbledon set the standard. And there the code of spectatorship was perfected. While the players, dressed in white to symbolize
their distance from dirty work, served and volleyed, the spectators sat
in utter and complete silence. The pleasant twang of the strings was
interrupted only by the polite applause that demonstrated appreciation
of a well-played point. When not actually on the courts, "lady players"
had special seats next to the press gallery. It was observed that they
"clapped their hands loudest, stamped their feet and pounded on the
floor with their parasols most vigorously" when William Renshaw
scored, but decorum was not seriously endangered.[45]

Wimbledon was the model for European royalty as well as for the
children of America's robber barons. A photograph published in *Outing* in 1899 shows the spectators at a tournament in Bad Homburg.
A set of eight princes, princesses, dukes, and duchesses is sitting in a
row of chairs placed on both sides of the umpire's perch.[46]

The proportion of male to female spectators in the aristocratic row
of chairs at Bad Homburg was typical of the American country club
as well. The club's protective environment encouraged female spectatorship (and participation). An article on the country club as a "national" institution had a suggestive subtitle: "Where Woman Is Really
Free."[47] The point was plain enough; only when "rougher elements"
are barred from entry can respectable women feel at ease. Generally,
in the lithographs and photographs of the age, there is an obvious
correlation between dress and the number of female spectators. When
the men appear in frock coats and top hats, there are usually large
numbers of women in bustles and feathered hats. Where the men
wear caps, female spectators are few.

If the country club represented an elitist extreme on the spectrum
of social exclusion and inclusion, the race track fell somewhere in the
middle. On the one hand, entrepreneurs were motivated to persuade
men and women of the upper and middle classes that their tracks were
as safe and pleasant as a college campus or a country club. On the
other hand, entrepreneurs knew that many men, not all of them from
the lower classes, sought an escape from domesticity and enjoyed the
rough folkways of the turf. Was Newmarket to be the model or Derby
Day at Epsom? Some entrepreneurs opted for exclusion, some for
inclusion, and some for indecision.

About the sport's potential popularity, there was never any doubt.

When spurred by intersectional rivalry as well as their owners' personal pride and monetary investment (in the form of a wager), Peytona and Fashion ran one of the most famous races in American history. The *New York Herald* for May 5, 1845, screamed the story:

THE GREAT CONTEST
BETWEEN THE NORTH AND THE SOUTH
PEYTONA, THE SOUTHERN MARE
VICTORIOUS
TREMENDOUS EXCITEMENT ON THE RACE COURSE
IMMENSE CONCOURSE OF PEOPLE

The article told how the first train had left from Brooklyn at 7:00 A.M., how more than three thousand people had crossed South Ferry before 8:00 A.M., how people drove out to Long Island in "cabriolets, chariots, drays, wagons, and every description of vehicle," how, in the vicinity of the track, private homes were turned into dram shops and the area swarmed with people selling brandy and lemonade, oysters, and oranges. Thirty thousand spectators jammed the stands and guards struggled with gate-crashing rowdies who eventually "attacked and carried the outer wall, thirty feet high, by escalade." The invaders' "chums" already in the stands pulled the newcomers up as the next in line pushed from below. Once the guards halted the influx, rowdies roamed about "like a tribe of Bedouins around a doomed caravan." The spectators ate, drank, bet, watched Peytona win both four-mile heats, and left in good humor. That night, New York's hotels were full and "many strangers must have been bedfellows."[48] The Currier and Ives print commemorating the race, *Peytona and Fashion*, shows a few women scattered among the male spectators.

The introduction of the parimutuel system of betting in the 1860s and 1870s further increased the entrepreneur's economic prospects (and aroused the ire of middle-class moralists, for whom the bookie was as unsavory as the pimp). Whether or not the spectators at suburban tracks were nostalgically reminded of rural fairs, as at least one historian has suggested, they were unquestionably eager to line up at the windows and to lay money on their choice to win, place, or show.[49] Some members of the American elite emulated the Restoration aristocrats who kept the rabble away from Newmarket. Leonard

Jerome, a founder of the American Jockey Club, arranged for the construction in New York City of Jerome Park in the same year, 1866. The track had a dining room, ballroom, and overnight accommodations. When it was opened on October 25, Ulysses S. Grant was in attendance (as was Josie Wood, the town's premiere madame). The American Jockey Club attempted to bar rowdy elements and the grandstand was reserved for club members, which brought complaints from the popular press. The *New York Clipper,* for instance, was sarcastic: "From this sacred spot the respectable public are tabooed, and none but the sweet scented and kid glove subscribers can enter."[50]

Most English and American tracks were less exclusive. One pillar of the new American elite, William H. Vanderbilt, went to the Derby in 1877 and wrote "that the sight of three hundred thousand people looking at a horse-race was worth . . . a trip across the ocean," but he seems to have been impressed by the sheer size more than by the colorfulness of the crowd.[51] Vanderbilt left it to the sharp-eyed French historian Hippolyte Taine to sketch a scene as carnival-like as when Charles Dickens described it:

> There were bohemians everywhere, singers and dancers grotesquely disguised as Negroes, there were archers and riflemen, charletans . . . selling watches, quill games, stick games, musicians of every kind. [It was a] day when everything is permitted, a debauch to end a year of restraint.[52]

In the United States, entrepreneurs had to persuade middle-class legislators as well as the middle-class public that the tracks were not simply a magnet for gamblers, pickpockets, cutthroats, prostitutes, and their helpless victims. Persuasion often failed. The New Jersey legislature, for instance, closed Monmouth track in 1894 and saved the community of Asbury Park from women "who never see the light of day."[53] (How exclusively nocturnal prostitutes were able to appear at the afternoon races was never explained.) Reform was the price of survival. How were owners to persuade middle-class men that it was safe to bring their sisters, wives, and daughters to the track? One traditional technique was, of course, to create a separate section for female spectators, which was done, for instance, at the Union Course in New Orleans. The lovely women whom the members of the club

invited to the track were said by the French visitor Salomon de Rothschild to have been more admired than the fine horses who were the
ostensible occasion for the outing.[54]

As a solution, however, sexual segregation has a serious disadvantage. It tends to separate the men from the women they were encouraged to bring with them. In the long run, the economically
rational response was to convince the affluent, who had the largest
sums to wager, that a day at the races was, like a day at Coney Island,
a riskless adventure. Most American entrepreneurs did as their English
cousins had done—they raised the price of admission and employed
the police to discourage well-heeled hoodlums. In America as in England pickpockets and untrustworthy tipsters continued to ply their
trade, gate-crashers were still a problem, and alcohol was deemed
necessary for full enjoyment of the turf; but modern horse racing was
not plagued by serious disorders. If most women continued to stay
away, it was because Fortuna had no charms for them, not because
they feared for their lives.

Unless of course they were invited to some of the more provincial
tracks. Conditions there were rough and ready. At a Virginia fair of
1888, one observer found a "plank fence surrounding a sandy patch
of ground, a half-mile track full of holes, a gaunt edifice purporting
to be a grand-stand." The motley crowd included a "haughty old
Southerner side by side with a foxy gambler; a rowdy Britisher cheek-
by-jowl with an 'old-time nigger.'" A night spent in a room with six
people in three beds did not improve the writer's mood.[55] Another
observer commented on provincial Irish races, where fights broke out
and experienced bystanders had to calm the female spectators: "Oh!
it's nothing—don't be afraid—only just the Doolan and Murphy factions having their annual little bit of 'divarshun'—they always have a
fight on Race day."[56]

The French of la belle époque also took to the races. (It was they
who invented the parimutuel system.) The aristocratic track at
Longchamp was opened in 1857 and immediately became an essential
part of la vie parisiènne.[57] By 1903 Le Jockey Club was providing a
splendid Tribune des Familles, where Anglophile duchesses and
countesses might sit and catch a glimpse of England's sport-obsessed
King Edward VII.[58] Elegant men and women placed their bets and
admired each other's fashionable attire. Pastel crinolines and parasols

made a colorful impression and quite a number of the French elite posed, whether they knew it or not, for the brushes of Edouard Manet and Edgar Degas. Meanwhile, the touts and the con-men were tolerated as long as they behaved themselves discreetly. Here too, higher charges for the better seats allowed the classes to sort themselves out.

There is evidence that the American races attracted black as well as white enthusiasts (as they had in colonial times). A writer for *Outing* asserted in 1903 that the New York races attracted "all kinds of humanity of both colors and sexes."[59] In Louisiana and other Southern states, race tracks—like most other public facilities—had segregated stands. At the automobile races in Savannah, Georgia, blacks were not allowed to sit in the grandstand, but no one was able to prevent them from lining the road to watch the horseless carriages thunder by.[60] The openness of those pre-Indianapolis-500 days was found in Europe too; photographs taken in 1905 show French peasants waiting patiently by country roads for a glimpse of the drivers.[61]

IV ENGLISH AND AUSTRALIAN CRICKET

Within the world of cricket, social class is the single variable that best predicts the probability of spectator violence. Since the early nineteenth century, English cricket has been associated with Oxford and Cambridge, with gentlemanly conduct and aristocratic status. Indeed, it takes an Oxford or Cambridge accent to scold loutish behavior with classically proper elitist disapproval: "That's not cricket."[62] Given the upper-class bias of the Marylebone Cricket Club, we should not be surprised that it was among the first organizations to institute a whole set of measures to control the crowd. In 1864, the club's secretary, R. A. Fitzgerald, announced the future employment of off-duty policemen and the institution of gate money. Henceforth, admission cost a shilling for those on foot, two shillings sixpence for those mounted, five shillings for those in two-wheeled carriages, and ten for those who arrived in four-wheeled conveyances. For the immensely popular Eton–Harrow game, the MCC charged two shillings sixpence for those on foot and proportionally higher prices for the others. Needless to say, the spectators were well above the poverty line.[63]

Those who were wealthy enough to own carriages and to pay shillings for an afternoon of cricket were also affluent enough to dress well and vain enough to want others to admire their finery. Articles in fashionable magazines like *Belgravia* opined that many of the spectators seemed to think of themselves as the spectacle.[64] It was an opinion about motives that had been voiced by Roman poets and it was certainly not implausible.

Although the MCC enlarged its stands at the end of the 1890s to hold as many as 30,000 spectators, historians agree that crowd control was not a problem; "Victorian cricket crowds behaved very well indeed."[65] Disorder was "generally verbal rather than physical."[66] The generalization holds for American cricket spectators, if one allows for an element of uninhibited democratic expressiveness. On at least one occasion, during the English tour of 1858, the American fans demonstrated their approval of thirteen-year-old George Newhall's bowling by firing their pistols in the air, but these improper Philadelphians were not accused of threatening the opposing side.[67] There was more acrimony and animosity voiced at American than at English cricket matches, but the crowds remained relatively decorous even in the United States.

Differing with Wray Vamplew's emphasis on economic reasons for the good conduct of cricket fans, Keith A. P. Sandiford notes that the crowds for club and village cricket were certainly less affluent than those at Lord's, and yet "there is still no evidence to show that they were any harder to control."[68] In county cricket as at Lord's, in America as in England, the middle and upper classes set the tone. There was little effort to lure the lower classes from their pubs and music halls. Those who administered the game simply renounced the economic principle of profit-maximization that might have led them to seek larger and more socially heterogeneous crowds. As P. F. Warner announced in 1912, "cricket is not a circus, and it would be far better that it should be driven back to the village green, where it found its origin, than yield a jot to the petulant demands of the spectators." Displeased sensation-seekers were advised to stay at home, "and the game will be none the worse for their absence."[69] Small wonder that cricket has long since ceased to be the most popular of British ballgames.

The decisive role of social class can be seen clearly when one contrasts the history of English with that of Australian cricket. In a full-length study of the latter, Richard Cashman has described the displacement of the patrician spectators of the early nineteenth century by the more plebeian crowds of the 1880s and after. In the first half-century of the game, the Members of the Club were in control. When gate money was first taken, in 1856, the Melbourne Cricket Club charged a shilling for entrance to the grounds, approximately a sixth of a worker's daily wages. For the First Test against England in 1877, a seat in the grandstand cost a prohibitive four shillings.[70] The *Melbourne Argus* noted that the Members' Reserve was "gay with the bright dresses of hundreds of ladies," but the "Outer" remained almost exclusively male until the 1970s. As the game grew increasingly popular, the "larrikins" (rough young men) began to invade the pitch and to cause delays in the game. On February 8, 1879, some two thousand larrikins stormed the grounds of the Sydney Cricket Club and roughed up the visiting English team. While middle-class fans strove to maintain the English tradition of polite applause for both sides, lower-class fans of the Outer developed a lusty countertradition of "barracking" friend and foe alike. Newspapers complained about the "unmanly behavior" of the "roughs" who jeered to unsettle the players, but the male preserve of "The Hill" at Sydney Cricket Ground reveled in the fine (and sometimes in the gross) art of comic insult and invective. Indeed, the stentorian wit of the most famous of all Australian fans, Stephen Harold Gascoigne, earned him a place in the *Australian Dictionary of Biography*![70]

After a period of relative order in which rugby and Australian Rules Football attracted the lion's share of lower-class spectators, cricket in the 1970s recovered its place as the nation's most popular spectator sport. (A 1983 McNair Anderson poll placed it slightly ahead of tennis and Australian Rules Football.) The revival of interest, however, came not through the efforts of the traditional clubs but as a result of commercially sponsored World Series Cricket. In 1977, private television's Channel 9 seized the initiative from the Australian Broadcasting Company and offered the public a new kind of mass-appeal cricket marked by one-day matches, night games, colored uniforms, close-up shots on TV, "honey shots" of attractive female fans, and magazines telling of the players' private lives (with more than a hint about their private parts). Survey data indicate that the new audience for cricket is younger, less affluent, more "ethnic," less well informed about the game, and—predictably—more given to chanting obscenities, invading the pitch, flinging beer cans, and scuffling with policemen.[71]

Since lower-class cricket crowds of the 1920s and 1930s were "well-behaved" chaps who "never invaded the field to protest or to congratulate" a high-scoring batsman, since there was an increase in the more moderate forms of disorder in the 1960s (before the advent of World Series Cricket), one cannot attribute *all* contemporary differences between English and Australian cricket crowds to the fact that the latter have been, like Australian society generally, more plebeian. Nonetheless, the contrast between Lord's and the Sydney Cricket Ground certainly corroborates the argument that social class is a crucial determinant of spectator behavior.[72]

V THE PEOPLE'S GAME

In the early nineteenth century, English football was still what it had been in medieval times, a "through and through game of the people . . . more than frowned upon as a pastime for gentlefolk."[73] The upper classes often watched but seldom admired the spectacle. In his *History of Derby* (1817), William Hutton mocked a football player "chaired through the streets like a successful member [of Parliament] although his utmost elevation of character was no more than that of a butcher's apprentice."[74] Within a generation, the game was transformed by the sons of those who mocked. In 1848, fourteen young men from Eton, Harrow, Rugby, Winchester, and other "public schools" agreed upon the Cambridge Rules (of which no copy exists).[75] In 1863, the "old boys" of Oxford and Cambridge formed the Football Association. The Bolton Wanderers, who won the first Cup Final in 1871, included four former Harrovians, three Etonians, and one man each from Westminster, Charterhouse, Oxford, and Cambridge.[76]

But soccer quickly underwent a second transformation. The schoolboys' modern form of the ancient village Shrovetide game began to attract large numbers of lower-class players and spectators. The graduates of Eton and Harrow found themselves playing clubs formed by the employees of the North Staffordshire Railway Company, the

Woolwich Arsenal, and the Thames Iron Works. (These clubs eventually became Stoke City, Arsenal, and West Ham United.) Aston Villa FC was formed in 1874 from a Bible Class at Villa Cross Wesleyan Chapel, but a butcher provided the playing field and a publican the dressing room. Beginning in 1847, a series of parliamentary factory acts freed workers from Saturday-afternoon labor. There was also an "undoubted improvement in real wages," which increased the workers' "discretionary spending power."[77]

Soccer crowds grew accordingly. They were often as large as 20,000 in the 1870s and 50,000 in the 1890s. For the Cup Final of 1923, 200,000 overflowed the capacity of Wembley Stadium. By the end of the century, the sport had become, once again, what it was in the Middle Ages: "the people's game." In 1901, *The Athletic News* concluded condescendingly that soccer, above all other games, "gladdens the hearts of the toilers."[78] As one historian of nineteenth-century leisure remarks, "middle-class claims for their own impact on the game have had more influence on the historiography of football than they have had on its practice."[79] Like music halls and the pubs, soccer games were an important part of what might be called "proletarian leisure." Such leisure was a means of "preserving the identity of a working class" and resisting middle-class "cultural hegemony."[80]

The coalminers and millhands who trudged over to the stadium to watch their mates at play expected to enjoy themselves in ways boisterous and uninhibited. Newspapers, which had in the 1840s published condemnations of folk football as "the assembling of a lawless rabble," began in the 1880s to carry disapproving notices of unruly soccer crowds.[81] The response of the Football Association was the familiar one: segregated seats, gate money, turnstiles, security guards. The date of Aston Villa's decision to charge gate money, 1874, coincides almost exactly with the end of free entry to race tracks.[82] Gate money had to be high enough to dissuade rowdies and low enough not to exclude the "respectable poor," who were assumed to have the sixpence necessary for entry and enough internalized middle-class morality to keep from wrecking the place. For the cheapest ticket, the spectator stood on earthen mounds or in terracing, perhaps under cover, perhaps not. The segregation achieved by differential pricing can be seen at Manchester United's grounds, Old Trafford, where, in 1910, it cost sixpence to enter the stadium but five shillings for a reserved seat in the center stand.[83] Needless to say, few manual workers wanted to lay out five shillings and risk a snub besides when they were able to stand with their chums for one tenth as much. That the workers *did* have sixpence to pay is certain. There is no doubt that by 1915 the "majority of those who went to watch professional football matches were working class in origin, occupation and life style."[84] They were skilled workers, foremen, tradesmen, clerks, and minor administrators.[85] Unlike the major cricket grounds, only two of which were in lower-class neighborhoods, nearly all the soccer stadia were built in what we might anachronistically call the "inner city." The location encouraged lower-class attendance and gave the upper and middle classes additional reason for staying away.

There is no dearth of evidence to prove that rowdy behavior persisted despite the clubs' attempts to quell it. When Preston North End beat Aston Villa 5–1 in 1885, there was a famous riot, vividly described by an eyewitness:

> Drummond . . . was assaulted by a young, well-dressed fellow who gave him a half hit and shove, saying "Oh, here's one of them." He was hemmed in and most unmercifully kicked, struck at, and poked . . . in the ribs with sticks. . . . The distance from the tent to the field gate is about 80 yards. The driver started at a brisk trot to cover this distance, and earth, small stones, rubbish of all sorts, began flying about our heads. When about ten yards from the gates, a gang rushed up and closed them. We were thus brought to a standstill in the midst of 2000 howling roughs. Thicker and faster came the stones, showers of spittle covered us; we were struck at over the side with sticks and umbrellas, and at last a big missile flew past my ear and caught Ross . . . on the side of the head, smashing his hat and down he dropped.[86]

When Blackburn insultingly fielded its second team on Christmas Day in 1890, Darwen took *its* first team off the field and sent in the reserve, whereupon the crowd rioted, uprooted the goalposts, and smashed windows. Referees frequently had to run the gauntlet of disgruntled spectators. In 1895, they were assaulted in Wolverhampton and Woolwich and splattered with mud at Sheffield. At the Scottish Cup Final of 1909, when Glasgow's Celtics (Roman Catholic) met Glasgow's Rangers (Protestant), spectators invaded the pitch and burned the goalposts and the nets. "A few policemen attempted to stem the flow but

they were beaten savagely."[87] The *Leicester Daily Mercury* described
the helplessness of the firemen who attempted to put out the blaze:

> When the barricading was broken down, the rioters piled the debris,
> poured whisky over it, and set the wood ablaze. The flames spread to
> the pay-boxes, which were only some 20 yards from a large tenement
> of dwellings. Great alarm prevailed, particularly when the firemen were
> attacked by the mob, and prevented from extinguishing the fire, for no
> sooner had they run out the hose than the crowd jumped on it, and,
> cutting it with knives and stones, rendered the efforts of the firemen
> useless. The woodwork of the boxes was completely destroyed, leaving
> only the corrugated iron roofs and lining, which were bent and twisted
> into fantastic shapes.[88]

Casualties included 138 people taken to Victoria Infirmary, among
them 58 policemen.

It is hardly surprising that soccer stadia did not attract large numbers
of female fans, but a few young women of the lower classes did accompany their fathers, brothers, and boyfriends to the terraces. Their
behavior seems to have been dismal. A letter to the *Birmingham Daily
Mail* from "A Citizen of Handsworth" expressed outrage at the sight
of "crowds of young girls, about 17 years of age, and also of youths
who were in such a state as to be a disgrace to a respectable citizen.
Some were rolling about the pavement utterly helpless and seemed to
have hardly the strength to do anything but curse, swear and endea-
vour to sing."[89] Alas, it is unclear whether the outraged citizen was
upset by the mere presence of teenage girls or because they were as
drunk and disorderly as the boys.

One modern authority concludes with a sigh that the working class
did "seem, on the whole, to have been supporters of a side rather than
lovers of the game for its own sake."[90] This judgment is mild compared
with that rendered by upper-class commentators of the 1890s. Discussing "The New Football Mania" in *Nineteenth Century*, Charles
Edwardes wrote, "The multitude flock to the field in their workaday
dirt, and with their workaday adjectives very loose on their tongues."[91]
And their workaday, or holiday, propensity to express frustration with
sticks and stones rather than with letters to the *Times* caused considerable upper-class concern.

The officials of the Football Association were forced to admit to

themselves that some of the spectators' expressions of anger were justified. In the early years of the sport, games rarely began on time and
referees were often drunk and incompetent. If one paid one's hard-
earned money, one expected the owners to hold up their end of the
bargain. The authorities bestirred themselves to remove some of the
immediate causes of spectator dissatisfaction. Both the Football Association and the openly professional Football League (founded in
1888) insisted that games start on time whether the stands were full
or not. Teams were required to be at full strength. Failure to comply
meant a fine of 250 pounds, i.e., the equivalent of gate money from
10,000 spectators. Chronically incompetent referees were disciplined.
Clubs were warned that it was their responsibility to control the spectators and stiff sanctions were imposed when the clubs were deemed
negligent.[92] As the clubs invested in larger stadia and expected increased gate money, closure was a serious penalty. In 1895, four
grounds were closed by the Football Association; in 1896, ten; in 1897,
six. The situation may have improved. In the years 1910–1912, only
four grounds were closed by the Football Association.[93] It is also possible that the perceived improvement was illusory. In Leicestershire,
for instance, there were five times as many "pitch invasions" in 1908–
1914 as in 1894–1900, when the situation was supposed to have been
at its worst. Of fifty-five incidents of local disorder reported in the
Leicester Daily Mercury for the years 1894–1914, only *three* appear
in the minutes of the Football Association. If Leicestershire was typical
of the rest of England, the authorities in London simply did not realize
how prevalent the disorders were.[94]

In the years between the wars, disorders at British soccer matches
continued. In 1930, for instance, the ground of the Glasgow Rangers
was closed "owing to the unruly conduct of their supporters during
the match with Northampton Town."[95] In 1934, a train was trashed
by Leicester City fans on the way home from a game in Birmingham:
"Windows were smashed, seats cut and torn, and the leather window-
straps slashed with knives."[96] On the whole, however, "the balance of
evidence for the period suggests that the rate of disorderliness was
declining."[97] In support of this conclusion, Eric Dunning and his
associates cite the increasing attendance of women at soccer matches.
Reporting on the 1927 Cup Final at Wembley, the *Leicester Mercury*
noted that "a remarkable feature was the number of women who had

accompanied their husbands and sweethearts. Many mothers carried babies in their arms."[98] Two years later, the same newspaper estimated that at least 50 percent of the railway passengers bound for the Cup Final were women.[99]

It is likely that many if not most of the women were the wives and daughters of lower-class men. By the 1920s, many middle-class Englishmen had long since abandoned soccer and adopted rugby football instead. In 1871, only eight years after the foundation of the Football Association, Rugby Football Union was formed. Unfortunately for those who sought a socially exclusive sport untainted by commerce, some members of the lower classes began to play rugby and to receive the economic assistance without which they could not have played. In order to reimburse the players for travel and "broken time" (i.e., time lost from work), the clubs needed more than the donations of middle-class sponsors. In 1895, twenty-two clubs from the Midlands, all of them committed to taking gate money, broke away from RFU to form Northern Rugby Football Union, which in 1922 became Rugby League. Still struggling to uphold the ideal of unpaid amateurism, still resisting "spectator-oriented professional sport," RFU remained an elitist institution into the 1960s.[100] Welsh amateur rugby has always had problems with unruly spectators, even in the 1880s, when visiting players who defeated the home team might, in the words of one aggrieved local newspaper, be "hustled and pushed, hooted and pelted with clods, mud and even stones." English rugby spectators were, however, a fairly orderly lot (at least until the 1960s).[101]

By the end of the nineteenth century, Association Football had become the world's most popular ballgame, exported from the British isles by colonial administrators, soldiers, engineers, teachers, and missionaries. The French took a while to overcome their traditional disdain for sports, but youths from four Parisian lycées (Carnot, Condorcet, St. Louis, Rollin) founded Le Racing-Club de France in 1882 and Le Stade Français a year later. Both clubs emphasized track and field in the summer and rugby in the winter. As rugby made headway among the upper classes, soccer caught on among the workers. Although it never quite rivaled the popularity of cycling, soccer became an important part of French lower-class culture. The "turbulent legacy" of traditional village football was bequeathed to modern spectators and "violence amongst the crowd was common from the start of the modern game."[102] Harassment of the players was common. When national pride was at stake, as it was when France played Scotland on New Year's Day in 1913, the spectators rampaged, stormed the pitch, and attacked the referee, who was saved by the police and players "and later smuggled out of the ground to avoid groups of angry French supporters baying for his blood." Some of the rioters went to the offices of *L'Auto* and blocked rue Montmartre for several hours until "they were finally dispersed by mounted police and soldiers with fixed bayonets."[103] In 1924 *La Nouvelle Revue du midi* complained,

> There is a new phenomenon in France: the "supporter." He will endure wind, rain and freezing temperatures to see his team. Capable of sudden and dramatic changes of mood, he abandons all critical or common sense and identifies himself with his side by wearing its colours, bawling out its songs and beating up the supporters of rival teams when the opportunity presents itself.[104]

Richard Holt, the historian of French sports, concludes that such behavior was a continuation of traditional behavior: "In town and country, youths who had formerly faced each other in open combat in the fields and market places began to congregate in the local stadium with broadly similar ends in view. . . . As a whole, spectator sports were less violent than former collective rituals."[105]

Once again, it is useful to look comparatively at the "same" sport. Although soccer is almost universally associated with the lower classes, the United States provides an instructive exception. American soccer, which was traditionally a sport for lower-class "ethnics," became popular in the 1970s when upper-middle-class Americans cast about for a ballgame suitable for boys who were under seven feet in height and weighed less than two hundred pounds. The recently defunct North American Soccer League managed to attract large numbers of these Americans. Among its fans, 74 percent were college-educated and 45 percent of them were women. It is therefore hardly an accident that the NASL was troubled by far less spectator violence than England's Football League, France's Fédération Française de Football Association, or Germany's *Bundesliga*.[106] The inability of the NASL to appeal to a larger audience than the upper middle classes may also explain why the outdoor league collapsed in 1985, although the indoor version continues.

VI THE IRISH AND OTHER BASEBALL FANS

On the whole, professional team sports in the United States have not created the problems of crowd control that they did in late-Victorian England or that they do today in Britain, Germany, Italy, Brazil, and a host of other countries at various points in the process of modernization. Although American journalists have made much of ugly behavior at recent baseball games, the generalization about relatively orderly American crowds holds even though baseball is a sport which has for over a century been more popular with blue-collar workers than with the leisure class.

Contrary to the misinformation that places the game's beginnings in bucolic Cooperstown, baseball was from its origins a part of urban culture.[107] Derived from the British children's game of rounders, baseball began to assume its modern form in New York in the 1840s.[108] By 1860, there were dozens of clubs in New York, four in Chicago, nine in New Orleans, and one in San Francisco. The first players and spectators were distinctly middle-class. "Far from attracting fans from all social ranks, New York's sports spectators prior to the Civil War came from no further down the social scale than the more prosperous members of the middle class."[109] Baseball was less elitist than cricket, but it was not yet "the national game." The Civil War accelerated the geographical diffusion of the game and it became popular with those who learned it while wearing the blue or the grey. In the postwar period, baseball far outstripped cricket (which had been quite popular in the East as late as the 1850s). Those who thronged to see the games of the National League, founded in 1876, were a very different demographic lot from those who had come out to watch the amateur teams of the prewar period. The leisure class spurned the baseball diamond. Photographs in the lavishly illustrated *Book of Sports* (1901) showed the American elite on the courts and links of their country clubs, but not a single illustration caught them at the ballpark.[110] The "national game" was not for them. In an age when the college-educated spectator waited eagerly for the football season and a chance to return to *alma mater* for the "Big Game," factory hands and office clerks sang "Take Me Out to the Ball Game" and clambered aboard the trolley that did just that.

It has been difficult, however, for poets and novelists in love with baseball and even for those trained as professional historians to acknowledge that "our national game" has attracted a predominantly lower-class audience.[111] In 1883, the *Boston Globe* commented that "every class, every station, every color and every nationality will be found at a ball match," but such comments cannot be taken at face value.[112] Skepticism is also appropriate in regard to Albert G. Spalding's self-serving claim that the supporters of his Chicago White Stockings came from the city's elite: "no theater, church, or place of amusement contains a finer class of people than can be found in our grandstands."[113] It was, of course, precisely because the urban elite was *not* found in the grandstands, much less in the bleachers, that Spalding and his fellow promoters struggled through the 1880s and 1890s to improve the public image of their investment. One reason for the National League owners' opposition to the upstart American Association was that the owners of the rival league sold beer at the ballpark, scheduled Saturday games, and charged twenty-five cents for admission (compared to fifty cents for most of the National League); these were all measures designed to tighten the game's hold on the skilled and unskilled workers who were its primary audience.[114]

In the United States, a class analysis of almost any social phenomenon can usefully be supplemented by an ethnic analysis, and baseball is no exception. Irish-American and German-American owners and players were disproportionately prominent in the post-Civil War years, and disproportionate numbers of these ethnic groups flocked to cheer for Michael Kelly, Honus Wagner, and others simultaneously representing memories of the old country and adaptation to the new. George Seymour comments in his multivolume history of the sport that the fans of these early years were "a very good cross section of the population," but he adds that the Irish and the Germans were the "most ardent baseball followers."[115] Both groups appear in a vignette from H. L. Mencken's autobiography; of his father's loyalty to the Baltimore team, Mencken wrote, "When it was on the road he would slip away from his office in the late afternoon to glim the score at

Kelly's oyster house in Eutaw Street."[116] For a fictionalized account
of a game he attended in 1909, Rollin Lynde Hartt invented "Mickey
O'Hooligan" as the archetypal fan. It was a likely choice. Boston's
Irish may have been better bred than Mr. O'Hooligan, but they were
fanatic enough to persuade Arthur Soden that it was a sound investment to pay "an unprecedented $10,000" to bring fabulous Michael
Kelly to the Braves in 1887.[118]

Baseball was especially dear to the hearts of the era's mostly Irish
political bosses, who catered to the needs of the needy and found their
most faithful followers among the immigrant groups. In Boston,
Michael T. McGreevey opened a saloon called "The Third Base" and
organized a fan club to boost the Braves. When the team swept the
1914 World Series from the Philadelphia Athletics, the "Royal Rooters" were joined at the ballpark by Mayor James Michael Curley,
former mayor John F. ("Honey Fitz") Fitzgerald, Governor David
Walsh, and a host of other Irish-American fans (and voters).[119] By the
1920s and 1930s, Tony Lazerri and Joe DiMaggio were playing major-
league baseball, for the Yankees no less, and Italian-Americans in the
bleachers were able to cheer with extra enthusiasm for a *paisano* on
the field. In 1941, 8 percent of all major leaguers were Italian-Americans, twice the percentage in the population as a whole, and there
is no doubt that Italian-American spectators were also overrepresented
in the stands.[120] The dreams and aspirations of youthful Jewish fans
have been nicely dramatized in two recent novels: Eric Rolfe Greenberg's *The Celebrant* (1983) and Robert Mayer's *The Grace of Short-
stops* (1984). Since both novels are set before the debuts of Hank
Greenberg and Sandy Koufax, the Jewish hero-worshippers idolize
Christy Mathewson and Pee Wee Reese. *Faute de mieux?* Between
the coming of racial segregation in the 1890s and the integration of
the National League in 1947, black fans chose between the games
offered by the exclusively white major and minor leagues, where they
were sometimes welcomed as spectators, sometimes not, and the contests of the Negro National League (1920) or the Negro American
League (1937), which fielded great players like Cool Papa Bell, Josh
Gibson, and Judy Johnson, but suffered from generally poor facilities
and frequently erratic schedules.[121]

At the earliest games played by the New York Knickerbockers, there
were ladies present (whose delicate complexions "were protected from

the sun by a colored canvas pavilion"). In the antebellum South, there were "commodious tents for the ladies spread under the umbrageous branches of the fine old live oaks."[122] As baseball became more popular, the percentage of women in the crowd diminished. The steelworkers and teamsters who knocked off early on Saturday in order to go directly from work to the ballpark did not, as a rule, bring their wives or girlfriends. When photographs of the crowd show men in caps more numerous than men in hats, few women are to be seen.[123] Of course, there have always been exceptions to the rule—women who knew every batting average on the team and cheered themselves hoarse every time their favorite slugger batted one out of the ballpark— but the impressionistic evidence of the nineteenth century agrees with the statistical surveys of the present: the "national game" has flourished with markedly more male than female support. An excursion photograph of Boston's "Royal Rooters," taken in September 1897, shows not a single female fan bold enough to accompany her husband, brother, or father to Baltimore.[124] Given the folklore of the game, which associates the players with tobacco juice, beer, mangled Lardneresque English, and Ruthian dalliance with "baseball Annies," it is small wonder that middle-class women have always shown resistance to the "national game." In addition to genteel repugnance, many women were fearful of what the *Boston Herald* called "baseball rowdyism."[125]

Realizing and lamenting the fact that half the population was staying away from the game, the National League, and then the American, made major efforts to entice women through the turnstiles. That there *were* turnstiles was important. At the first annual meeting of the National League, in 1877, it was agreed that attendance was to be tabulated by the new device and that visiting teams were to get fifteen cents of the standard fifty-cent admissions charge. A seat in the bleachers then cost an extra dime, a seat in the grandstand an extra quarter. While few who favored such charges justified them publicly as a means to screen out the less "respectable" lower classes, some segments of the press complained that few workers were able to pay for tickets, which cost the equivalent of roughly 20 percent of a day's pay.[126] Hoping to replace the *Lumpenproletariat* with the ladies, the baseball magnates instituted "Ladies' Days." The Knickerbockers began in 1867 to set aside the last Thursday of each month as Ladies'

Day, "at which time members [of the club] were requested to invite their wives, daughters, and girl friends. . . . When the professionals took over the game, the owners soon adopted the practice."[127] The custom was to admit the ladies free if accompanied by a "gentleman" (defined as a paying male). At least one ballpark constructed a special entry that led from the carriage park to the grandstand "so that ladies could reach their seats without passing through boisterous crowds."[128]

Ladies' Days had the full support of the press, which lauded the presence of "the fairer portion of creation, whose presence ever gives additional zest and luster to all amusements."[129] Some journalists expressed the fond hope that the women whom the rowdies frightened away might yet become the means by which the savages were tamed. The *New York Chronicle* opined that "the presence of an assemblage of ladies purifies the moral atmosphere" and represses "all the outburst of intemperate language which the excitement of the contest so frequently induces."[130] The influential *Sporting News* noted with evident satisfaction that men were "more choice in the selection of adjectives" when the women were present.[131]

When women did take to baseball, it was not uncommon for their motives to be questioned (as have the motives of female spectators since Roman times). Heywood Broun's novel *The Sun Field* (1923) describes a Vassar-educated journalist's initial antipathy for the game. She overcomes her dislike when she falls in love with a player "with a line from his shoulder to the tip of his fingers as fine as anything in Greek sculpture," but it is difficult to know how many real women were converted to the old ball game by philhellenic eroticized aestheticism.[132]

VII FIGHT FANS

If baseball has appealed to relatively few female spectators, prizefights have been even less popular. Although the women of eighteenth-century England's lower classes turned up for (and even participated in) pugilism, nineteenth-century and early-twentieth-century women seem to have lined up in a phalanx to express not lack of interest but positive repugnance. The fight fans pictured in George Bellows' lurid pictures, *Both Members of the Club* and *Dempsey and Firpo*, are all men. Indeed, it is a hackneyed theme of popular literature that the fighter's girlfriend and mother kneel down and beg for their loved one to hang up his gloves before he is battered senseless. If female fight fans tended to be prostitutes or gangster molls who rather liked the ring's sweaty aura of ostentatious masculinity, it was partly because they, unlike their sheltered middle-class sisters, were already accustomed to a good deal of daily violence.

Nineteenth-century and early twentieth-century fights were no place for a lady. Middle-class opinion held that they were no place for a gentleman either. For most of the nineteenth century, prizefights were illegal in England and America. In addition to disliking the inherent brutality of the sport, proper Victorians feared the ever-present possibility of mob violence. Ironically, illegality meant that the police were not available to control the crowd. In fact, it was often the unwanted arrival of the constables which set off the riot.

Another motive for middle-class disapproval can be glimpsed in a Royal Commission report of 1842, which complained of Warwickshire coalminers leaving the pits five or six times a summer to see a fight.[133] Some Englishmen felt that leisure was for the leisure class (and some Puritanical souls were so committed to the work ethic that they felt that *no one* should waste time at play).

While nineteenth-century fight fans came mostly from the lower classes, there were some bouts which apparently aroused the interest of just about everyone. Typically, it was nationalism which overcame genteel dislike of professional fisticuffs. On the eve of the Civil War, as angry Southerners gathered to consider secession, James C. Heenan of the United States invaded England to challenge Tom Sayers for $1,000 and the championship of the world. The *New York Times* thought that the fight excited all classes, "eclipsing the Charleston Convention and throwing completely into shadow all political themes."[134] This was also the surprised judgment of Salomon de Rothschild.[135] The fight, which took place on April 17, 1860, was stopped in the 42d round and declared a draw, which allowed the British to claim victory for Sayers and the Americans for Heenan. "Throughout the land—in respectable Victorian homes, as in respectable Victorian newspapers—millions who normally ranked pugilists with common criminals hailed an illiterate bruiser as a national hero." On April 28, the *Vanderbilt* docked in New York with two tons of

English newspapers. The next day, the *New York Herald* ran seven columns on Heenan's heroic feat.[136] Currier and Ives produced an unrealistic print, *The Great Fight for the Championship*, in which the spectators—all men—wear top hats and sit stiffly a good ten yards from the ring. When George Eliot's stepson wrote home to say that he had pummeled his landlord as Sayers had Heenan, there was no need to explain the allusion. Everybody knew about "the fight."[137]

Such attention from the respectable world was unusual. Where prizefights were not illegal, they were lamented and disparaged. Around John L. Sullivan, the "Boston Strong Boy," controversy swirled:

> A braggart, a brawler, and a drunkard throughout most of his career, he squandered his earnings and ten years after his last fight was forced to file for bankruptcy. But he counted presidents and crown princes among his friends and admirers.[138]

Irish-American politicians were eager to bask in Sullivan's fame. Mayor Hugh O'Brien and seven other members of Boston's City Council showed up in 1887 when the pugilist was presented with a magnificent diamond-studded gold belt. The *Evening Transcript*, which represented Brahmin upper-class Boston, was appalled at the Mayor's "amazing performance."[139] While the "shanty Irish" idolized Sullivan as one of their own, the "lace-curtain Irish" who read *Donahoe's Magazine* distanced themselves from him; *they* saw Sullivan not as a symbol of Erin's manhood but rather as a reminder of the unflattering stereotypes they had labored to overcome.[140] When Sullivan lost his heavyweight crown to James Corbett in 1892, the *New York Times* crowed that "the dethronement of a mean and cowardly bully as the idol of the barrooms is a public good."[141]

As far as respectable opinion was concerned, championship bouts were bad news, but club fights were even worse. They were part of the lower-class male subculture symbolized by *The Police Gazette*, whose publisher, Nat Fleischer, was one of the prize ring's most faithful publicists. No one has bettered Paul Gallico's description of the cultural contrast between the fight crowd and the tennis set:

> One afternoon you might be at the tennis tournament at Forest Hills,

between matches drinking an iced tea at little iron tables set out on the close-clipped green lawn, beneath gay, colored umbrellas, surrounded by beautifully dressed women and soft-spoken men in summer flannels; and the next you might find yourself sitting at a spotted, rickety wooden table in a frowsy, ribald fight camp, gagging over a glass of needle beer and eating a steak sandwich, surrounded by lop ears, stumblebums, cheap, small-time politicians, fight managers, ring champions, floozies, gangsters, Negroes, policemen, and a few actors thrown in for good measure.[142]

Despite (or perhaps because of) their association with a violent subculture of masculinity, the championship fights of the 1920s became fashionable. Suddenly, the "flappers and philosophers" immortalized by F. Scott Fitzgerald put down their tennis rackets and rushed to the ringside. The first of the fights which "everyone" had to see was an international encounter, the mismatch between Jack Dempsey and Georges Carpentier at Boyle's Thirty Acres, Jersey City, on July 2, 1921. For the event, George "Tex" Rickard built stands for over 90,000 people. The celebrities present included not only the big names of "show biz" but also such aristocrats and plutocrats as Vincent Astor, Henry Ford, Joseph W. Harriman, John Ringling, John D. Rockefeller, Jr., Kermit Roosevelt, William H. Vanderbilt, Harry Payne Whitney, and the Prince of Wales. The press estimated that 2,000 women were present, including Alice Roosevelt Longworth. Many of the same names appeared in the press reports of the Jack Dempsey–Gene Tunney fight of September 23, 1926. Their heirs, literal and metaphorical, purchased ringside seats to "be there" for the fights of Joe Louis and Muhammad Ali.[143]

The enthusiasm of lords, ladies, and robber barons for bare-knuckled and gloved brawlers has been shared by men of letters from Byron's day to Norman Mailer's. Writers as different as George Bernard Shaw, Bertolt Brecht, Ernest Hemingway, and Jean Cocteau have been fight fans. Although Americans might imagine that American novelists have been especially susceptible to the lure of the ring and the roar of the crowd, French scholars are just as convinced that *their* authors have had a special relationship to pugilism.[144]

White support for black fighters is a very recent phenomenon. The worst outbreaks of sports-related violence in American history have occurred when racial partisanship intensified the emotions of the fans. On July 4, 1910, when Jack Johnson faced James Jeffries, Reno, Nevada, was a powderkeg. The spectators were asked to check their guns at the gate. The clearly partisan band played "All Coons Look Alike to Me," and Johnson was greeted by racial slurs. As word of Johnson's easy triumph over the "Great White Hope" was telegraphed around the nation, the response was violent:

> In Houston, Charles Williams openly celebrated Johnson's triumph, and a white man "slashed his throat from ear to ear"; in Little Rock, two blacks were killed by a group of whites after an argument about the fight in a streetcar; in Roanoke, Virginia, six blacks were critically beaten by a white mob; in Norfolk, Virginia, a gang of white sailors injured scores of blacks; in Wilmington, Delaware, a group of blacks attacked a white and whites retaliated with a "lynching bee"; in Atlanta a black ran amuck with a knife; in Washington . . . two whites were fatally stabbed by blacks; in New York City, one black was beaten to death and scores were injured; in Pueblo, Colorado, thirty people were injured in a race riot; in Shreveport, Louisiana, three blacks were killed by white assailants. Other murders or injuries were reported in New Orleans, Baltimore, Cincinnati, St. Joseph, Los Angeles, Chatanooga, and many other smaller cities and towns.

Reno itself was fairly quiet.[145]

Among Afro-Americans, Johnson became a folk hero comparable to the legendary John Henry. When Johnson returned to Chicago after the fight, he was greeted by 10,000 blacks and by the 8th Regiment Band playing "There'll Be a Hot Time in the Old Town Tonight." In North Carolina, Negroes sang, to the tune of "Amazing Grace,"

> Amaze an' Grace, how sweet it sounds,
> Jack Johnson knocked Jim Jeffries down.

Another song, popular a few years later, was often sung by "Leadbelly" (Huddie Ledbetter); it imagined Johnson mocking the sinking *Titanic*, whose captain had allegedly refused to let the black champion book passage on the doomed ship.[146]

Outbreaks of ring-related racial violence decreased in the 1920s when Jack Dempsey and other champions "drew the color line" and refused to risk their crowns against black challengers, but when Joe Louis won the title in 1937 similar outbreaks occurred, and they have occurred ever since (but never on the scale of 1910). When Louis defeated Primo Carnera in 1935, the *Pittsburgh Courier* reported, "Harlem is hilarious with joy."[147] When he defeated Max Baer, the novelist Richard Wright described the exuberance of Chicago's blacks, who "seeped out of doorways, oozed from alleys, trickled out of tenaments, and flowed down the street; a fluid mass of joy."[148] Since Louis, often introduced patronizingly as "a credit to his race," was most definitely not a "bad nigger" of the Jack Johnson variety, his reign was considerably more acceptable, if not exactly popular, among white fans. In 1938, the reluctance of white spectators to accept a black representative of masculine valor was diminished, but definitely not eliminated. When Louis sought to avenge his 1935 loss to Max Schmeling, who was loaded down with the heavy burden of Adolf Hitler's best wishes, Louis had the endorsement of Franklin Delano Roosevelt, who invited him to the White House. An amazing 64 percent of all American radios were tuned in on the evening of June 22 and all but the most incorrigible racists were symbolically in Louis's corner.[149] As the German approached the ring, patriotic spectators screamed curses and pelted him with trash.[150] By knocking Schmeling out in 124 seconds, Louis became the first black boxer accepted as an idol by large numbers of white Americans.

The Brown Bomber's significance for black Americans can scarcely be overestimated. Lena Horne, then singing with Noble Sissle's band, has described her feelings as Joe Louis lost to Schmeling in their first encounter:

> We had the radio on behind the bandstand and during the breaks we crowded around it to hear the fight. I was near hysteria toward the end of the fight when he was . . . badly beaten and some of the men in the band were crying. . . . Joe was the one invincible Negro, the one who stood up to the white man and beat him down with his fists. . . . But this night he was just another Negro getting beaten by a white man.[151]

For the black bourgeoisie as well as for those trapped in the ghetto, for Afro-Americans as different as Maya Angelou, Ralph Bunche, Duke Ellington, Richard Wright, and Malcolm X, the sharecropper's son was a hero.

VIII SOCIAL CLASS AND SPECTATOR BEHAVIOR

The years from Victoria's coronation in 1837 to the outbreak of war in 1939 saw the emergence of modern sport as a mass phenomenon. While the perennial tendency to separate the social classes at their play was certainly not eliminated, as the spread of the socially discriminatory country club attested, there were also integrating forces at work. Whether the egalitarian ideals of democracy or the commercial possibilities of capitalistic exploitation were stronger is impossible to say because democratization and commercialization both impelled sports in the direction of more widely inclusive participation and spectatorship. In most sports, the gates were thrown open (and now there *were* definitely gates) to women as well as men, to the poor as well as the rich, to black as well as white (but not yet on equal terms). The problem for the sponsors and purveyors of modern sports was not to keep the mob away but rather to transform it into a crowd of enthusiastic but nonetheless well-behaved (or at least nonviolent) spectators. One way to achieve this was to preach the doctrine of fair play, good sportsmanship, and gentlemanly spectatorship. This was done in schools and universities, in the press, and in juvenile literature. Another means to the end was to construct stadiums and arenas to which access was strictly controlled and within which social classes tended to be separated by different ticket prices. If these measures proved inadequate, promoters and sponsors relied on the police, off-duty or dispatched by the authorities.

A less frequently discussed factor deserves more detailed comment. The economic and temporal costs of travel to away games were, even in an age of rail transportation, relatively high when measured against the wages of the average working man. The youthful apprentice who was passionately eager to stand up for the London-based Tottenham Hotspurs simply did not have the means to take off to the Midlands to scuffle with the misguided fans of Manchester United. This geographical factor certainly helps to explain why, despite the informality of an officially egalitarian society, lower-class American spectators were more pacific than their British and French counterparts. The enormous distances between the rival franchises of professional team sports must have reduced the level of spectator violence. The railroad network of the Northeast was in place by the late nineteenth century and was, indeed, a prerequisite for the establishment of baseball's National League in 1876, but few supporters of the New York Giants were able to follow the team on trips to Chicago or St. Louis. The Giants and the Brooklyn Dodgers were the only teams whose supporters were liable to encounter each other with any regularity. The reputation of the proverbial Dodger fan doubtless has something to do with this proximity. Even today, in an age of jet travel, only the wealthiest fans are ready to pay transcontinental airfare simply to root for the home team away. The tendency of American distances has been to separate the fans of rival teams.

In the United States as in Great Britain, local rivalries are often the fiercest and it is precisely at the local level that American sports have been most violent. When proximity exacerbates racial, religious, and class differences, which is often the case in American cities, clashes have been so extreme that spectators are now barred from many high-school football and basketball games. As modern communication and transportation bring us all closer together, the effects of distance are diminished. Eric Dunning notes that England's soccer hooliganism became a serious social problem in the late 1950s when "younger fans were less restricted to their immediate localities. In growing numbers they were enabled, by the improved, cheap transportation system and their capacities to pay, to travel regularly all over the country in support of their teams, thus spreading the incidence of violence and vandalism at matches."[152]

Above and beyond these sports-specific factors there was the general tendency of "the civilizing process." Throughout Western society, behavior in public places has been—at least until recently—characterized by a general decrease in expressive violence. While the instrumental violence epitomized by depersonalized modern warfare has been on the rise, spontaneous outbreaks of uncontrollable rage have been waning.

Looking back on the period from the perspective of the late twentieth century, one might conclude that the tumult and disorder of

Victorian days was far less than it might have been given the political, economic, and social exploitation of those on top. Dunning and his associates have estimated that there were over 2,000 cases of spectator misconduct at English soccer matches in the years 1908–1914, but this scary number means that for all of England there were 8.8 incidents a week.[153] When one considers that hundreds of thousands of lower-class spectators jammed the terraces weekly, one might well conclude that English miners, longshoremen, truckdrivers, and factory hands were a rather respectable lot of good chaps who had actually internalized a large measure of middle-class restraint. It is true that Victorian enthusiasts were naïve to think that sports taught "fortitude, gentleness, meekness, and fair play."[154] They were probably wrong to think that developments in sports were a major force in bringing about the greater restraint and civility of life in the Victorian and Edwardian ages, but the least one can say is that sports were involved in the same sorts of transformations as the rest of society. There is no reason to doubt that modern sports, despite considerable residual violence, contributed their bit to the "civilizing process."

II
Contemporary Spectators

FIVE
MEDIATED SPECTATORSHIP

I SHIFTING METHODOLOGICAL GEARS

THE SPORTS SPECTATORS of the 1930s took the streetcar or the subway to the stadium, bought a ticket at the kiosk, and made their way through the turnstile. Fifty years later, the spectators either have a season ticket or, in the case of one-time events, dial Ticketron (or its equivalents) for a computer-assisted reservation. If assured of a place to park, they are more likely to drive than to take public transportation. Where spectators once came dressed in straw hats or derbies, or in white dresses and feathered hats, their grandsons and daughters are likely to show up in blue jeans and leather jackets or in shorts and T-shirts. Baseball fans are liable nowadays to loll barechested in the sun and even Wimbledon crowds are liable to cause grim lips among the straitlaced.

Spectators of the 1930s knew that each sport had its season. Today's fans can look forward to, or dread, the day when soccer, football, baseball, basketball, hockey, golf, and tennis compete simultaneously for their attention. Although the phenomenon has not yet afflicted Europe, American spectators experience anew the kind of organizational instability that marked the first decades of modern sports: "gypsy" franchises that move suddenly from one city to another, entire leagues that appear, announce their challenge to the established circuits, and collapse. Wholly new sports, like hang gliding, float into place along with modern versions of the martial arts, like judo and karate. Pseudosports like Roller Derby have suddenly attracted immense numbers of lower-class female fans and have just as suddenly disappeared, leaving behind banked tracks and a film with Raquel Welch.[1]

Among the established sports, there are constant shifts in relative popularity. Professional football, American style, became far more popular in the postwar period than it had been. In the same years, basketball arenas began to dot the European landscape and American blacks suddenly found themselves household names in cities like Milano and Napoli. Tickets to women's gymnastics became intensely sought-after Olympic prizes and club fights now attract crowds so small that some have begun to fear (and others hope) that pugilism might die a natural death.

How can any scholar, immersed in modernity's plethora of data and buffeted by a welter of contradictory trends, tendencies, and fads, sensibly discuss anything as complex as sports spectatorship in the latter half of the twentieth century? How can one avoid both the Scylla of triviality (the economics of the concessions booth) and the Charybdis of otiosity (a sport-by-sport and country-by-country analysis of the demographic composition of the contemporary sports crowd)? The dilemma is familiar. Equally familiar is the response. We seek the field of investigation that seems important to us, devote years to our research, and hope that others will agree that the game was worth the candle.

Since most of the basic patterns of spectatorship were established by the end of the 1930s, what are some of the fundamental questions to be asked about contemporary sports spectators? Four questions seem to justify sustained consideration. (1) What have been the consequences of modern communications, especially television? (2) Has sports spectatorship become, as Neo-Marxist critics allege, the newest "opiate of the masses," dulling sensibilities, inducing apathy, and distracting energy from necessary political engagement? (3) Has the level of spectator violence begun to arise again after centuries of decline? (4) What are the actual and the ideal motivations of sports spectatorship? Although it turns out, not unexpectedly, that these questions are related, I shall discuss them separately in this and the next three chapters.

II MODERN SPORTS JOURNALISM

Now that an entire generation has grown up assuming that life without television is an impossibility, it may be useful to remind ourselves that sportscasting began with radio, not with TV, and that sports journalism in print is older still. A few comments on sports magazines and on the golden age of radio sports are in order.

Beyond the obvious fact that the audience for the earliest printed reports had to be literate (or to rely on someone able to read aloud), we know next to nothing about those who read early periodicals like *The Sporting Magazine* and *The Spirit of the Times*. Internal evidence, always circumstantial, suggests a fairly affluent and educated audience able to understand literary references and Latin tags but also cognizant of the Fancy's fancy slang. Presumably, the purchaser of such a journal was not destitute, but even this is a presumption; twentieth-century fans have been known to deprive themselves of "necessities" in order to buy tickets to a game. Since the tastes and preferences of the readers inevitably exert strong pressure on the editors, one can assume that early-nineteenth-century British and American readers were especially enthusiastic about horse races, field sports, and pugilism. By the middle of the century, popular journals in the United States featured stories about baseball while their British and German counterparts opted for soccer and French periodicals began to follow *le vélocipède* on its merry career. By the end of the century, there was an audience for magazines like *Outing*, which reported on regattas and Derby Day, on bicycle tours of the Far East, and hunting expeditions in the Wild West.

Since different sports appeal to different social strata, the spectrum of specialized magazines corresponds to the class structure of modern society, but it should be emphasized that the readers of sports magazines are, in general, likely to be better off economically than the average person. While 9 percent of upper-class Germans read the distinguished intellectual weekly, *Die Zeit*, 7 percent of them also read Germany's most popular sports magazine, *Der Kicker*.[2] Statistics on the readership of *L'Equipe* also indicate an appeal to the advantaged members of French society.[3] *Runner's World* reports periodically on the advanced education and affluence of its readers.[4] It is no surprise when *Boating* boasts that 73 percent of its subscribers are college-educated, but *Bowling*, struggling to convince advertisers that *its* subscribers are *not* all waitresses and housewives, claims 55.6 percent of them are college-educated, which suggests that American bowlers are better educated than golfers (*Golf Digest*'s subscribers are a mere 52 percent college-educated).[5]

No periodical which pretends to cover sports in general has ever devoted as much attention to female as to male athletes. Popular journals appealing to the lower classes, like *The Police Gazette*, were to be found not on the library tables of elegant homes but rather in bars, barber shops, and fire stations. *Their* readership was predominantly male (and their interest in women's sports tended to be confined to voyeuristic accounts of "lady" wrestlers). General sports magazines appealing to the better educated and more affluent devote more space to women's sports. From the 1880s to the 1920s, *Outing* published numerous essays reporting on and strongly advocating women's participation in sports; from 1954 to the present, *Sports Illustrated* has gradually increased its coverage of, and its covers featuring, women's sports. It seems reasonable to assume that significant numbers of middle-class and upper-class women once perused *Outing* and now read *Sports Illustrated*. In fact, women now account for approximately 13 percent of *Sports Illustrated*'s readership. The similarity of European to American patterns of readership is striking; in 1962, 18 percent of the readers of *L'Equipe* were women.[6] A decade later, a German scholar of the sporting press reported identical results: 18 percent of the German readers were women.[7] The readership of Rio de Janeiro's *Jornal dos Sports* is 19 percent female, which seems remarkable in a society even more patriarchal than those of Europe and North America.[8]

Inevitably, journals specializing in male-dominated sports like soccer have mostly male readers. *Fussballwoche* has eleven male readers for every female.[9] This seems appropriate for a game played mostly by males, but other statistics require interpretation. Although *Boating* reports that 97.7 percent of its subscribers are male, one cannot conclude that only a handful of women actually read the magazine; one must assume that many women who love to sail are content to have their male relatives do the actual subscribing. One's suspicions about a mismatch between reported data and the real world increases when *Bowling* maintains that only 17.6 percent of *its* readers are women.

If we look not at the gender of the subscribers but at the reading habits of the public at large, we have a somewhat different picture. Scientific survey data indicate that 43 percent of all German men but only 14 percent of the women read about sports (which corresponds to the fact that 39 percent of the men and only 11 percent of the women actually attend sporting events on a regular basis).[10] *These* credible data imply that one-third of the readers of German sports magazines must be women.

Adolescents are the age group most likely to participate in sports and they are certainly readers of sports magazines, but they are less likely than their more financially secure elders to be subscribers. The median ages for subscribers are: *Boating* 46 years, *Golf Digest* 39.8 years, *Bowling* 26.1 years. Since *Bowling* also asserts that there are as many five-to-eleven-year-old bowlers as there are those over fifty years of age, one must distrust either one's impressions or the stereotype-shattering statistics.

Although we have some data on the social class, gender, and age of the sports-magazine readers, we skate toward thin ice when we speculate about their racial identity. The evidence is almost entirely inferential. Since the racial minorities of Europe and the United States are less likely, for economic as well as cultural reasons, to participate in sports, it is probable that they are also underrepresented as readers. Then, too, racial minorities are in general less literate than the white majority. On the other hand, the salience of sports heroes for disadvantaged groups is a reason for general magazines, like *Ebony*, to pay what may seem disproportionate attention to athletic achievement.

On the whole, scholars (as opposed to advertisers) know little about the readership of sports magazines. This should not surprise literary historians because it is a truism among them that there is almost no empirical evidence pertinent to the readers of fiction about whom scholars have been making confident statements for approximately two hundred years. What we do know about sports-magazine readers tends to come from internal evidence (the literary scholar's favorite source) or from self-interested surveys conducted with an eye on advertisers. The internal evidence may or may not tell us something about the readers: do teenagers focus on stories about teenagers? are essays about women's sports read only by women? The survey data, which many editors are reluctant to release, are a help, but skepticism is called for.[11] An editor must be superhumanly honest to report to potential advertisers that his readers are young, poorly educated, and unemployed. It is best to admit that our picture is a blurred one.

III RADIO SPORTS

Some of the same methodological problems appear when we look at radio. The medium was most deeply involved in sportscasting in the 1930s and 1940s, after which time it more or less abandoned the national market to television, while still playing an important role in broadcasting games of local franchises. Since statistically sophisticated audience surveys were practically unknown in radio's heyday, and we seldom have a record now of what was actually said then, we know even less about the radio fan than about the newspaper and magazine reader. The A. C. Nielsen Company has made a science of finding out exactly who is tuned in to what television program, but one can only conjecture about the radio audience of the twenties, thirties, and forties.

On July 2, 1921, the era of network sports broadcasting was inaugurated when RCA's WJZ broadcast the Dempsey–Carpentier fight from Boyle's Thirty Acres in Jersey City. A month later, on August 5, KDKA Pittsburgh did a play-by-play of the Pirates versus the Phillies at Forbes Field. [12] There must have been some initial skepticism about the receptivity of the audience. Listening to a game of baseball or soccer is obviously a mild form of sensual deprivation. Skepticism proved unfounded. Millions of people tuned in to hear the crack of unseen bats and to hear about the hooks, jabs, and uppercuts of invisible boxers. Two years after Dempsey battled Carpentier, an estimated two million people heard the Firpo–Willard fight. By 1927, fifty million listened to Graham McNamee's blow-by-blow account of the second Dempsey–Tunney bout. [13] German fans had to wait until 1925 for "live" broadcasts; in July of that year Sender Muenster reported on a crew contest and then, in November, a soccer match between Arminia Bielefeld and Muenster Preussen. [14] Because the BBC had signed restrictive contracts with the news agencies, British listeners had to wait until 1927 for the first running commentaries on sports. [15] Some hallowed British institutions, like the Henley Regatta, resisted the temptation even then and opted for exclusivity. The National Olympic Committee of the Netherlands refused to allow broadcasts from the games held at Amsterdam in 1928 and financial problems hindered broadcasts of the games from Los Angeles in 1932, but the Berlin Olympics of 1936 provided the basis for a "monumental radio show."[16]

Inevitably, at least in the United States and other countries choosing privately owned rather than state-run broadcasting, corporate sponsors moved in to exploit the commercial possibilities of an eager audience. By 1934, Henry Ford paid $100,000 for the rights to baseball's World Series. By 1945, all the clubs had overcome their initial reluctance to "give away" their product. By that time, sportscasters like Mel Allen (the New York Yankees) and Red Barber (the Brooklyn Dodgers) had become local heroes whose voices were instantly recognized by millions of people.

Assuming correctly that the sports audience was predominantly male, the Gillette Safety Razor Company played a major role in sports-related radio advertising. Brewers were quick to follow.[17]

The impressionistic evidence from Europe indicates the same demographic pattern as in the United States. Radio audiences were disproportionately male. Unless this audience was a sociological anomaly within the structure of organized sports, the audiences contained disproportionately few older people, poor people, and members of racial or ethnic minorities.

Radio differs from the print media in many ways. One important difference is its immediacy. Most newspapers are read within the space of a few hours, but it is impossible to imagine that millions of readers have ever read their papers at *exactly* the same moment. With radio, however, we can be sure of simultaneity: apart from the possibilities of taped replay, everyone listens at the same time. This may seem like an obvious and trivial point to make, but it is a point which helps to explain regional and national outbursts of sports-related violence. Radio made it possible for millions of people simultaneously to experience the thrill of a game. Radio made it possible for *all* black Americans to exult while Joe Louis pounded his white opponents. Small wonder that celebrations broke out across the length and breadth of the land. Small wonder that some of them turned violent. Had radio rather than the telegraph flashed the news of Jack Johnson's victory over Jim Jeffries in 1910, the appalling toll of killed and injured would probably have been even higher than it was.

On a smaller scale, radio made possible the kind of instant citywide celebration of victory by the local college team or professional franchise. In a model study, a pair of political scientists have shown how the broadcast of an away-game triumph set the stage for a celebration, how the radio announcement of the team's arrival time enabled thousands of physically distant people to converge upon the airport, how radio in a certain sense *caused* the violence that ensued when the celebration became too boisterous.[18] Each season now brings repetitions of the pattern.

IV THE WIDE WORLD OF TELEVISION SPORTS

Television represents—at least at present—the ultimate stage of mediated experience (and the last word in audience monitoring).[19] Indeed, the illusion of immediacy is so powerful that today's journalists can plausibly tell us that we are really *there*. Whether one agrees or disagrees with Marshall McLuhan's notorious theories about "hot" (radio) and "cool" (television) media, one fact is indisputable: the new electronic medium displaced the radio in the lives of sports fans.[20] In the 1930s radio was an essential part of almost everyone's daily life; by the end of the 1940s, the average American listened to the radio for only twenty-four minutes a day.[21]

Although the French began to experiment in 1935 with a transmitter placed upon the Eiffel Tower, the first regular telecasts began in Berlin on January 15, 1936.[22] The Olympic Games, held in Berlin that summer, became the world's first major television event, in which 150,000 people were able to watch the flickering picture transmitted to 27 *Fernsehstuben* ("TV locales") scattered through the city.[23] The BBC began to experiment with television in late 1936 and covered the Oxford–Cambridge boat race of 1937.[24] The United States entered the era of sports television on May 17, 1939, when NBC affiliate W2XBS New York sent Bill Stern to telecast a baseball encounter between Columbia and Princeton on the former's field.[25] An estimated two hundred sets were already in place in the New York area.[26] The poor quality of the picture disguised the potential of the medium, but NBC was pleased enough with the outcome of the experiment to offer the viewers a boxing match, two weeks later, in which Lou Nova defeated Max Baer and thus won the dubious privilege of facing Joe

Louis. Further telecasts followed in 1940, but the immense popularity of televised sports came after the war, when larger screens, improved pictures, closeups, slow motion, color, instant replays, and split screens provided an experience rivaling and in some ways surpassing that to be had in the stadium.

In the earlier years of televised sports, however, technical limitations strongly influenced the networks' selection of events to be offered to the public. The large size of the baseball field and the smallness of the ball and the swiftness of its motion, plus the fact that the ball is likely to go in one direction while the runner goes in another, make the game relatively unsuited for television. Boxing, on the other hand, seemed ideal for the TV camera, which could be trained on two men in a small space. The result was a glut of matches, which reduced the live audience at Madison Square Garden by as much as 80 percent and eventually provided the television viewers with more fisticuffs than they wanted. (In 1952, boxing was able to attract 31 percent of the prime-time audience; by 1959, the share had sunk to 10.6 percent and the networks began to bail out.)[27]

Initially, no one seemed to realize what the new medium was destined to do to sports as an institution. The Fédération Internationale de Football Association, which sponsors the quadrennial World Cup soccer championship, gave away the rights to its 1954 spectacle in Bern, Switzerland, and considered itself lucky to get the publicity.[28] Forty-five stations in eight European countries allowed most of the continent to watch the German team carry off the trophy. In 1982, FIFA received over one hundred million German marks for radio and TV rights.[29] Avery Brundage, president of the International Olympic Committee from 1952 to 1972, doubted that the networks would be willing to pay for the rights to the games. (When he discovered that the contrary was true, he was far-sighted enough to worry about the impending transformation of "amateur" sports by the influx of huge sums of media money.)[30]

Brundage was unquestionably wrong about the reluctance of the networks to pay. After experiments with the winter games in Cortina d'Ampezzo in 1956 proved the feasibility of Olympic television, the National Olympic Committee of Italy sold the rights to the 1960 games, which were held in Rome. NBC agreed in 1961 to pay

$600,000 for the rights to the 1964 games in Tokyo. Although European networks, including those of the Soviet bloc, have paid millions of dollars for television rights, the commercially operated American networks are the major source of this particular variety of Olympic gold. For the Olympic spectacles of 1984, Eurovision managed to come up with less than $20 million while ABC paid $92 million for the winter games in Sarajevo and $225 million for rights to the summer games in Los Angeles. ABC spent an additional $100 million to produce its coverage. The huge investment was economically sound. The network found sponsors who were ready to pay as much as $520,000 a minute for the right to interrupt the athletic action with their advertisements. While the runners, swimmers, and gymnasts reaped their golden, silver, and bronze harvest, ABC gleaned an estimated $650 million. (Olympians like Carl Lewis, Edwin Moses, Mary Decker, and Joan Benoit have also earned hundreds of thousands of dollars as a result of their vividly televised performances in Los Angeles.) Supported by the sale of TV rights, direct contributions from some of the nation's largest corporations, and an army of volunteer workers, the financially astute organizers of the Los Angeles games closed out their affairs with a net profit of approximately $250 million, the first surplus since the last time the Olympics had been staged in Los Angeles in 1932. Whether or not ABC will recoup the $309 million it has offered for the winter games in Calgary in 1988 remains to be seen (as is the case with NBC's similar offer for the 1988 summer games in South Korea), but the offer itself is evidence that the most experienced of Olympic televisers have faith that the bubble is not going to burst—at least not yet.[31]

At the dawn of the Age of Television, the owners of American sports franchises were no more prescient than Brundage was. Their initial reaction was to protect their "gate" from the threat of "free" entertainment at home. They sought, at a very minimum, to prevent the transmission of home games. There seemed to be good reason for apprehension. Minor-league baseball attendance declined from a peak of 42 million in 1949 to a scant 10 million twenty years later, at which time fifty-one leagues had shrunk to twenty. In England, the introduction of the new medium seemed to threaten the end of professional soccer as a spectator sport. The attendance figures in table 1 tell the story.[32]

Table 1	
Attendance at British Soccer Matches	
SEASON	ATTENDANCE
1948–1949	41,250,000
1960–1961	28,500,000
1982–1983	18,750,000

There was no guarantee that TV would not have a similar effect on American football attendance. When the Los Angeles Rams of the National Football League allowed their games to be televised in 1950, their attendance plummeted from 205,109 the previous year to 110,162. When home games were blacked out in 1951, attendance figures bounced back.[33] It was not until the arrival of Alvin "Pete" Rozelle as NFL commissioner in 1960 that suspicions were overcome and the league became firmly committed to television.[34]

For their part, the networks were also surprisingly slow to consummate the marriage that has transformed the world's spectator sports. In retrospect, the hesitation of the networks seems almost comical. DuMont, which was then a serious rival to the major networks, televised five NFL games in 1951 and twelve (plus the championship) in 1954, for a mere $95,000! Only two years later, CBS paid over a million dollars for the season. By the 1980s, the NFL's annual Super Bowl was attracting over 130 million viewers, more than half of the entire population of the United States. Commercials cost $800,000 a minute and "cabinet members, corporate executives, and celebrities of all sorts vied for the tickets." In 1982, the NFL played hard to get and was cajoled with the promise of two *billion* dollars over five years, a sum so enormous that the three major networks agreed to share the rights (and the costs). Under this contract, each team was guaranteed $15,000,000 a year before the first ticket was sold. In 1983, baseball, despite its unsuitability for the screen and its alleged demise as the "national game," was still attractive enough for the networks to pool their resources and sign a four-year contract for one billion dollars.[35] In comparison, the sum of 38,000,000 marks paid by the German TV networks for rights to the 1974 World Cup, which was hosted by the Deutscher Fussball Verband, seems like a real bargain (but one must remember that the publicly owned German networks had to carry their advertisements indirectly, by training the camera on advertisements displayed in the stadia).[36]

For the owners of American sports franchises, infusions of television money make a life-or-death difference. Challenging the established NFL, the American Football League was on the brink of bankruptcy in 1964 when television came galloping to the rescue. The situation was a rather dramatic one. On January 24, 1964, CBS unexpectedly outbid NBC and won the rights to do the NFL games. Two hours later, NBC offered the AFL $42,000,000 for a five-year contract. With this bankroll, the league was able to offer Joe Namath, the first of its superstars, $420,000 over three years, the first of the extravagant salaries.[37] The AFL lived to merge with the NFL in 1966 (thanks also to a generous antitrust exemption granted by the sports-obsessed United States Congress). Last-minute rescues make good TV shows, but bad business. Before it played a single game of its first season, the United States Football League had already arranged to sell TV rights to ABC for $9,000,000 and to Cable TV's Entertainment and Sports Network (ESPN) for $11,000,000.[38]

Televised sports can also make, and perhaps break, a network. In 1959, NBC decided to discontinue prizefights, which had lost most of their TV popularity, but which the Gillette Company wished to continue to sponsor. Louis Maxon, whose advertising agency handled the Gillette account, called ABC's Thomas Moore and offered him Gillette's entire TV advertising budget of $8 million. With the windfall, ABC was able to acquire the rights to intercollegiate football from the National Collegiate Athletic Association (NCAA). Under the direction of Roone Arledge, ABC's sports division went on to purchase the rights to professional golf and a variety of amateur sports then controlled by the Amateur Athletic Union (AAU). These rights enabled the network in 1961 to inaugurate the technically innovative and spectacularly successful series, *Wide World of Sports*, which entranced its 25,000,000 viewers with slow motion, zoom lenses, stop action, hand-held and underwater cameras, mug shots, and split screen, with track meets, cliff divers, and the stunts of R. C. "Evel" Knievel. The next step in ABC's drive to TV sports hegemony came when the network bought the rights to the 1968 Olympics for $7 million. (The games, held in Mexico City, were the first covered by means of satellite transmission.) A year later, ABC launched the prodigiously successful series, "Monday Night Football." It was Arledge who introduced "honey shots" of attractive female spectators and who established Howard Cosell as "the man you love to hate," the volubly opinionated sports commentator simultaneously most liked and disliked by TV fans. It was also Arledge who defied the International Olympic Committee in 1968 and sent Cosell to interview Tommie Smith after his clenched-fist Black Power demonstration and it was Arledge who decided at Munich in 1972 that pony-tailed Olga Korbut was the gymnast most likely to attract American viewers to what was, until then, an almost unknown spectator sport. (When Korbut slipped, fell, and wept, Arledge ordered a close-up and sent "a shudder of empathy through America.")[39] In 1976, shortly after the Montreal Olympics, ABC topped CBS for its share of the TV audience *for all shows.*[40]

The popularity of televised sports has also had an enormous influence, mostly nefarious, upon intercollegiate athletics. Although complaints about the commercialization of campus sports are a century old, television has drastically upped the ante. More than school pride is at stake when TV appearances can bring a school as much as a million dollars (and make its athletic recruitment infinitely easier). In 1983, NBC paid $7 million for a single event—the Rose Bowl. In 1984, the NCAA, which oversees and vainly attempts to control collegiate sports, was busy distributing some $60 million a year to its members when the University of Georgia and the University of Oklahoma, unhappy about their share of the money, sued successfully to break up the NCAA's monopoly.[41]

As the universities' sports programs become increasingly dependent upon TV revenue, paid directly or distributed through athletic conferences and the NCAA, coaches come under increased pressure to put together bowl-bound telegenic teams. When success can bring adulation and a quarter-million-dollar-a-year contract while failure brings contempt, contumely, and dismissal, the temptation to win at any price is hard to resist. Coaches demand more and more of "student-athletes" who are recruited with less and less regard for the NCAA's mostly unenforced rules. The athletes are well aware that many coaches and alumni have broken the rules in order to recruit them and keep them in school. (Cash delivered in a shoe box and a grade of "A" for a course not taken do stimulate awareness.) The "student-athletes" cannot be severely blamed if they decide that they are badly rewarded for their athletic efforts. They become prime targets for gamblers who prefer fixed games to the charms of Lady Luck. Since most of the abuses from which we presently suffer date from the 1890s, it is obvious that television has not created them, but television, and the spectators who turn their sets on every autumnal Saturday, have made the disease incurable.[42]

If tens of millions of ordinary Americans were not as sports-obsessed as their political representatives in Washington, manufacturers of automobiles, beer, and computers would not purchase halftime spots at $15,000 a second. Quite plainly, however, major corporations—the only ones that can afford largess on this gargantuan scale—are persuaded that these millions of dollars are well spent, and the A. C. Nielsen Company assures them that they are correct. In the 1970s, 31 percent of the nation's viewers watched ABC's Monday Night Football, listened to the histrionics of Howard Cosell, and—presumably—rushed out the next day to purchase whatever products appeared between the plays. That the viewers did *not* rush to work the next day can be seen in the fact that Tuesday supplanted Monday as the peak of absenteeism in Detroit's automobile factories.[43]

Since most Europeans watch state-run rather than commercial television networks, the economics of sports and the mass media are less clear than in the United States. What *is* clear is that sports are as attractive to European as to American viewers. In fact, some data indicate that German television offers its viewers as much sport as do the American networks—i.e., about 10 percent of the total program content, while the figures for French and British television has soared as high as 15 percent (RDF) and 25 percent (BBC).[44] In Germany, soccer matches can draw upwards of 80 percent of the audience and track-and-field meets, a rarity on American television, can attract as many as 36 percent of the viewers.[45] The Olympic Games are even more popular than in the United States, which means that Eurovision (the organization formed by the Western European networks) is ready to pay sizable amounts of the taxpayers' money for the right to offer the quadrennial spectacle to the French, the Germans, the Italians, etc.

Now that most American sports leagues (including the major collegiate sports conferences) have become dependent upon television money, subtle and not-so-subtle changes have occurred. When the networks commit themselves to handing over billions of dollars, there is an explicit or implicit expectation that he who pays the piper will at least be allowed to request the tune. Examples of influence are many. Athletes have accepted the fact that they must shoot their baskets or trade their punches at times suitable for East Coast viewers. The Ali-Foreman fight took place at 2:00 A.M., the Ali-Bugner fight at 6:00 A.M. Baseball players shiver their way through the World Series because the networks want them to play during prime time—i.e., evenings. Popular golfers tee off in prime time while the unknowns drive and putt through morning mists and evening shadows. Soccer matches are sprinkled with penalties and "injuries" so that the advertisements can be inserted. Boxers toy with their opponents for round after round for the same reason. There is talk of "adjustments" in the daily schedule of events in Seoul in 1988—to provide the American viewers with prime-time coverage of their favorite sports.

Just as significant is the change in the economic status of the players. While the great athletes of the past often received princely salaries, e.g., Babe Ruth's $80,000 a year in the midst of the Great Depression, the stream of network gold that has poured into the hands of contemporary owners has aroused passionate demands that at least some of the flow be diverted into the pockets of those who put their bodies on the line (and on the screen). It is inconceivable that basketball players performing in arenas holding 15,000 spectators could earn $500,000 a year if their owners did not have lucrative television contracts. On March 4, 1985, the cover of *Sports Illustrated* listed the names of thirty-six baseball players earning over a million dollars a year. No matter how many fans throng to see the Phillies, no matter how many hot dogs they consume, they alone are too few to pay Mike Schmidt's $2,130,000. At best, ballpark spectators have become the equivalent of studio guests; at worst, they are background, mere television props.

Does any of this bother the television viewer? Ironically, three quarters of the fans questioned in a 1983 poll complained about the high salaries that their addiction has made possible.[46] When athletes go on strike, no matter what the cause, in Europe as in the United States, the fans almost invariably side with the owners. Disgruntled, they gripe loudly about high salaries and greed, yet they have only themselves to blame. If Marvin Hagler earns $7 million a year as the best middleweight in the business, it is because the American people have made their values known—whether they realize the fact or not. If Americans supported opera as they support spectator sports, tenors and mezzosopranos would have incomes comparable to those of boxers and basketball players.

Although occasionally bothered by the modern players' business acumen, American spectators acquiesce supinely in the advertisers' interruptions of the game. If sports spectacles are a species of drama, as numerous theorists have proclaimed, they are unquestionably mutilated dramas whose mutilation arouses little protest. Edwin Cady's comment is unusual: "The cameras and directors fragment, skew, and impoverish the potential esthetic experience. . . . The television fan does not know the game; he has never seen it."[47] Popular programs like ABC's *Wide World of Sports* or German television's *Sport Aktuell* shift disruptively from sport to sport and oscillate between gymnastics and a demolition derby. What does the popularity of such programs say about theories of "dramatic unity"? About the psychology of the viewer? Have commercial radio and television "programmed" their American audience to expect and enjoy experiences that a theatergoer would find absolutely intolerable? These are questions which have been scarcely raised, much less answered.

It is somewhat easier to say that *some* sort of satiety or disillusion has begun to set in. During the 1984 football season, all three networks suffered a decline in the Nielsen ratings. CBS was down 16 percent while ABC and NBC were down 6 percent and 4 percent. Over a five-year period, telecasts of the NCAA basketball final, the Super Bowl, college bowl games, the Indianapolis 500, the Masters golf tournament, the Kentucky Derby, and Wimbledon all attracted a diminishing number of viewers. Network executives like Arthur Watson of NBC and journalists like William Taafe of *Sports Illustrated* attribute the dropoff to the glut of televised sports available to the beleaguered (in several senses of the word) fan. In the ten years between 1973 and 1983, CBS more than doubled the hours of sports it offered the public and the three networks together boosted their sports telecasts by 63 percent. This suggests saturation. On the other hand, the 1984 Super Bowl had the 11th largest audience in American history and the Los Angeles Olympics averaged 23.5 percent of the prime-time viewers. While there has certainly been a dip in the curve, the graph of TV sports popularity does not yet prove that the public's hunger has finally been sated.[48]

It is much easier to indicate who watches what. On the whole, American viewers prefer sports to newscasts, documentaries, situation comedies, and every other standard category except "movies."[49] German viewers seem to rank their preferences differently; 66 percent of them told pollsters they were very interested in newscasts and only 44 percent admitted to a strong interest in televised sports. (Since people tend to give socially acceptable answers to pollsters' questions, and Germans still tend to believe in high-mindedness, some skepticism about German viewing habits is necessary.)[50]

Men watch more TV sports than women do. In the United States, 90 percent of the former and "only" 75 percent of the latter say they watch.[51] For some sports, like football and basketball, the gender gap is very large, which is why one rarely sees a halftime ad for perfume. In 1963, when the A. C. Nielsen Company began to provide advertisers with precise and accurate data on the demographics of TV sports, the five most popular sports all showed a preponderance of male viewers even though women make up a slightly larger percent of the total U.S. population (see table 2). Twenty years later, in its survey of the 1983 season, the A. C. Nielsen Company found a very similar pattern (table 3).[52]

There are, of course, some spectator sports which attract more women than men. Although track and field is not as popular in the United States as in Europe, women made up a larger share of its amall 1969–1970 audience than men did. In 1980, women were more likely than men to have watched ABC do the Winter Olympics from Lake Placid, a very popular event which drew an average audience of 21.6 percent of all TV households (compared with 44.4 percent for the

Table 2
Percent of 1963 TV Audience Made Up of

SPORT	ADULT MALES	ADULT FEMALES	TEENAGERS	CHILDREN
Football	50	27	11	12
Boxing	46	37	7	10
Baseball	44	33	10	13
Bowling	44	37	8	11
Golf	38	29	11	22

Table 3
Average 1983 TV Audience as Percent of U.S. Population

SPORT	ADULT MEN	ADULT WOMEN
NFL Football	16.3	7.4
USFL Football	6.1	2.6
NCAA Football	11.2	5.1
Baseball	9.0	5.2
NBA Basketball	6.3	2.6
NCAA Basketball	5.5	2.6
Golf	3.9	2.7
Tennis	2.1	1.9
Bowling	4.6	4.1
Auto Races	6.9	2.7
Horse Races	6.9	6.7
Boxing	4.9	2.2

NFL Super Bowl and 32.8 percent for the World Series).[53] In 1983, more women than men watched CBS do the NCAA gymnastics championships.

One reason for the popularity of gymnastics among women is, of course, that the sport has almost as many female champions as male. (Men have more events.) In general, men are more likely to watch men perform while women are a more reliable audience for female athletes. There may, however, be some erosion of this gender-determined pattern as females are increasingly accepted as authentic athletes and not as "bimbos" or "cheesecake." Shortly before the Los Angeles Olympics of 1984, both men and women who were asked to name members of the American team were more likely to respond with "Mary Decker" than with any other name; both men and women indicated that they looked forward most intensely to the gymnastics contests.[54]

In regard to the gender of TV spectators, European data strongly confirm the American pattern. In Norway, 64 percent of the men and only 49 percent of the women follow the country's most popular sports telecast. Norwegian women, however, are more likely than men to watch gymnastics and swimming.[55] In Germany, 75 percent of the men and 52 percent of the women are regular consumers of TV sports. Soccer is "seen gladly" by 86 percent of the men (and a surprising 52 percent of the women) while the proportions are reversed for the second most popular sport, figure skating (81 percent of the women, 58 percent of the men). Considering the American preference for team sports, one should note that the Germans polled indicated that skiing, gymnastics, and track and field were what they most wanted to see after their lust for soccer and figure skating was satisfied. Since German television is state-run and not dependent on commercial sponsorship, there is no guarantee that the spectators will actually see what they most want to see. In 1974, for instance, the two networks (ARD and ZDF) telecast 44 soccer shows that captured an average of 36 percent of all sets and 22 tennis shows (a miserable 4 percent of all sets). Women clamoring for figure skaters had to be content with 10 shows.[56]

Television has had a mostly unnoticed effect on the age of the fans who actually go to the sports events. Photographs prove beyond question that pretelevision crowds for baseball, cricket, and soccer were composed mostly of adults. When, however, the television camera zeroes in on the spectators, one sees a much younger crowd. This perception is amply supported by an admirably detailed study of the soccer crowd in Cologne, West Germany, where 52.6 percent of those who show up in the stadium, fair weather or foul, are twenty-one or younger. (And 88.2 percent of them are male.) Clearly, the older fans of 1.FC Koeln have decided that it is easier to turn on the TV set than to battle the traffic on Aachenerstrasse or squeeze into the streetcar for Muengersdorf.[57]

It is no surprise that social class also makes a difference in the audience. Almost from its origins in the 1840s, baseball has attracted lower-class fans. In Europe, despite its derivation from games played at Oxford, Cambridge, and the elitist "public schools," soccer is identified as the "people's game." American football was once strongly associated with institutions of higher education, but the advent of television has unquestionably made a difference. Certainly, the stereotypical image of the football fan has changed: the college boy in raccoon coat and with a whisky flask in his pocket has been replaced by the truckdriver in his T-shirt and with a beer bottle in his hand. Conventional imagery set the collegian in the stadium, where he cheered drunkenly for his team, while the truckdriver was plopped down before the television screen, where he cheered drunkenly for his team.

The new stereotypes are exaggerations. The traditional associations bear up rather well. In fact, A. C. Nielsen Company's data reveal that televised baseball consistently attracts a disproportionate number of the poor and the elderly while football telecasts continue to appeal to younger and wealthier spectators. Precise survey data also confirm the conventional wisdom which says that bowling is for the workers. Economic relationships are neatly captured in the price tags; although the average audience for bowling is 42 percent of that for NFL football (6.6 percent versus 15.8 percent of all households in 1983), bowling's commercials cost less than one sixth as much as football's.

The European situation is unambiguous. Cycling remains immensely popular and lower-class French and Italian fans continue to be mad about the *Tour de France* and the *Giro d'Italia*. The television audience for tennis and golf is growing, but these sports are still perceived as expensive elitist pastimes of very little interest for ordinary men and women. Although numerous Europeam intellectuals have fallen in love with soccer, as many once did with boxing, televised soccer continues to be "the people's game." Since other European intellectuals are convinced that soccer is also the people's ruin, it is to their critique of modern sports that we now turn.

SIX

DEHUMANIZED SPECTATORS?

I THE NEO-MARXIST INDICTMENT

ALTHOUGH IT IS UNUSUAL to denounce museum-goers for not painting still-lifes and bad form to fault concert audiences for not playing the harpsichord, it is quite common, even for those who are enthusiastic about sports, to criticize spectators for athletic inactivity. Why are they up in the stands rather than down on the field? Worse yet, why do they swill beer before the boob-tube when they might jog euphorically through the leafy woods? "Telecasts of professional team sports," writes an economist, "have become the opiate of millions of American households."[1] Less pithy than Marx's original formulation but no less emphatic. As a team of social psychologists has remarked, "The discussion of spectatorship amounts to a nearly universal condemnation of the phenomenon."[2] When the critics disapprove of sports as well as of sports spectators, the judgment can be savage, as a few words from Eugene Bianchi attest: "More than 25 million Americans fostered their own dehumanization each weekend last fall as fans of big-time football. Fixed to TV sets or huddled in the great arenas across the land, the spectators reinforced in themselves the worst values of our culture."[3]

Bianchi writes as a Christian moralist in the tradition of Tertullian and the other Fathers of the Church who turned their patristic wrath against the circus and the gladiatorial games of imperial Rome. The most detailed criticism of sports spectators comes, however, not from the churches, which have generally made their peace with whatever happens in sports, but from the Marxist tradition, which has, especially in its Neo-Marxist variant, developed a full-scale indictment of the alleged dehumanization of both athletes and spectators.

The Marxist and Neo-Marxist critiques of modern sports are related but nonetheless distinct. While Marxist scholars, both European and American, have condemned the obvious racism and commercialism and the putative militarism, nationalism, and imperialism of "capitalist" sports, they have *not* rejected sports as such. Quite the contrary. As the enthusiastic endorsement of sports by all Communist governments has amply demonstrated, Marxism has had a kind of love-is-blind infatuation with modern sports. Once society evolves from the capitalist to the socialist stage, its contradictions are said to disappear and sport becomes an instrument in the creation of what Marxist scholars enthusiastically refer to as "New Socialist Man." They eagerly announce the good news that the Soviet Union has moved beyond mass sport to "universal sport," a phenomenon described as "a humanistic model, in accordance with the authentic and essential needs of people."[4]

The affirmation of sports extends, in the Soviet Union, to the spectators as well. This group, predominantly male in the Soviet bloc as in the West, is said by Soviet scholars to learn lessons in citizenship through its role as sports spectators. Since Soviet sports are presented at "a high ideological and educational level," they can strengthen the will and encourage the fans to "express themselves and find confirmation." Spectatorship creates community.[5] Since Soviet society has overcome class conflict, there is no reason for spectator violence. Spokesmen for the German Democratic Republic come to the same happy conclusion.[6]

This benign view of sports is not shared by the Neo-Marxists. In their view, "Modern industrial society . . . is now in the process of attempting to colonize the individual world of dreams and leisure through the medium of sports."[7] For Neo-Marxist critics, sports are an affliction, they are "the capitalistically deformed form of play."[8] Although Neo-Marxist analysis is usually limited to the United States and Western Europe, its proponents insist that their indictment is valid for the sports of the Communist world as well as for capitalistic societies.[9] In their view, Russians and Poles should join Americans and Britons in a rejection of modern sport and in an affirmation of spontaneous play.

At the risk of simplification, the Neo-Marxist indictment of spectator sports can be summed up under three counts.

1. *Capitalist society is characterized by a division of labor in sports as well as in other sectors.* Division of labor determines that a handful of highly paid but nonetheless exploited professional athletes perform,

while millions of spectators sit passively or restrict their exercise to fetching food from the refrigerator or the concessionaire. "The spectacle of professional athletic experts has reduced the individual in North American mass society to passive emulation."[10]

2. *Both active and passive sports participation stabilizes the capitalist system.* According to this considerably more serious charge, sports, by diverting potentially revolutionary energies away from political action, distract the exploited masses in the classic *panem et circenses* manner. The protest against political and economic injustice is drowned out by the spectators' mindless screams of ecstasy and rage as they identify with the gridiron gladiators and the stock-car drivers.

3. *Spectator sports function cathartically.* This charge, distinctly neo-Marxist rather than Marxist, sees sports as emotional safety valves for the potentially dangerous aggression created by the repression of capitalist society. This charge requires explanation.

Drawing upon Freud as well as Marx, in the manner of Theodor Adorno, Herbert Marcuse, and others of the famed *Institut fuer Sozialforschung* in prewar Frankfurt, Neo-Marxist doctrine holds that capitalist society requires the repression and sublimation of sexual energy. The sexually repressed worker sublimates his erotic energies into productive labor, which brings in great profits for the capitalist owner. The psychological mechanisms of repression and sublimation are, however, imperfect. There is always the danger that the repressed energies cannot be totally sublimated in work. Unsublimated energies are potentially explosive and must be dealt with. Surplus repression which cannot be transformed into economic productivity benefiting the ruling class builds up frustration and threatens to upset the entire system of economic exploitation and political control.

Enter sports. They serve to drain away, in a kind of secondary sublimation, that extra portion of repressed sexual energy which cannot be profitably utilized in the primary sublimation of the economic system. Within the confines of the stadium, sports permit this secondary sublimation which is, in practice, the release of the repressed in the form of physical aggression: "The aggression derived from sexual repression can thus be released through athletic achievements and competitions. . . ."[11] In addition to this catharsis, there is displacement. The rage and anger which should be directed against the ruling class is turned instead against the opposing team. The loyalty and emotional involvement which should be part of the worker's class consciousness is perversely wasted on the athlete's teammates.

The psychological mechanism of identification completes the process. Through the mechanism of identification, the spectators in the stands and before the flickering TV sets join vicariously in the violent release achieved by the players on the field. Drained of all hostility by the spectacle of aggression, the fans are devoid of any interest in political action. They are apathetic, infantilized, cretinized; in a word, dehumanized. The catharsis is complete. Sport is capitalism's safety valve.

This, in an abbreviated form if not exactly in a nutshell, is the three-part Neo-Marxist indictment of the allegedly dehumanized sports spectator. It is, curiously, an indictment which does *not* focus upon the outbursts of spectator violence which have been important themes of "bourgeois" sports sociologists (but *that* is the theme of the next chapter).

II DO THE WATCHERS ALSO DO
WHAT THEY WATCH?

Although there are surprisingly few direct investigations of sports spectators, numerous studies have demonstrated a strong correlation between active and passive sports participation, at least in the United States and Western Europe. Contrary to the widespread assumptions of Neo-Marxist and other moralists, there is no simple dichotomy between watchers and doers. Those who participate directly in sports are much more likely than nonparticipants to be spectators, both in person and through the electronic media. Some examples from Europe, where empirical studies of sports are far more numerous than in the United States, are appropriate. Of 482 vocational students in Bremen, 21 percent of those who *participate* in sports at least thrice weekly *attend* sports events at least once a week while only 2 percent of the athletically inactive attend that often.[12] In other words, the athletically active are more than ten times as likely to attend sports events as are the inactive. In a study of 942 Swiss workers aged 20 to 65 years, another scholar found that "those active in sports, old as well as young, were to a highly significant degree more likely to attend sports events than were those who were not active." While 14 percent of the athletically active went to the stadium or field at least once a week, only 3 percent of the others did.[13] German women in general are unlikely to read the sports section of the newspaper, but the majority of those active in tennis or on women's soccer teams do— still another indication of the correlation of active and passive participation.[14]

Looking at the participants to see how many are spectators is one approach; surveying the spectators to count the participants is another, complementary approach. Active participants are invariably a minority of the total population of any given modern society, so that they are very likely to attend sports events does *not* in itself mean that most spectators are also active participants in sports; but numerous empirical studies indicate that the spectators are indeed more likely to be participants than are their fellow citizens who avoid the spectator's role. Even in soccer, where the ratio of active to passive participation is much lower than in most other sports, studies confirm this relationship. For example, as many as two-thirds of the Danish soccer spectators are themselves active players.[15] In Hamburg, Germany, one scholar reported that 66 percent of his sample of soccer fans played the game and 60 percent of the cycling spectators also cycled (with even higher percentages for those who watched swimming, tennis, team handball, and weightlifting).[16] Among the male fans at the games of 1.FC Koeln 63 percent "are or were active soccer players." The German author emphatically rejects the theory of the inactive spectator: "Soccer fans are incomparably more active than the average German."[17] Since young people do more sports than older people, it fits the pattern of empirical results that a study of teenage soccer fans in Nuernberg found that 67.3 percent claimed to do sports at least once a week.[18] (Appropriately enough, German soccer fans have founded their own Fussball-Fanclub-Verband, which sponsors an annual tournament in which *they*, the fans, are the players.[19]

An Italian historian seems to feel that he has exposed the lethargy of the fans when he reports on a poll taken in 1963, which found that two-thirds of the readers of the *Gazzetta dello Sport* and *Tuttosport* "do no sports at all." Since only 4 percent of the Italian population of that time participated in sports, the historian might better have acknowledged that the fans are roughly eight times as likely to be active as those who do *not* read the sporting press.[20] Finally, after an unusually careful study of Norwegian adolescents, Svein Stensaasen concludes that "clearly significant relationships appear at all grade levels between frequency of active sport participation and frequency of attendance at sport contests as spectators." These correlations hold up for the relationship between participation and TV spectatorship as well—i.e., those "who are most often active in sport also tend to be those who most often watch sport on TV."[21]

Similar results have been obtained in North America. In Alberta, Canada, 88 percent of Edmonton's hockey fans participate in sports at least once a week.[22] In a study of American college students, Gerald Kenyon and Barry D. McPherson found that "the more the individuals enacted primary sport roles, the greater their interest in other facets of sport, and therefore the greater their consumption of sport."[23] American spectators at the 1976 Olympics in Montreal are no exception to the rule; 84 percent of the men and 75 percent of the women claimed they participated in some sport on at least a weekly basis.[24] Those with money enough to attend the Olympic Games are obviously not a very representative sample of the general population, but the spectators at baseball games—a group in which the lower classes are still overrepresented—are almost as active. Surveys at Boston's Fenway Park and at Yankee Stadium found that 63 percent of the Red Sox and 62 percent of the Yankee fans considered themselves active athletes.[25]

Clearly, one cannot take all such claims at face value, but most of the evidence seems to point in the same direction. Even if the claims are exaggerated by respondents who know that participation is supposed to be a good thing, the exaggeration is not likely to be greater than that which occurs when 30 percent of the entire U.S. population describes itself as athletically active. In other words, if we compare self-reported activity with self-reported activity, baseball fans are more than twice as likely as the average American to be sports participants. It is quite likely that a study of spectators at a golf or tennis match would establish that 75 percent or more of the spectators are active players of the game they love to watch. Since sports spectators are on the whole younger than average, some of this greater activity can be attributed to youth, but the empirical data cannot be interpreted as a sign of a watcher/doer dichotomy.

This result should not surprise anyone who has not deduced the contrary from a chain of theoretical assumptions. Why *shouldn't* someone who plays a game be more interested in watching it than someone who doesn't? Why *shouldn't* the observation of skilled performance lead to emulation rather than to apathy? The isolated attempts to summon up empirical data to prove the contrary suffer from methodological weakness. There is, for instance, a Spanish psychologist's report that the spectators of Madrid are athletically inactive. This allegation is based on the fact that 60 percent of his sample watched sports more often than they participated in sports.[26] Watching more than doing hardly seems the criterion to employ in order to discover whether or not spectators are inactive. Such an approach would surely come to the gloomy conclusion that violinists who play two hours a day are passively involved in music because they listen to National Public Radio's *Morning Pro Musica* for five hours a day. There is simply no good reason to doubt that it is "those who participate most actively in outdoor sports who are likely to be spectators as well."[27]

III DOES SPECTATORSHIP DIVERT
FROM POLITICS?

The second count in the Neo-Marxist indictment is less easily dismissed. Spectator sports *do* divert people from political action in the obvious sense that three hours spent watching the Super Bowl or the *Fussballweltmeisterschaft* or the *Tour de France* are quite obviously three hours unavailable for the picket line or the protest march. The dedicated revolutionary will take Lenin as his model—Lenin loved chess but refused to play the game because pushing pawns to capture knights deflected him from the task of urging peasants to expropriate landlords. If, however, our approach to politics is somewhat less ascetic than Lenin's, if we allow for moments of recreation as well as moments of commitment and engagement, the empirical data tend to invalidate the Neo-Marxist argument.

Much of the evidence depends on the already established relationship between watching and doing. A number of Austrian, Canadian, Danish, East German, West German, and Swiss studies have com-

pared athletically active to athletically inactive populations and found
that activity in one area correlates with activity in other areas while
the athletically inactive are likely to be just that—inactive.[28] These
empirical studies also indicate that the athletically active are more
likely than their inactive counterparts to be involved in politics. These
studies did not ask directly whether or not the *spectators* were more
culturally active than the rest of the population. Therefore, despite
the clear connection between watching sports and doing sports, we
cannot use studies of the athletically active and inactive to prove that
the spectators are also culturally active. There is, however, an empirical investigation which found just that. Young spectators were more
likely than other Swiss youths to listen to the radio, read, dance, listen
to jazz, visit with friends and family, and to go out for a glass of beer.
In brief, "Sports spectators can be characterized as definitely gregari-
ous."[29]

Confronted with the empirical data, the argument about apathy
falls apart. Obviously, there are people obsessed, as Lenin was, by a
single passionate goal from which they will not swerve, but they are
hardly typical of the world's *homme moyen sensuel*. No doubt, many
of those unenthusiastic or even hostile about sports spectatorship are
avid harpsichord players or numismatologists or environmental activ-
ists, but many of the uninterested are like the schizophrenics studied
by a group of American psychologists; they neither watch nor do sports
because they are not much interested in *anything* outside of their own
troubled psyches.[30]

IV DO SPECTATORS EXPERIENCE CATHARSIS?

The third charge of the indictment, that spectator sports function
cathartically to provide capitalism with an emotional safety valve, is
the most difficult to deal with because acceptance or rejection of the
charge depends largely on whether or not one is persuaded of the
general validity of the catharsis theory.

There is some evidence to indicate that the players themselves are
frequently less aggressive after the game than they were before (an
effect most probably attributable to the amount of energy expended
during the physically exhausting encounter), but there is a rare con-

sensus among non-Freudian social psychologists apropos of the alleged catharsis experienced by the sports spectator. This consensus derives from two types of experiment. In the first type, spectators are tested with pencil-and-paper or projective techniques before and after they attend athletic events of various sorts. In one study, for instance, obliging football fans submitted to interviewers who asked them thirty-six questions from the Buss-Durkee Hostility Inventory. The authors used the same technique to test spectators at a gymnastics meet. They concluded that there was no support whatsoever for the catharsis theory. Indeed, the scores tended to show increased rather than diminished aggressiveness after the sports event—even when the fan's favored team won. For the Army–Navy football game, the mean score rose from 11.20 (pregame) to 13.40 (postgame); for the Army–Temple gymnastics meet, scores rose from 12.00 to 12.71, which, while not statistically significant, was in a direction that casts doubt about the catharsis theory.[31]

One of the authors replicated the test in England, at the University of Lethbridge, where students filled out the questionnaires before and after they watched contests in wrestling, ice hockey, and swimming. The results once again called into question the assumption that sports events foster "goodwill and warm interpersonal relations."[32] Almost identical results were obtained from two very similar studies using the Thematic Apperception Test (TAT) and sentence-completion techniques to test the aggressiveness of football, basketball, and wrestling spectators at the University of Maryland. Analyzing the data gathered by these projective techniques, the author of the first study concluded austerely, "The results of the study do not support the cathartic or purge theory of aggression. Actually, the significant increase in the number of aggressive words after the football and basketball contests seem [sic] to support the contention that the viewing of violent or aggressive acts tends to increase the aggressiveness of the viewer."[33]

The second type of test is one developed by Leonard Berkowitz and his associates. Although the experiment has been performed in many variations, including those popularized by Stanley Milgram in *Obedience to Authority* (1969), one basic form is a comparison of responses of subjects to violent and nonviolent films. For instance, the subjects of the experiment see either a travelogue or a filmed boxing match. The subjects are then tested for their willingness to express their aggressiveness in an action against another person. This willingness is measured by the amount of electric shock the subjects *think* they administer to another person in what they *think* is an experiment to test the effect of punishment on learning. (There is actually no electric shock administered, but the naïve subject is unaware of this.) Subjects who observe the boxing film are significantly more willing to administer a dangerously high level of electric shock than are subjects who see films of a travelogue (or a track meet, a tennis match, a baseball game, etc.)[34] A logical inference from this entire series of experiments is that the alleged catharsis achieved by watching sports does not occur. The implication is rather the opposite: aggression can be learned and watching sports is one way to learn it.[35] As a German scholar concluded after studying 205 soccer fans, "Latent tension is neither repressed [*gebunden*] nor channeled but rather intensified and activated."[36]

Despite the unusual agreement among psychologists that there is little evidence to support the catharsis theory, a revisionist approach may lend some support to the Neo-Marxist argument about sports and social stability. In a remarkable essay by Norbert Elias and Eric Dunning, "The Quest for Excitement in Unexciting Societies," it is hypothesized that there is a direct relationship between the routinization of daily life in modern industrial society and the prevalence of sports like soccer, rugby, hockey, and American football: "in the more advanced industrial societies of our time, compared with societies at an earlier stage of development, occasions for strong excitement openly expressed have become rarer."[37] Although Elias and Dunning clearly espouse a sophisticated version of the catharsis theory in their essay, they emphasize not the passivity and infantilization of the spectator but rather the active expression of a variety of emotions. Games like football provide Saturnalia-like occasions for the uninhibited expression of emotions which are tightly controlled in our ordinary lives. The role of shouting, screaming, arm-waving spectator is an alternative to the more restrained roles of parent, employee, and civilized citizen. There may not be a catharsis in the sense of a purgation that produces calm and tranquillity, but this sort of spectatorship certainly provides the alleged "occasions for strong excitement openly expressed."

   Although Elias and Dunning do not explore the possibility, their essay can turn one's attention to collegiate sports, where the roles of student and spectator co-exist in what often seems like paradoxical juxtaposition. American high schools and colleges have always been agencies of socialization dedicated largely to the nurture of rational behavior. In football's collegiate heyday, from the 1880s to the 1950s, American colleges were institutions which emphasized discipline and self-control. Students, drawn mostly from the upper and middle classes, were supposed to study. It was nonetheless always expected, since boys will be boys even when they are Amherst Men, that they would exhibit the exuberance associated with adolescence. College sports, especially football, provided a regular and socially sanctioned occasion for displays of manly courage, outbursts of drunken revelry, transgressions of the dean's rules and regulations, and the release of whatever impulses these rules and regulations had, from Monday through Friday, suppressed. And, once the student had graduated, the force of nostalgia conspired with the calendar (games are played on weekends, when middle-class citizens turn from labor to leisure) to give football a special place among the many versions of the emotional "time-out." The catharsis, if there is one, is achieved not by passive spectatorship of the sort displayed by psychological subjects viewing a film but by active participation in the extended repertory of roles associated with a football weekend. The proper time to measure levels of hostility and aggression is not immediately before and after the game itself but before and after the lengthier period of time which frames the entire sports experience. The sedentary viewing of the contest is liable to terminate in increased hostility and aggressiveness even when the "sedentary" spectator jumps up and down and screams for the home team, but an active part in the larger drama of a "big weekend" may allow the release of emotions in a wide range of behavior including pregame levity, frenzied cheering during the game, and post-game carousing. The game itself figures as the occasion, sometimes perhaps even the pretext, for various activities frowned upon when not associated with sports. In this wider sense, some modified version of the catharsis theory may be valid. Exciting the spectator and then providing for the release of normally proscribed and inhibited behavior, the spectator sport may indeed function as a safety valve, and thus, in this sense, support the Neo-Marxist argument that spectator sports can, by their diversion of aggression and their controlled release of frustration, stabilize the social system.

There is, however, an irony which should not go unnoticed. Whether stimulated by the excitement of spectatorship or allowed by social conventions to release at sports events frustrations accumulated elsewhere, the fans do sometimes run wild. Spectator violence occurs and the safety valve turns out to be almost as destructive as the exploded boiler. While Neo-Marxists have minutely anatomized the apathy and infantilization which do not exist, they have more or less ignored spectator violence, a phenomenon closely associated with the lower classes. In other words, spectator sports, which are after all a part of proletarian as well as bourgeois culture, may actually do what Marx wanted to be done—heighten class consciousness and intensify class conflict. While middle-class spectators run through the antics of their institutionalized "time-out," lower-class fans may be stimulated to rebel if not to revolt against the social system which exploits them. Their sparks of rebellion, however, can all too easily disappear from scholarly sight under the thick ideological blanket of Neo-Marxist rhetoric. It is time to look more closely at spectator hooliganism.

SEVEN
SPECTATOR HOOLIGANS

I REPORTS OF KILLED AND WOUNDED

HAS THERE BEEN a reversal in the "civilizing process"? Have the measures taken by Victorian and Edwardian entrepreneurs become inadequate to control the modern crowd? Are we now in for a new age of spectator violence? It is hard to avoid that impression. American journalists have documented destructive behavior by drunkenly obscene spectators and British newspapers describe sports-related vandalism in terms reminiscent of the decline and fall of the Roman Empire. Headlines in the *Bild-Zeitung* and other European newspapers are equally scary. Italian reporters refer to the fans as *tifosi* (i.e., those infected with typhoid fever) and the Italian fans seem determined to make the sportswriters' military metaphors literal: a bomb was thrown at one of Verona's soccer matches (it failed to go off).[1] The Brazilian press conveys the same grim picture: stadia have moats, fences, armed guards, and attack dogs to separate the spectators from the players and from each other.

Historians of the contemporary scene can gather more than enough hard evidence to prove that sports-related violence does occur on an alarming scale. The most violent explosions of spectator hooliganism have not been ignited by the most violent sports. The 1910 championship bout between Jack Johnson and Jim Jeffries led, as we have seen, to a national orgy of violence, but post-World-War-II fight fans have apparently learned how to riot without actually killing anyone. One might expect that ice hockey's legitimate (within the rules) and illegitimate (outside them) violence has stimulated mayhem among the spectators, but such disorders as have taken place—e.g., the Montreal Riot of 1955—have seldom if ever resulted in fatalities.[2] Fatalities *did* occur immediately before a cricket match in Calcutta in 1968 when six people were trampled to death by fans fighting for tickets to India versus Australia, but the vast majority of the deaths occurring before, during, or immediately after sports events are associated with soccer football.[3] A selective recital of the calamities can be appalling.

In 1964, Angel Eduardo Pazos, a Uruguayan referee, disallowed an equalizing Peruvian goal toward the end of a match against Argentina. The Peruvian crowd rushed to the seven-foot-high steel-link fence topped with barbed wire, and broke through it. Simultaneously, they set fire to the stadium. The police responded by hurling tear gas into the crowd, which intensified the panic. The fans struggled to leave through the stadium's tunnels, but three of the seven doors were tightly locked. Hundreds were crushed to death. Estimates of the loss of life vary from 287 to 328.[4] In 1967, there was a somewhat less bloody aftermath to a match between the Turkish rivals Kayseri and Sivas. By the time the army restored order, 42 people were dead.[5] In 1968, 71 died in Buenos Aires after a group of thugs caused a stampede by throwing burning newspapers at spectators exiting on a winding stairway.[6] Three years later, a similar catastrophe occurred in Glasgow's Ibrox Park, when the Rangers equalized against their crosstown rivals, the Celtics; fans who had begun to leave in discouragement turned around and tried to push their way back into the stadium; 66 of them died.[7] When Brazil won the World Cup in soccer in 1970, two million people took to the streets to greet the returning team; the celebration left 44 dead and 1800 injured.[8] In 1974, forty-nine people were killed in Cairo when the Egyptian officials sold 100,000 tickets and then moved the game to a stadium that held 45,000 people.[9] An English fan was stabbed to death at a Blackpool game in 1974. In Germany, in 1979, a fan of Schalke 04 died when he slipped and fell while brawling. Two years later, in Saarbruecken, three intoxicated fans from Homburg were thrown out of a bar and expressed their annoyance by beating a passer-by to death.[10] Despite extremes of verbal violence, Italian fans have infrequently murdered one another, but an enthusiast waving the wrong flag was fatally stabbed in Milan in 1984.[11]

British soccer has made a special contribution to spectator violence. After supporters of the Tottenham Spurs rioted in Rotterdam in 1974, "football hooligans" became an international phenomenon feared throughout Europe, where authorities soon made it clear that the Union Jack was no longer a welcome sight in continental stadia. As preparations were under way for the 1982 World Cup, Bert Millichip, chairman of the Football Association, expressed sympathy for the Spanish hosts:

> the Spaniards, without doubt, are nervously contemplating the arrival of ferocious gangs of moronic louts from this country who find the game of football such a convenient platform from which to launch and display their show of naked and uncontrolled aggression. Nothing can prevent this invasion. Tickets or no tickets, they'll be on the boat to Bilbao, get drunk, wreck the boat and then get drunk in Bilbao and wreck that. They might get shot, but that is their problem.

The police in Bilbao indicated preparedness: "It is not our policy to use our guns except in extreme circumstances. We prefer to use methods of rubber bullets, water cannon, tear gas, the baton and swift arrest."[12]

Although the British "hooligans abroad" supported their national team, they did not leave their local animosities behind them. Chelsea fans, who are among those noted for "pathological displays of fascist regalia," taunted their Tottenham rivals:[13]

> Spurs are on the way to Auschwitz.
> Hitler's gonna gas 'em again.
> You can't stop 'em,
> The yids from Tottenham,
> The yids from White Hart Lane.[14]

The wonder is not that there was considerable spectator violence in Bilbao and other cities but that no one was killed.

In May of 1984, a fan from the Tottenham Hotspurs was shot and killed after a match in Anderlecht in Belgium. A little more than a year later, Liverpool's "hooligans abroad" took the ferry to Belgium for the European Cup Final (Liverpool versus Juventus of Turin); they attacked the Italian fans, pushed them up against a brick wall, which crumbled, they pinned others beneath a fallen fence. The *New York Times* for May 30 reported forty dead and more than a hundred injured. British teams were banned from continental play.

In comparison to such horror stories, American sources have little to report. One scholar has calculated that there were 312 sports-related riots in the United States between 1960 and 1972 (table 4).[15] While none of these American riots and acts of individual violence has escalated to the levels reached by soccer hooliganism abroad, they are clearly a cause for concern.

Some of the worst riots have occurred at the high-school level, especially where racial tensions aggravate traditional rivalries. When Washington's public and mostly black Eastern High School met private and mostly white St. John's High School in football on November 22, 1962, there was sporadic violence throughout the game. There were both black and white victims, but only about 20 percent of the 50,000 spectators were white, and black boys were said to have been the aggressors in most cases. When the game ended with St. John's ahead by a score of 20–7, an estimated 2,000 black youths began indiscriminately attacking white spectators, whom they kicked, punched, and struck with bottles. Five hundred people were injured.[16] An equally notorious and frequently cited riot took place at Schaefer Stadium in Foxboro, Massachusetts, on October 18, 1976. The riot is memorable not because 49 people were arrested nor because two people died of heart attacks. It was the obscenity of the behavior which appalled. "As an ambulance attendant fought to save one of the dying heart attack victims with mouth-to-mouth resuscitation, someone urinated on his back."[17] Apart from those killed in the aftermath of the

TABLE 4
Sports-Related Riots, U.S., 1960–1972

SPORT	NUMBER OF RIOTS
Baseball	97
Football	66
Basketball	54
Hockey	39
Boxing	19
Motor Sports	12
Horse Racing	11
Golf	4
Soccer	3
Wrestling	3
Track and Field	2
Tennis	2
TOTAL	312

Johnson–Jeffries fight of 1910, few Americans have actually been killed in spectator violence. Most of the disorders have involved fists, sticks, stones, cans, and bottles.[18] There have, however, been some fatalities. In 1977, a football fan gunned down three persons at Denver's Arabian Bar because the TV set had been turned off in the midst of the Broncos–Colts game. Two years later, Raymond L. Wilson, denied admission to a Super Bowl TV party at a bar in Louisville, returned with a 45-caliber submachine gun and opened fire on the partygoers. In each shooting, one person was killed, two wounded.[19]

Spokesmen for the Soviet bloc routinely maintain that *their* spectators are well-behaved, but visitors to Moscow and Leningrad are warned by their Intourist guides not to attend soccer matches, where high spirits are often sent even higher by vodka. Westerners unfortunate enough to have been in the People's Republic of China in the summer of 1985 were attacked on the streets when the Chinese soccer team lost an important international match. The newspapers of the German Democratic Republic report that "drunken youths en route to away games have trashed trains and bothered, threatened, and physically attacked their fellow passengers." Although one cannot judge a nation's spectators on the basis of a single work of art, it should nonetheless be noted that Hannes H. Wagner's painting, *Fans*, which hangs in the *Rathaus* in Halle, portrays the East German spectators as a moronic mob. If no fatalities have been reported by the sports sociologists of the USSR and its allies, credit should probably go to the police rather than to the soccer crowds.[19]

II PRELIMINARY ASSESSMENT AND THEORETICAL MODELS

How serious is the problem of spectator violence? Since many of the horrendous examples are familiar ones repeatedly cited, it is important to emphasize that most of the deaths were accidental. In nearly every instance of multiple fatalities, panic either created or magnified the catastrophe. While thuggery was often (not always) the cause of the panic, very few deaths occurred because one person intended to kill another. These remarks are not meant to exonerate sports spectators who stab and merely wound or to excuse those who threaten, intimidate, insult, shove, push, bruise, or urinate upon their fellows. Bestial behavior is bad news whether it happens in the subway, in a darkened alley, or in the gymnasium; but we must guard against exaggeration.

The initially frightening demonstration of Neo-Nazi identification on the part of young people in various countries turns out, upon inspection, to be troubling but not terrifying. The kids don't know what the symbols mean and don't care. What they *do* know is that the swastika and the shouts of *"Sieg Heil!"* horrify the people whom they want most to horrify. As one astute student of the German scene has written, "The youths who scream, 'Send Schalke [fans] to Auschwitz,' don't really know what happened there, but they know that something horrifying must have taken place and the word 'Auschwitz' alone is enough to bring out aggression, rage, and similar reactions in many people."[20]

Has spectator violence gotten worse? When we think back on the behavior of ancient, medieval, and early modern sports spectators, there does not seem to be reason for alarm about the present situation. There are signs of an increase of sports-related violence in societies where violence of all sorts is on the increase. When a society is torn apart by social conflict, conflict will occur in conjunction with sports as it does in conjunction with everything else, including rock concerts and religious services. Given the level of racial, religious, class, ethnic, and ideological conflict in the modern world, we ought to be amazed that the vast majority of contests are as pacific as they are. A team of psychologists specializing in sports spectatorship has come to the startlingly unorthodox conclusion that "dubious taste and misconduct" are the exception and that "the typical sports fan manages his or her emotions admirably. He or she may yell and stomp the ground, but, after the game, he or she usually will be no more vicious than after an exciting movie or a stimulating concert."[21] If most sports events take place in a relatively irenic atmosphere, part of the credit must go to institutions of social control (like ticket-takers and policemen) and part to the behavioral code internalized by the overwhelming majority of modern fans, according to which cheering and jeering are legitimate but physically injuring is not.

Spectator hooliganism is localized and closely related to social class. It occurs often in soccer, baseball, and boxing, seldom in cricket, rugby, and tennis. As a defender of British soccer has remarked of the stadium at Liverpool: "The Kop is not a members' enclosure at Ascot." The same authority has argued there is far less violence than one might think from newspaper headlines and two-minute TV reports.

> Week by week the Sunday and Monday morning papers suggest a Saturday afternoon scene somewhere between the storming of the Bastille and a civil rights march in Alabama, and round about Wednesday [they] report the squalid little magistrates' court cases which follow the apparent mayhem: three or four skinny 17-year-olds in London, half a dozen more in Liverpool, a couple up in Newcastle, another two or three in Manchester.[22]

Among the German hooligans as among the British, the threat of physical violence is far more common than the actuality. When interviewed by two scholars, a nineteen-year-old miner admitted that he and other supporters of Schalke 04 had been in a few fights with "provocateurs" from Dortmund, but he shrugged the encounters off as "puberty's by-products."[23] The behavior of American sports spectators has not been studied as thoroughly as that of the "football hooligans" of Britain and Germany, but there is evidence that they, too, are more bark than bite. One research team, investigating the phenomenon at the height of public concern, attended forty major-league baseball games and witnessed thirty-nine fights, hardly frightening when one considers the hundreds of thousands of people present.[24]

Sensationalist journalism can create an "amplification spiral" in which simplification, exaggeration, and stigmatization bring about panicky cries for immediate police action.[25] The British press, which defines people by what they *are* rather than by what they *do*, contributes to the image of "the football hooligan as a new folk devil."[26] Referring to "teenage thugs" and "mindless moronic maniacs," the press blames the hooligans for driving away the women and children who in point of fact seldom if ever were an important part of the soccer crowd.

Why do the fans behave violently? Sociologists and social psychologists have attempted to find an explanatory model for sports riots. They have looked to a wide range of theories for help: (a) the "contagion theory" put forth by Gustave LeBon in 1895 and subsequently popularized by Robert Park, E. W. Burgess, and Herbert Blumer,

(b) the "value-added theory" of Neil Smelser, and (c) the "emergent norm theory" of Ralph Turner and Lewis M. Killian.[27]

There is a vast body of literature devoted to what Gustave LeBon referred to, quite simply, as "the crowd."[28] This line of argument, commonly referred to as the "contagion model" of collective behavior, holds that individual identity disappears into the collective identity and that rationality dissolves into the hysteria of the crowd. In one of the very first essays devoted to the "Social Psychology of the Spectator," George Elliott Howard posits a subconscious self that emerges as the fans become part of "a composite social-psychic personality." Although Howard has some upper-class doubts about the phenomenon, he claims no immunity: "Who of us has not shared in the hypnotic frenzy, the mob-hysteria, of the 'bleachers' if not of the 'grand-stand'?"[29] Two generations later, a typical application of crowd theory to sports spectatorship refers to the "infantile men in the crowd, with primitive reactions," subject to "collective hysteria."[30]

The term "contagion" implies that irrationality spreads like disease. In Elias Canetti's ideosyncratic version of this theory, "the mass" is described as if afflicted not by some contagious disease but by a form of madness. Men in crowds are like those possessed by demons.[31] Theorists of this school tend also to emphasize the negative. The loss of self can indeed be frightening, as can be seen in many examples from Canetti's *Masse und Macht*, but the temporary merger of the impotent self with the collective power of the crowd can be exhilarating.

It is also easy to overstate the degree to which sports spectators abandon their individual selves. Spectators *do* often behave collectively in ways they shun individually; not many people scream themselves hoarse in their living rooms. Still, most fans are conscious of the canons of civility as they relate to spectatorship. Hooligans are relatively rare, even in England, in comparison to the huge numbers of self-disciplined men and women who attend sports spectacles. Finally, no theory of collective behavior is adequate that cannot explain why some spectators applaud politely and others set the stadium on fire. The generalizations of the LeBon-Canetti tradition tell us little about the variety of different behaviors exhibited by the groups and individuals who make up "the crowd."

The "contagion model" is in considerable disrepute these days, but

Smelser's theories are widely accepted and frequently referred to in the field of sports studies. They stipulate a causal sequence consisting of (a) structural conduciveness (state of affairs which encourages or discourages disorder), (b) structural strain, (c) the growth and spread of generalized beliefs, (d) precipitating factors, (e) mobilization of participants for action, and, finally, (f) the restoration of order by the operation of social control. None of these factors, taken alone, adds much to our sense of why riots take place. The first and second tell us that there must be something about a society which makes collective behavior likely. The third claims that ideas matter. The fourth points to some event which seems to have triggered the disorder. The fifth and sixth inform us that some people riot and others stop them. The crucial element in Smelser's "value-added" model is his notion that there is "a temporal sequence of activation of determinants," i.e., a necessary causal sequence.[32] In Cyril White's cogent summary:

> Each determinant is seen as prior to and operating within the scope established by the earlier and more general determinants. Each determinant is viewed as a necessary but not sufficient condition for the occurrence of an episode of collective behavior. However, taken together in logical order, the necessary conditions constitute the *sufficient* condition for its occurrence.[33]

After looking closely at a series of sports riots, White concluded that the model worked well but that the sequence was not always what it was supposed to be. Since the sequence is the essence of the model, which otherwise consists in a collection of generalities, one might fairly conclude that the model is a failure. Having looked at dozens of episodes other than the three White selected for his test cases, I confess to a disappointed conviction that Smelser's contribution is not very helpful. Since Smelser specifically defined collective behavior as behavior that is "not institutionalized behavior," he apparently excluded sports festivals from the kinds of occasions his model was meant to cope with. There is good reason to abandon the doomed attempt to find a single scientific formula for sports-related spectator violence.[34]

Turner and Killian are more eclectic, and more helpful. They approach the problem of collective behavior, *including* that associated with sports, by combining work done in anthropology, psychology, and sociology. Their specific contribution is a very complicated tax-onomy of different kinds of collective behavior; their essential point is that collective behavior "seems to be governed by norms that are not envisaged in the larger society and may even modify or oppose these broader norms."[35] Within the crowd are "emergent norms" gov-erning what looks from the outside like lawlessness. The Turner-Kil-lian approach is very like that used by Peter Marsh and his Oxford associates in their study of English "soccer hooliganism" (but the Ox-ford group does not refer to Turner and Killian or use their particular terminology).[36]

Although one can undoubtedly learn a great deal about sports spec-tators from the theorists of collective behavior—especially from "emer-gent-norm" theorists—I am convinced that one comes closest to understanding the causes of spectator violence by examining (a) the historical context of the behavior and (b) the standard sociological variables of age, gender, and—especially—social class.

III WHO THEY ARE AND WHY THEY RIOT

Who then are the hooligans and why do they behave as they do? It is only a small simplification to say that in all modern industrial societies the typical spectator hooligan is a young lower-class male, frequently but not usually unemployed. Of 497 people arrested in the North of England for soccer-related violence, only one was female; 59 percent of the arrested were under twenty-five years of age and only two of the 497 were occupationally classified by the police as "professional/managerial."[37] In another sample of 652 offenders ar-rested by London's Metropolitan Police in 1974–1976, 99.2 percent were male and the five females arrested were charged with the minor offenses of obstructing the police, obstructing the highway, or using insulting words. The average age of the group was 19 years. The younger members were by far the most violent. While only 7.7 percent of the arrests were made for assaults on the police, 66 percent of these assaults were committed by those under 21. As for social class, 68.1 percent of the arrested were manual workers, 12 percent were un-employed, 10 percent were schoolboys.[38] German scholars, who have studied the problem extensively, draw the same demographic picture. In Cologne, for instance, the police have identified a "hard core" of troublemakers, 71 percent of whom are minors.[39]

American evidence is more impressionistic, but what data exist corroborate the evidence from abroad. Of the 101 people arrested the first night of Pittsburgh's tumultuous celebration of the Steelers' 1975 Super Bowl victory, 95 percent were male and 86 percent were twenty-five years old or younger. While the police may be predisposed to nab young men rather than young women, they are also predisposed to grab blacks rather than whites. The fact that 91 percent of those arrested were white suggests that the paddy wagons collected a truly representative sample of the drunk and disorderly celebrants. Social class was not recorded, but it is a safe bet that the disadvantaged were statistically overrepresented. They, far more than the rest of us, really need something to celebrate.[40]

The disadvantaged classes are also given to behavior which the upper and middle classes, differently socialized and with more to lose from a rocking boat, simply misinterpret. Much of the behavior which the press castigates as "moronic" or "mindless" is actually purposeful and ritualized. "Senseless" conduct often makes excellent sense if one looks at it from the right perspective. Peter Marsh and his associates have attempted to see hooliganism as the hooligans see it. They have employed a set of concepts very like the Turner-Killian "emergent-norm" model, which asserts that what looks like deviant behavior from the point of view of the dominant culture may actually be the creation of a new set of norms. Abhorred disorder may be a new order in the making. From this perspective, one has a very different view of the "chaotic" stadium terraces where lower-class kids stand to cheer the home team and taunt the "wankers" from everywhere else. What looks like random disorganization from the outside reveals itself as behavior closely governed by "rules of disorder." "Life, as it is lived in classrooms and on the [stadium] terraces, has almost none of the characteristics of anarchy and impulsiveness that are often attributed to it." Deviant from the point of view of the dominant middle class, the hooligans have their own social system with a gamut of recognized roles: novice, rowdy, chant leader, "aggro leader," organizer, "nutter," scapegoat. Most "fights" remain verbal with rituals of belligerence carefully designed to allow the "combattants" to be restrained by their friends. "There is a . . . consensus that there are limits beyond which one should not go."[41]

German hooligans do not seem to be very different. There is the same variety of roles (leader, assistant, chant-leader, "tough guy," clown) and the same preference for verbal rather than physical assault, for carnival-like rather than criminal behavior.

> On the periphery of *Bundesliga* football a youthful subculture has developed. Self-organized and not controlled by society's institutions, it has its own norms, symbols, designations, and rituals. As it represents and defends its territory within the curves of the stadium, it generally, collectively, and demonstratively represents and defends itself against the world outside.[42]

The members of this subculture are comparable to the punks and rockers who have appeared everywhere in industrial and postindustrial society.

While Marsh and his associates are certainly correct to say that one must understand what sports hooliganism means to the hooligans, there is still reason to be skeptical of the additional argument that the violence consists almost entirely of ritualized words and gestures. There are far fewer dead and wounded than some alarmists have led us to expect, but there are still far too many to ignore. Critics have also pointed out that the youths studied by Marsh were supporters of Oxford United (not one of the most violence-plagued clubs) and also that one cannot extenuate physical violence by referring to its symbolic, ritualistic functions.[43]

Acknowledging the violence which has occurred, and building upon the work of Norbert Elias, Dunning has referred to the distinction between "segmental" and "functional" bonding (forms of social organization roughly equivalent to Ferdinand Toennies' *Gemeinschaft* and *Gesellschaft* or to Emile Durkheim's *mechanical* and *organic* solidarity). Modern society, according to this persuasive analysis, is characterized by a governmental monopoly on legitimate violence, by a complex division of labor and a resultant "lengthening of the chains of interdependence," and by an emphasis on competition and achievement. Modern society's prototypical middle-class citizens relate to each other impersonally, functionally, on the basis of their social roles. In their world, "self-control is an essential precondition for the maintenance and growth of the differentiation of functions." The modernization of traditional societies leaves sports like rugby, soccer, and boxing as "a social enclave in which specific forms of violence are socially defined as legitimate."[44] The lower classes, however, continue to demonstrate many of the characteristics of "segmental" (i.e., premodern) society. "Internally, their members remain locked in social figurations that are reminiscent in many ways of the preindustrial forms of segmental bonding and that correspondingly generate acute forms of aggressive masculinity."[45] These norms stress toughness and an ability to fight. Since these norms differ markedly from those "currently dominant in society at large," acting upon them will "incur condemnation from socially dominant groups."[46] Rampaging "skinheads" are a highly visible group. Inevitably, some "disaffected youths from 'respectable' working-class and middle-class backgrounds" will turn to the hooligans as their role models.[47]

Dunning's views fit nicely with those of a number of analysts in Britain and Germany who have stressed the obvious fact that the lower classes have traditionally admired physical toughness. Witty (or even stupid) invective can win prestige, but a "hard one" needs handy fists, and a set of chains is not a bad idea either. One has to be able to "take it" and "dish it out." In such a subculture of physical violence, sports hooliganism is nothing out of the ordinary.[48] It is, on the contrary, a means to establish one's status and identity. As a team of German scholars notes, courage, strength, toughness, and the ability to bear pain are prized by lower-class adolescents. "The fan that hasn't been injured physically is simply no fan at all."[49]

If we accept the notion of violence as an acceptable response on the part of young lower-class males, why should the game of soccer call forth such intense displays of what the British call "aggro"? One reason, which Dunning has stressed, is that soccer football's masculine norms dovetail nicely with the norms of the deviant subculture: toughness, aggressiveness, strength, stamina. Ian Taylor has developed a complementary argument to the effect that British (and presumably other) workers feel that "their" game has been taken away from them. The owners, who were once local businessmen anxious to stay on neighborly terms with the fans, are now wealthy industrialists whose "significant others" are likely to be Members of Parliament or film stars. Players, who once joined the fans in the pub for a pint or two, now spend their time with other celebrities.[50] "Hooliganism comes out of the way in which the *traditional* forms of football watching encounter the *professionalization* and *spectacularisation* of the game."[51] To these explanations, one should add that the crowd-control measures begun in the nineteenth century—fences, tickets, turnstiles, segregated seats, moats, attack dogs, policemen—have intensified the sense of estrangement felt by young men (and women) who simply want to let themselves go. Build a cage to hold a person and that person is likely to act like a caged animal.

Rejecting most of Taylor's argument, Garry Whannel has noted correctly that the lower classes lost control of "their" game at least fifty years before the resurgence of spectator violence in the 1960s.[52] His point is certainly valid, but one can still ask if the angry young men of modern industrial society *know* that their feelings of deprivation and denial are nothing new? Although their sense of history may not be very developed, they presumably realize that their fathers and grandfathers played and watched soccer games. They can still feel it to be *their* game, and in a certain sense it is. If we mix our metaphors to make our point, we can say that the soccer grounds are their turf. Let the high and mighty take notice.

IV THE CAUSES OF SPECTATOR VIOLENCE

Conventional wisdom often seeks the causes of spectator violence in the nature of the sport—legitimately and illegitimately violent sports are said to encourage violent spectators. Historically, as we have seen, this factor has turned out to be much less important than assumed. As the examples of gladiatorial games and chariot racing demonstrated, the most violent sports do not necessarily have the most violent spectators. National character is still another often-cited factor. Although Danish soccer stadia have had their tumults too, the Danes have not yet shown the kind of frenzied spectatorship demonstrated by the Italians and the Brazilians. The British example, however, reminds us that the concept of national character may be a will o' the wisp. At any rate, soccer hooligans do not *seem* to be given to the laconic understatement said to characterize the English. Social class certainly accounts for more of the observed variation in sports-related behavior than national character does. It seems to be the case in *all* modern societies that upper-class and middle-class spectators can normally be counted on to exercise more self-restraint than their less privileged and somewhat differently socialized lower-class compatriots. Age is another very important demographic variable. As we have seen, the nearly universal availability of television has encouraged older men and women to stay away from the stadium and still follow the game. Those who attend the event are, therefore, disproportionately young. As every sociologist and psychologist knows, adolescence is a troubled period in which the propensity to commit acts of expressive violence, and not just sports-related violence, peaks.

The historical context and even the historical moment must also be considered. Modern communications make it all but impossible not to be aware of major sports events. Modern transportation makes it easy to attend. Modern communications, once again, guarantee coverage, often instantaneous, of whatever violence occurs. The "spiral of amplification" is at work.

It also seems reasonable to assume that societies under stress will suffer more from violence of every kind, including spectator violence. (This simple wisdom seems to be the basic element of Smelser's model of collective behavior.) It also seems reasonable to expect that societies characterized by a variety of ethnic and religious differences will have to be either very civilized or very tightly controlled from above if they are not to suffer periodic outbreaks of expressive violence, including spectator violence. Finally, unless Norbert Elias is completely mistaken about the existence of a "civilizing process," modern men and women are now (or at least have been) far less given than formerly to spontaneous outbursts of expressive violence. Whether or not the secular trend is about to be reversed, no one knows. If soccer hooliganism represents the residual behavior of lower-class youths who are not yet—but eventually will be—"civilized," then spectator violence will decline and perhaps even disappear. If, however, spectator violence is merely one aspect of a general reversal of the "civilizing process," then the riots and rampages of spectator hooliganism are an ominous portent of hard times to come.

EIGHT
MOTIVATIONS ACTUAL AND IDEAL

I METHODOLOGICAL QUALMS

WHY DO PEOPLE WATCH athletes perform and teams compete? There is quite obviously no simple answer. If one attempts, moreover, to specify, to analyze the various motives that make spectators into fans of this or that sport, the task of interpreting becomes awesomely difficult and the opportunities for writing nonsense become practically infinite. Although I am well aware of the dangers as well as the delights of speculations about motivation, I have attempted to suggest some of the specific motives that brought men and women to various sports at various moments in history. It is perhaps appropriate, in coming to a conclusion, to speculate more generally about motivation. Needless to say, such speculation can never have the precision and degree of reliability we expect from data produced by the A. C. Nielsen Company.

There are at least two problems with the evidence at hand. (1) It is mostly subjective. (2) Too much of it comes from the twentieth century. There is not much that one can do about the first problem. Psychologists have done their best to study human motivation objectively, and their best will have to be good enough until scientists can be at least as clear about the mind as about the body. There is even less that we can do about the second problem, which is one that historians have always faced. Since almost no one in the past, other than a handful of moralists like Seneca and Tertullian, devoted much time to the psychological analysis of sports spectatorship, historians must infer motivation from contemporary attributions and from recorded behavior. We must assume that medieval and modern psyches are different but nonetheless comparable. A researcher can always take comfort from Robert Frost's meditation on those who look out to sea:

> They cannot look out far.
> They cannot look in deep.
> But when was that ever a bar
> To any watch they keep?

Within the limitations, one has plenty of evidence in the form of scholarly monographs like Arnold Beisser's *The Madness in Sports,* personal testimonials like Robert Heilman's "An Addict's Memoirs and Observations," novels like Frederick Exley's *A Fan's Notes,* and poems like "The Base Stealer" and "The Pitcher," both by Robert Francis. Sociologists and psychologists have also relied on interviews, which are useful, and on questionnaires, which are not. (The difficulty with questionnaires is that motivational categories overlap and are seldom mutually exclusive; how can one reasonably choose between "I go for the fun of it" and "I go to be with friends" when part of the fun is to be with friends?)[1]

II ACTUAL AND IDEAL MOTIVATIONS

Why then *do* people watch? No matter how complex the response to this five-word question, no answer will be universally valid. Some answers will seem to have very little to do with sports and it is just as well to admit this from the start. Not all spectators at sports events are *sports* spectators. By this apparently paradoxical remark I mean to refer, for instance, to dandies of both sexes who strut and preen about the venue and never glance at the game, to hooligans who show up simply because they want to bash someone, to policemen sent to round up the bashers, to spouses dragged by spouses to an afternoon of tedium, to parents who come because someone must, to lovers seeking the privacy of a public place, and to all others whose motives are extrinsic to sports per se. In saying that not all sports spectators are there for the athletic encounter, I mean also to refer to voyeurism. After centuries in which moralists on one side ranted about the sexuality displayed in sports and moralists on the other side denied the sensual attractiveness of youthful bodies in motion, Edgar Friedenberg let the cat out of the psychological bag. He openly acknowledged the excitement he felt at the sight of young boys playing and affirmed the presence of "a strong and pervasive erotic strain in the human response to athletic spectacles."[2] In asserting that such all-too-human motives are, strictly speaking, not motives for sports spectatorship, I do not mean for a moment to deny their importance, only to insist, once more, that simple answers are impossibly reductionist.

If we come a little closer to sports as the motive rather than as the milieu or the occasion or the pretext, we can disentangle some important threads from the web of motivation. If the runner's stride (and agonized grimace), the gymnast's vault (and forced smile), and the goalie's save (and muddied brow) are not forms of art, they certainly arouse in us emotions related to those we experience when we listen to one of Bach's cantatas or contemplate a still life by Chardin. Unquestionably, there are physical performances that live in the memory like the lines of a poem. We all have our cherished images: Jesse Owens dashing his way to immortality, Carleton Fisk winning one for the Red Sox, Ludmilla Tourescheva swinging and bounding around the uneven bars, Billie Jean King rushing the net. It is nonetheless doubtless true that sports are not, despite assertions and even books to the contrary, a form of art. They are demonstrations of possibility but they are not, strictly speaking, interpretations of the human condition or the natural world.[3] Still, as the German novelist Peter Handke has pointed out in a brilliant essay on the appeals of soccer, there are those unfortunate souls for whom sports may be the "only contact with the aesthetic."[4]

The line between sport and art wavers uncertainly. The line between sport and religion is equally hard to draw. The hardy travelers who sailed and trudged to the ancient Olympics witnessed athletic performances that were also religious rituals. The runners were human but they were also representations of the gods. Modern sports spectators live in a predominantly secular age, but there are clearly analogues to ancient ritual in secular sports festivals like the Olympic Games.[5] We have our sports heroes, just as the Greeks did, and metaphor permits us to do figuratively what they did literally, to speak of athletes—at least of some of them—as gods. It is admittedly a different kind of piety that brings us to the stadium, the pitch, the grounds, and the courts, but there are those, like the dazzled fan of Nebraska football, who say, "When the team comes running on the field and the band strikes up 'Dear Old Nebraska U' the tears damn near scald my cheeks. It's life's ultimate experience."[6] (And then there is the Italian soccer fan who says that victory for Roma is like a night in bed with his favorite filmstar.[7]) We can debate Michael Novak's proposition that sports have become a substitute for conventional religious faith, but how else can we understand the Nebraskan's ecstatic tears or the remark of an adolescent German girl who shocked her pious mother by saying of the local soccer team, "The HSV is greater than God"?[8] When we speak lyrically as Novak does (at epic length) about the "sacred trinity" of baseball, basketball, and football, we indulge ourselves in hyperbole, but the fact remains undeniable that many (by no means all) sports spectators experience something akin to worship.

Without denying the differences between the sacred and the secular realms, we can recognize a mythic dimension to sports which adumbrates a world apart from the rationalized abstractions of modernity. "Sports," writes Michael Real drawing on the insights of Mircea Eliade, embody "the sacred cycle of mythic time" and provide "a needed psychic relief from the tedium of western linear time."[9] Like primitive myths of eternal return, sports too have their seasons ever new, their history which repeats itself every year. Their newness-sameness offers the spectator a strange sense of continuity within change. "Other interests and persuasions," writes a confessed sports addict, "faded with the years, were replaced by new ones that took their turns and then receded. But sports formed the connective tissue that bound me to the fragments of my youth, and it was only through sports that I could retrace my steps."[10]

On quite another and less exalted level, modern spectators often experience attenuated analogues to the political motivations that once were part and parcel of sports contests. When the rulers of ancient Egypt bent their bows and sent their arrows through sheets of bronze, they enacted a political ritual which visibly demonstrated their divine right to rule and their ability to defend the kingdom. Those who watched were presumably comforted and reassured.[11] When the rulers of medieval Europe were helped into their armor and hoisted upon their horses and cheered for their prowess in the tournament, the assembled lords and ladies, clerics and peasants, were consciously or unconsciously involved in a political drama. It is true that modern equivalents to such enactments are usually attenuated and often parodic. The parody can be grotesque, when the aged Mao swims down the river, or pathetic, when Ronald Reagan offers to arm-wrestle all comers, but it presumably stimulates in some modern men and women the reassurance conveyed by similar rituals in more traditional societies. Modern dictators are certainly eager to collect political prestige by staging extravagant sports spectacles and democratic leaders seldom miss an opportunity to throw out the first ball, to telephone congratulations to the winners, and generally to bask in the reflected glory of athletic achievement. Robert M. Levine has written well about the manipulation of the Brazilian masses by right-wing dictators who can present themselves as the sponsors of "our side." Fortunately, sport used as a political instrument is a double-edged sword. Since soccer is "virtually the only participant institution touching all Brazilians, whether rich or poor, it literally represents a barometer by which national pride, exuberance, frustration, rage and hope all may be measured."[12] While the "barometer" does not function as a safety valve, as claimed in the discredited catharsis theory, it *does* record frustration and rage as well as hope and national pride. Fans who associate their dictatorial leaders with losing teams can become disgruntled.

For many men and women, the motivation seems to have been at least partly economic. Probably every sport has, at some time, impelled some of the spectators to bet on the outcome. Large sums of money may not have changed hands because of croquet results, but over twenty national governments provide their citizens with the opportunity to gamble on soccer scores through organizations like Brazil's Loteria Esportiva, which took in $367,000,000 in 1977.[13] In Great Britain, one-third of the entire over-sixteen population avails itself of the opportunity to pick the winners and quit work forever.[14] One wonders, of course, if those who participate in the pool are really *sports* fans; many of them seem ready to buy a ticket in whatever lottery is available. Pushpin was as good as poetry to the utilitarian philosopher Jeremy Bentham and the exact count of a jug of beans is as good as the outcome of the World Cup for the fanatic gambler. Still, the impulse to wager on horses, dogs, automobiles, motorcycles, and airplanes is probably the dominant motive bringing the spectator out for a day at the races. (It is, I confess, a motive which I did not sufficiently heed in *From Ritual to Record*.) There are those who cannot enjoy a sports event if they have not bet on the outcome. They are surely motivated by more than the crass desire to pocket whatever sum the lucky wager earns. Sports have always provided the spectators with a chance to play a metagame of their own in which they test their abilities to back a winner in whatever game the metagame is based on.

Most spectators, uninstructed in the terminology of social theory, say simply that they "like to follow sports" or that sports give them a topic of conversation. They frequently mention reasons which psychologists usually categorize as "sociability" or, in the extensive German literature on the topic, *Geselligkeit*.[15] Exclusion from the world's quotidian chitchat can be painful. Everywhere in the modern world, sports are among the most common topics of conversation. *Not* to participate in the conversation is perceived as antisocial—i.e., to be a spoilsport. The Harvard professor without *some* shreds of information about the Red Sox, the Celtics, the Patriots, and the Bruins is as odd a bird as the Brazilian worker, one in a hundred, who doesn't want to hear about Fluminense or Botafolgo.

As considerations of inclusion in or exclusion from talks about sports suggest, there is also a psychological component at work. Beneath the religious, political, economic, and social motives, all of which have appeared historically with varying intensity and in various forms, there is the need of the observer to identify with the actor.

The process of identification is a complex one. It was remarked upon in psychoanalytic terms as early as 1929, when Sigmund Freud's translator, A. A. Brill, published his seminal article entitled, "The Why of the Fan." Modern industrial man, wrote Brill, is still "an animal formed for battle and conquest." Since only a few can participate in sports, which are a sublimation of aggressive instincts, the average man must watch:

> Let him identify himself with his favorite fighter, player or team. He will purge himself of impulses which too much dammed up would lead to private broils and public disorders. He will achieve exaltation, vicarious but real. He will be a better individual, a better citizen, a better husband and father.[16]

(Brill's assumptions about the spectator's gender were of course typical of his times.)

In its extreme form, commonplace in adolescent fantasy, the boundaries of the self become diffuse and one actually imagines onself as the admired other, running, jumping, throwing, catching. Adults too indulge in daydreams, but they are more likely to fall into the Walter Mitty Syndrome and to picture themselves as heroes rather than to confuse Self and Other. Still less extreme is the desire to model one's behavior on that of some sports idol (who thus replaces the idealized saints, warriors, poets, and entrepreneurs of the past). Finally, there is simply the moment of empathy signaled by gestures mimicking those on the field. We draw back our arm as the quarterback passes, we flinch when the pass-receiver is clotheslined. We glide grandly with the figure-skaters through their final dance. Identification can include elements of sadism and masochism as well as the desire to be one with noble souls whom we idolize. Vicariously, we can maul a staggered boxer or shudder to receive a knockout punch. We are what we watch.

Frederick Exley's novel, A Fan's Notes, seems almost to have been written to dramatize the possibilities (and limits) of just this kind of psychological identification. The New York Giants football team, proclaims the first-person narrator, "were my delight, my folly, my anodyne, my intellectual stimulation." The narrator's erotic and occupational fumbles are a stark contrast to the athletic achievements that mesmerize him. "It was very simple, really. Where I could not, with syntax, give shape to my fantasies, [Frank] Gifford could, with his superb timing, his great hands, his uncanny faking, give shape to his." The narrator cheered until Gifford "became my alter ego."[17]

In Exley's novel, identification fails to produce psychic health, but psychiatrist Arnold Beisser has published a true-to-life case-study showing how baseball fandom made it possible for "Benny," a fearful, uprooted, estranged young man living in the sprawling "nowhere city" of Los Angeles, to become part of a larger whole, to overcome his neuroses and "to relate himself to the members of his own family."[18] Score one for the Dodgers? From Beisser's psychoanalytic perspective, the rituals of spectator sports are the functional equivalent of the ceremonies binding together the members of traditional societies.

In Desmond Morris's The Soccer Tribe (1981) photographs are cleverly paired to imply that the spectators' clothing and accessories are comparable to the dress and regalia of primitive ceremonies. While it is an exaggeration to write (with tongue in cheek?) as if the fans really *were* members of a tribal society, there is unquestionably an analogical similarity. This is perhaps most obvious in Japan, where thousands of fans attend baseball games not simply with banners of the appropriate color but in complete baseball uniforms. Empathy can hardly go further.

Since sports spectatorship is usually a shared experience, whether we watch in the crowded stadium or before millions of TV sets all tuned to the same channel, individual identification inevitably becomes collective—whether the spectators appear in uniform or not. In the phenomenon that I have termed "representational sport," individual identification with the athletes and collective membership in the community combine. As Alan Ingham and Michael Smith remark, "Sport is . . . expected to provide the larger community with athletes who are perceived as the embodiment of a collectivity." The athletes are proclaimed representatives of a school, town, nation, race, religion, or ideology. There is, in short, an apparently irresistible impulse to allegorize the sports contest and to feel that collective identity is somehow represented by five or eleven or fifteen men or women doing something with a ball or a single powerful man doing something with his fists.

The playwright Maya Angelou tells how the poor blacks of rural Arkansas gathered at her grandmother's general store to listen to broadcasts of Joe Louis's fights. When Louis was in trouble, all the listeners were still:

> It was not just one black man against the ropes, it was our people falling. It was another lynching, yet another black man hanging on a tree. One more woman ambushed and raped. A black boy whipped and maimed. It was hounds on the trail of a man running through slimy swamps. It was a white woman slapping her maid for being forgetful. We didn't breathe. We didn't hope. We waited.[20]

Who has not felt as Maya Angelou did?

Although the example drawn from Angelou's autobiography demonstrates solidarity in the face of hostility, representational sport can also allay social conflict and bring hostile groups together in the community of fandom. Cities wracked by racial tensions can find moments of release in the joys of sports championship. On a larger scale, international sports encounters create national teams and bring the fans of Manchester United together with the fans of Chelsea Arsenal in their fervent joint desire to see the English side defeat the players from Milan, Turin, and Rome.[21] There are even faint signs that identification can take place across the lines of race or religion—so that Protestants *and* Catholics of Belfast cheer for the Catholic boxer Finbarr McGuigan and white Southerners root for black baseball players.[22]

There is, then, evidence to support Janet Lever's enthusiasm: "Sport promotes communication; it involves people jointly; it provides them with common symbols, a collective identity, and a reason for solidarity. . . . Sport is one institution that holds together the people in a metropolis and heightens their attachment to the locale." It is the modern analogue to traditional religious ritual.[23] In discussing sports as a creator of collective solidarity, Marxists make common cause with "bourgeois" scholars. While they are horrified by the commercialized sports spectacles of the United States, they delight in "socialist" sports spectatorship as a manifestation of classless collectivity and as a means of moral instruction.[24] For them as for us, representational sport is a basic element of social reality. It is quite impossible to imagine how we might get along without it.

There is, unfortunately, a negative side to this representational function. Representational sport can diminish as well as increase a sense of community. Psychologists who testify to the enhancement of school spirit after "our" team has thrashed "them" have also noticed a tendency to doff the totemistic sweatshirt when the team falters in defeat.[25] Representational sport depresses the vicarious losers and loosens the bonds of community. Partisans of the defeated side have been known to bicker among themselves over the causes of the defeat. This is doubtless a minor drawback. Most of us are flexible enough in our identifications to shrug off a vicarious loss by reminding ourselves with a sigh that it is, after all, only a game. It is even possible to take comic pleasure in defeat. New Yorkers supported the once-hapless Mets through thick and thin. The inept players "were just plain folks—stumbling, sandlot players who somehow got shifted, however inappropriately, into a big stadium."[26]

There are far more serious reasons to limit our enthusiasm for representational sport. One of its strongest attractions is its ability to present precisely defined dramatic encounters between clearly separate antagonists whose uniforms immediately mark them as "our side" and "their side," but this very clarity brings with it sport's susceptibility to debased Manichean allegory. The impulse to allegorize can degenerate to the point at which sports turn into show business and the grunters and groaners of professional wrestling caricature Good and Evil for an audience, mostly female, that seems to want its Morality Plays to be crassly physical.[27] Perhaps this is simply good fun enjoyed by those who have not lost their sense of ironic detachment. But for some, the identification with those who seem to represent them is clearly pathological. From Roman times to the present, sports history records occasional suicides (by those too psychologically bound to the losers to detach ego from object) and murders (by those who cannot bear to see their representatives lose). These responses are unquestionably ingredients in the brew of spectator violence. Some allegories are deadly.

It must also be said that representational sport can smash the fragile ethos of fair play. If fair play is on the ropes, it is representational sport, not money, which landed the hardest punch. Fame and fortune beyond the dreams of nineteenth-century athletes are now the prize for the physically gifted, but the fame is prior to the fortune. It is *because* millions of ordinary, and extraordinary, men and women feel themselves personally represented by sports heroes and heroines that they buy millions of tickets and turn on hundreds of millions of television sets. No fame, no fortune. Money alone is not the primary reason for the decline in the ethos of fair play. High-school basketball games are rarely lucrative, but watch the boys and girls on the floor give each other the elbow and listen to their parents and classmates in the stands taunt the hated rivals from the other side of town. The athletes themselves, whether high-school basketball players or Olympic cyclists or professional heavyweight boxers, realize that they represent their school, their town, their nation, their ideology, their race. The impulse to give someone the elbow, to take drugs, to get in one more punch after the bell has rung, becomes harder and harder to resist as the psychological drama of representational sport becomes more and more intense. And money does play an important role. When a deftly faked injury brings a penalty kick, when a penalty kick brings the world championship in soccer, when the championship means an entire nation gone mad with joy, when a nation gone mad with joy means a salary raise of a million pounds or marks or a billion lira, it takes a dedicated sportsman to resist. It takes some nice guy, doomed no doubt to finish last. Some loser, upper-class or middle-class or lower-class, but definitely not world-class.

Fortunately, there is no need to end in despair over the nasty aspects of representational sport. We must remind ourselves that the historical record contains good news as well as bad, fair play as well as foul. We must maximize the positive potentiality of representational sport and make the most of sport's propensity for bringing people together. We are accustomed to gathering selected athletes into new teams representing larger collectivities. Traditionally, these larger collectivities have been cities, nations, races, religions, and ideologies, but the largest of all human groups is *Homo sapiens* and the purest of all responses is the aesthetic one. If we really *need* to feel represented by athletes, we might think of them not as black or white or Protestant or Catholic or Russian or American but as men and women whose performances help existentially to define what it means to be human. In the immensity of astronomical space, we are alone on this tiny planet, on this spinning ball of earth. In that sense, all of us are on the home team. May the best person win.

Notes

INTRODUCTION

1. For Dunning's work dealing entirely or in large measure with sports spectators, see Eric Dunning and Kenneth Sheard, *Barbarians, Gentlemen and Players: A Sociological Study of the Development of Rugby Football* (Oxford: Martin Robertson, 1979); Dunning, "Social Bonding and the Socio-Genesis of Violence," in Alan Tomlinson, ed., *The Sociological Study of Sport* (Brighton: Brighton Polytechnic–Chelsea School of Human Movement, 1981), pp. 1–35; Dunning, Patrick Murphy, and John Williams, "Ordered Segmentation and the Socio-Genesis of Football Hooligan Violence," also in Tomlinson, *Sociological Study*, pp. 36–52; Dunning, J. A. Maguire, Patrick Murphy, and John Williams, "The Social Roots of Football Hooligan Violence," *Leisure Studies* (1982) 1(2): 139–156; Norbert Elias and Dunning, *Sport im Zivilisationsprozess* (Muenster: Lit-Verlag, 1983); John Williams, Dunning, and Patrick Murphy, *Hooligans Abroad* (London: Routledge and Kegan Paul, 1984); Dunning, Patrick Murphy, John Williams and Joseph Maguire, "Football Hooliganism in Britain before the First World War," *International Review of Sport Sociology* (1984) 19(3–4): 231–232.

1. GREEK AND ROMAN SPECTATORS

1. Wolfgang Decker, *Quellentexte zu Sport und Koerperkultur im alten Aegypten* (Sankt Augustin: Hans Richarz, 1975), p. 82.

2. Sir Arthur Evans, *The Palace of Minos*, 6 vols. (London: Macmillan, 1921–1935), 3, Plate XVI, p. 65.

3. Ingomar Weiler, *Der Sport bei den Voelkern der alten Welt* (Darmstadt: Wissenschaftliche Buchgesellschaft, 1981), p. 225; Jean-Paul Thuillier, "Les Sports dans la civilisation étrusque," *Stadion* (1981) 7(2): 188.

4. Gerhard Lukas, *Der Sport im alten Rom* (Berlin: Sportverlag, 1982), p. 14.

5. Bronislaw Bilinski, *L'Agonistica sportiva nella Grecia antica* (Rome: Angelo Signorelli, 1961), p. 18.

6. Hans-Volkmar Herrmann, *Olympia: Heiligtum und Wettkampfstaette* (Munich: Hirmer, 1972), pp. 61–199; Joachim Ebert, *Olympia* (Vienna: Tusch, 1980), pp. 19–31; E. Norman Gardiner, *Olympia* (Oxford: Clarendon Press, 1925), pp. 175–299.

7. Quoted by M. I. Finley and H. W. Pleket, *The Olympic Games* (New York: Viking Press, 1976), p. 54.

8. Willy Zschietzschmann, *Wettkampf- und Uebungsstaetten in Griechenland*, 2 vols. (Schorndorf, West Germany: Karl Hofmann, 1960–1961), 1:13.

9. Lucian, *Anacharsis*, A. M. Harmon, trans. (London: Heinemann, 1925), pp. 13, 15.

10. E. Norman Gardiner, *Greek Athletic Sports and Festivals* (London: Macmillan, 1910), p. 101.

11. Johann Heinrich Krause, *Die Pythien, Nemeen und Isthmien* (Leipzig: Johann Ambrosius Barth, 1841), p. xviii; see also Ludwig Drees, *Olympia*, Gerald Onn, trans. (New York: Praeger, 1968), p. 56; John Mouratidis, "Heracles at Olympia and the Exclusion of Women from the Ancient Olympic Games," *Journal of Sport History* (Winter 1984) 11(3): 41–55. For possible exceptions to the rules excluding female athletes, see Hans Langenfeld, "Griechische Athletinnen in der roemischen Kaiserzeit," in Roland Renson et al., eds., *The History, Evolution and Diffusion of Sports and Games in Different Cultures* (Brussels: Bestuur voor de Lichamelijke Opvoeding, de Sport en het Openluchtleven, 1976), pp. 116–125.

12. Hugh M. Lee, "SIG3 802: Did Women Compete against Men in Greek Athletic Festivals?" (unpublished paper).

13. Louis Robert, *Les Gladiateurs dans l'orient grec* (Amsterdam: Adolf M. Hakkert, 1971), p. 263; see also Alan Cameron, *Circus Factions* (Oxford: Clarendon Press, 1976), p. 205.

14. Roberto Patrucco, *Lo Sport nella Grecia Antica* (Florence: Olschiki, 1972), p. 21.

15. M. I. Finley and H. W. Pleket, *The Olympic Games* (New York: Viking, 1976), p. 57.

16. Nicolaos Yalouris, ed., *The Eternal Olympics* (New Rochelle: Caratzas Brothers, 1979), p. 37 (Plate 14); Ebert, *Olympia*, pp. 40–41 (Plate 76); see also Ingomar Weiler, *Der Agon im Mythos* (Darmstadt: Wissenschaftliche Buchgesellschaft, 1974), p. 267.

17. K. Palaeogos, "The Organization of the Games," Yalouris, *The Eternal Olympics*, pp. 112–113; H. A. Harris, *Greek Athletes and Athletics* (London: Hutchinson, 1964), p. 158; Manfred Laemmer, "Zum Verhalten von Zuschauer bei Wettkaempfen in der griechischen Antike," in Giselher Spitzer and Dieter Schmidt, eds., *Sport zwischen Eigenstaendigkeit und Fremdbestimmung* (Bonn: Institut für Sportwissenschaft, 1986), pp. 75–85.

18. Johann Heinrich Krause, *Olympia* (1838; Hildesheim: Georg Olms, 1972), p. 192; Krause's most useful source was probably Philostratus, *Imagines*; for a modern translation, see Philostratus, trans. Arthur Fairbanks (London: Heinemann, 1931), p. 151.

19. Walter Woodburn Hyde, *Olympic Victor Monuments and Greek Athletic Art* (Washington: Carnegie Institute, 1921); H. W. Pleket, "Zur Soziologie des antiken Sports," *Mededelingen Nederlands Instituut te Rome* (1974) 36:57–87; H. W. Pleket, "Games, Prizes, Athletes and Ideology," *Stadion* (1975) 1(1): 49–89; Horst Buhmann, *Der Sieg in Olympia und in den anderen panhellenischen Spielen*, 2d ed. (Munich: UNI-Druck, 1975); David C. Young, *The Olympic Myth of Greek Amateur Athletics* (Chicago: Ares, 1984).

20. Polybius, *The Histories*, W. R. Paton, trans. 6 vols. (London: Hutchinson, 1922–1927), 5:509.

21. Quoted by Harold Arthur Harris, *Greek Athletics and the Jews* (Cardiff: University of Wales Press, 1976), p. 89.

22. Martin Vogt, "Der Sport im Altertum," in G. A. E. Bogeng, ed., *Geschichte des Sports aller Voelker und Zeiten*, 2 vols. (Leipzig: E. A. Seemann, 1926), 1:161; Peter L. Lindsay, "Attitudes Toward Physical Exercise Reflected in the Literature of Ancient Rome," in Earle F. Zeigler, ed., *History of Sport and Physical Education to 1900* (Champaign, Ill.: Stipes, 1973), p. 179; Ludwig Friedlaender, *Roman Life and Manners Under the Early Empire*, J. H. Freese and Leonard A. Magnus, trans. 4 vols. (London: George Routledge and Sons, 1908–1913), 2:122; E. Norman Gardiner, *Athletics of the Ancient World* (Oxford: Clarendon Press, 1930), p. 49.

23. J. P. V. D. Balsdon, *Life and Leisure in Ancient Rome* (London: Bodley Head, 1969), pp. 324–326; Siegfried Mendner, *Das Ballspiel im Leben der Voelker* (Muenster: Aschendorff, 1956), pp. 91–93.

24. Balsdon, *Life and Leisure*, pp. 244–252; Michael Grant, *Gladiators* (London: Weidenfeld and Nicolson, 1967), pp. 7–27; Georges Ville, *La Gladiature en occident des origines a la mort de Domitien* (Rome: Ecole française de Rome, 1981), pp. 42–51.

25. Friedlaender, *Roman Life and Manners*, 2:40–90; Ville, *La Gladiature*, pp. 57–173.

26. Augusta Hoenle and Anton Henze, *Roemische Amphitheater und Stadien* (Zurich: Atlantis, 1981), pp. 55–59; Roland Auguet, *Cruelty and Civilization* (London: Allen and Unwin, 1972), pp. 32–36, 124–126; Balsdon, *Life and Leisure*, p. 268.

27. Ibid., p. 291.

28. Petronius, *The Satyricon*, trans. William Arrowsmith (Ann Arbor: University of Michigan Press, 1959), p. 42.

29. Grant, *Gladiators*, p. 31.

30. Georges Ville, *La Gladiature*, p. 262.

31. Suetonius, *The Twelve Caesars*, Robert Graves, trans. (Harmondsworth: Penguin, 1957), p. 75; P. S. Tumolesi, *Gladiatorum pari* (Rome: Edizioni di Storia e Letteratura, 1980), p. 157; see also Wilhelm Backhaus, "Oeffentliche Spiele, Sport und Gesellschaft in der roemischen Antike," *Geschichte der Leibesuebungen*, ed. Horst Ueberhorst, 6 vols. (planned) (Berlin: Bartels and Wernitz, 1972–), 2:208–209; Ward W. Briggs Jr., "Augustan Athletics and the Games of *Aeneid* V," *Stadion* (1975) 1(2): 267–283.

32. Horace, *Satires and Epistles*, S. P. Boyle, trans. (Chicago: University of Chicago Press, 1959), p. 216.

33. Balsdon, *Life and Leisure*, pp. 289–290.

34. Ville, *Le Gladiature*, p. 344.

35. Juvenal, *Satires*, Rolfe Humphries, trans. (Bloomington: Indiana University Press, 1958), p. 67.

36. Grant, *Gladiators*, p. 96.

37. Hoenle and Henze, *Roemische Amphitheater und Stadien*, pp. 17–18.

38. Tacitus, *The Annals of Imperial Rome*, trans. Michael Grant (Harmondsworth: Penguin Books, 1959), pp. 311–312.

39. Barry Baldwin, "The Sports Fans of Rome and Byzantium," *Liverpool Classical Monthly* (February 1984) 9(2): 29.

40. Traugott Bollinger, *Theatralis Licentia* (Winterthur: Hans Schellenberg, 1969), pp. 14–15.

41. Suetonius, *The Twelve Caesars*, p. 76.

42. Balsdon, *Life and Leisure*, p. 259; Alan Cameron, *Circus Factions* (Oxford: Clarendon Press, 1976), pp. 176–177.

43. Auguet, *Cruelty and Civilization*, p. 38.

44. Bollinger, *Theatralis Licentia*, pp. 6, 19.

45. Bollinger, *Theatralis Licentia*, p. 18.

46. Friedlaender, *Roman Life and Manners*, 2:62.

47. Horace, *Satires and Epistles*, p. 148.

48. Augustine, *Confessions*, E. B. Pusey, trans. (London: J. M. Dent, 1907), pp. 106–107.

49. Friedlaender, *Roman Life and Manners*, 2:43.

50. Balsdon, *Life and Leisure*, pp. 290–291.

51. Petronius, *Satyricon*, p. 43.

52. Dio Cassius, *Roman History*, E. Cary and H. B. Foster, trans., 9 vols. (New York: Macmillan, 1908–1913), 8:335; Ville, *La Gladiature*, pp. 263–264; Balsdon, *Life and Leisure*, p. 299.

53. Juvenal, *Satires*, p. 18.

54. Suetonius, *The Twelve Caesars*, p. 163; Auguet, *Cruelty and Civilization*, pp. 93–99.

55. George Jennison, *Animals for Show and Pleasure in Ancient Rome* (Manchester: University of Manchester Press, 1937), p. 52.

56. Suetonius, *The Twelve Caesars*, p. 167.

57. Cicero, *Twelve Orations*, cited by Hoenle and Heinze, *Roemische Amphitheater und Stadien*, p. 20.

58. Ovid, *The Art of Love*, Rolfe Humphries, trans. (Bloomington: Indiana University Press, 1957), pp. 164–165.

59. Seneca, *Ad Lucilium Epistulae Morales*, R. M. Gummere, trans., 3 vols. (London: Heinemann, 1917–1925), 1:30–31; the best discussions of pagan and Christian moral responses are Ville, *La Gladiature*, pp. 447–472; Werner Weismann, *Kirche und Schauspiel* (Wuerzburg: Augustinus, 1972).

60. Tertullian, *De Spectaculis*, T. R. Glover, trans. (London: Heinemann, 1931), pp. 271–273.

61. Salvian, *On the Government of God*, E. M. Sanford, trans. (New York: Columbia University Press, 1930), p. 160.

62. Georges Ville, "Les Jeux des gladiateurs dans l'empire chrétien," *Mélanges d'Archéologie et d'Histoire de l'Ecole Française de Rome* (1960) 72:289.

63. Novatian, *De Spectaculis*, G. F. Diercks, ed. (Turnholt: Brepols, 1972), p. 171.

64. Barbara Schrodt, "Sports of the Byzantine Empire," *Journal of Sport History* (1981) 8(3):51.

65. Balsdon, *Life and Leisure*, pp. 244–252.

66. Robert, *Les Gladiateurs*, p. 248.

67. Jerome Carcopino, *Daily Life in Ancient Rome*, E. O. Lorimer, trans. (New Haven: Yale University Press, 1940), pp. 214–215; other scholars estimate the capacity of the Circus Maximus at 150,000 to 190,000: Heinz Kindermann, *Das Theaterpublikum der Antike* (Salzburg: Otto Mueller, 1979), p. 124; Balsdon, *Life and Leisure*, p. 268; Friedlaender, *Roman Life and Manners*, II, 20.

68. Quoted in H. A. Harris, *Sport in Greece and Rome* (London: Thames and Hudson, 1972), pp. 221–222.

69. Cameron, *Circus Factions*, p. 219.

70. Quoted in Carcopino, *Daily Life*, p. 219.

71. See Hoenel and Heinze, *Roemische Amphitheater und Stadien*, p. 103, plate 71.

72. Alan Cameron, *Porphyrius the Charioteer* (Oxford: Clarendon Press, 1973), p. 1.

73. Balsdon, *Life and Leisure*, p. 314.

74. Harris, *Sport in Greece and Rome*, p. 215.

75. Suetonius, *The Twelve Caesars*, pp. 194, 214. Carcopino, *Daily Life in Ancient Rome*, p. 214; Balsdon, *Life and Leisure*, p. 260.

76. Carcopino, *Daily Life*, p. 217.

77. Cameron, *Circus Factions*, p. 231.

78. Ibid., pp. 50, 79.

79. Ovid, *The Art of Love*, pp. 109–110.

80. Ibid., p. 69.

81. Juvenal, *Satires*, p. 35.

82. Balsdon, *Life and Leisure*, p. 253.

83. Cameron, *Circus Factions*, p. 273.

84. Pliny, *Letters*, Betty Radice, trans. (Harmondsworth: Penguin, 1963), p. 236.

85. Stephen Hardy, "Politicians, Promoters, and the Rise of Sport: The Case of Ancient Greece and Rome," *Canadian Journal for History of Sport and Physical Education* (1977) 8(1):1–15.

86. Bollinger, *Theatralis Licentia*, p. 71.

87. Ville, *La Gladiature*, p. 445.

88. Cameron, *Circus Factions*, pp. 179–180.

89. Bollinger, *Theatricalis Licentia*, pp. 32–33; Cameron, *Circus Factions*, pp. 236–237; C. R. Whittaker, "The Revolt of Papirius Dionysius A.D. 190," *Historia* (1964) 12:363.

90. Ibid., pp. 348–369.

91. Rodolphe Guilland, "The Hippodrome at Byzantium," *Speculum* (1948) 22:676–682.

92. John Malalas, *Chronicle*, trans. Matthew Spinka and Glanville Downey (Chicago: University of Chicago Press, 1940), p. 111; Cameron, *Circus Factions*, p. 150.

93. Cameron, *Circus Factions*, pp. 277–280.

94. Ibid., pp. 20, 77, 284, 311.

95. Bollinger, *Theatralis Licentia*, p. 24.

96. Cameron, *Circus Factions*, p. 101.

97. See J.-P. Augustin and M. Berges, "Sports et société locale: le rugby à Bordeaux," in Christian Pociello, ed., *Sports et Société* (Paris: Vigot, 1981), pp. 337–351.

98. Cameron, *Circus Factions*, pp. 271n2, 296n1.

2. THE MIDDLE AGES AND THE RENAISSANCE

1. Roger Sherman Loomis, "Arthurian Influence on Sport and Spectacle," in Loomis, ed., *Arthurian Literature in the Middle Ages* (Oxford: Clarendon Press, 1959), p. 557.

2. Klemens C. Wildt, *Leibesuebungen im deutschen Mittelalter* (Frankfurt: Wilhelm Limpert, 1957), p. 6; Michael William McConahey, "Sports and Recreations in Later Medieval France and England" (Ph.D. diss., University of Southern California, 1974), p. 433; see also Franz Begov, "Sportgeschichte der fruehen Neuzeit," *Geschichte der Leibesuebungen*, Horst Ueberhorst, ed., 6 vols. (Berlin: Bartels and Wernitz, 1972–), 3:145–164; for instruction for the ways in which each medieval order was involved in the sports of the others, I am indebted to John Marshall Carter's *"Ludi Medi Aevi": Studies in the History of Medieval Sport* (Manhattan, Kansas: MA/AH Publishers, 1981).

3. J. J. Jusserand, *Les Sports et jeux d'exerice dans l'ancienne France* (Paris: Plon, 1901), pp. 12, 18.

4. Richard Barber, *The Knight and Chivalry* (Ipswich: Boydell Press, 1974), p. 193; see also Charles Homer Haskins, "The Latin Literature of Sport," *Speculum* (1927) 2:238: "The major sport of the Middle Ages was war, with its adjuncts the tournament, the joust, and the judicial duel."

5. Paul Meyer, ed., *L'Histoire de Guillaume le Maréchal*, 3 vols. (Paris: Renouard, 1891–1901), 3:74.

6. Stephen H. Hardy, "The Medieval Tournament," *Journal of Sport History* (Fall 1974) 1(2):96.

7. Jusserand, *Les Sports et jeux*, p. 58; Maurice Keen, *Chivalry* (New Haven: Yale University Press, 1984), p. 87.

8. Barber, *The Knight and Chivalry*, p. 191; Keen, *Chivalry*, p. 86.

9. Francis Henry Cripps-Day, *History of the Tournament in England and France* (London: Bernard Quaritch, 1918), p. 29.

10. Jusserand, *Les Sports et jeux*, p. 55.

11. Sidney Painter, *William Marshal* (Baltimore: Johns Hopkins University Press, 1933), p. 38.

12. Arthur B. Ferguson, *The Indian Summer of English Chivalry* (Durham, North Carolina: Duke University Press, 1960), p. 14; see also Sydney Anglo, *The Great Tournament Roll of Westminster*, 2 vols. (Oxford: Clarendon Press, 1968), 1:19–40; Maurice Keen, "Huizinga, Kilgour and the Decline of Chivalry," *Medievalia et Humanistica*, n.s. (1977) 8:1–20.

13. Jusserand, *Les Sports et jeux*, p. 73.

14. For the point system, see Joycelyn G. Russell, *The Field of Cloth of Gold* (New York: Barnes and Noble, 1969), p. 116; Joachim K. Ruehl, "Wesen und Bedeutung von Kampfsagen und Trefferzahlskizzen . . . ," *Sport zwischen Eigenstandigkeit und Fremdbestimmung*, pp. 86–112.

15. Quoted by Teresa McLean, *The English at Play in the Middle Ages* (Shooter's Lodge, Windsor Forest, Berkshire: Kensal Press, 1983), pp. 75–76.

16. Martin Hahn, *Die Leibesuebungen im mittelalterlichen Volksleben* (Langensalza: Hermann Beyer und Sohn, 1929), p. 56.

17. Ibid., p. 58.

18. F. K. Mathys, *Spiel und Sport im alten Basel* (Basel: Cratander, 1954), p. 15.

19. Austin Lane Poole, "Recreations," in A. L. Poole, ed., *Medieval England*, 2 vols. (Oxford: Clarendon Press, 1958), 2:623.

20. Illustrated in Horst Ueberhorst, ed., *Geschichte der Leibesuebungen*, 6 vols. (planned) (Berlin: Bartels and Wernitz, 1972–), 3:123.

21. John Stow, *Survey of London*, Charles Lethbridge Kingsford, ed., 2 vols. (Oxford: Clarendon, 1908), 1:268.

22. John Nichols, *The Progresses and Public Processions of Queen Elizabeth*, 3 vols. (London: John Nichols and Son, 1823), 2:302n2.

23. R. Coltman Clephan, *The Tournament* (London: Methuen, 1919), 76–78.

24. Keen, *Chivalry*, plate 21.

25. Painter, *William Marshal*, p. 59.

26. Kenneth Grant Tremayne Webster, "The Twelfth-Century Tourney," *Anniversary Papers by Colleagues and Pupils of George Lyman Kittredge* (Boston: Ginn, 1913), p. 230.

27. On Chrétien, see Larry D. Benson, "The Tournament in the Romances of Chrétien de Troyes," *Chivalric Literature*, Larry D. Benson and John Leyerle, eds. (Kalamazoo: Western Michigan University Press, 1980), pp. 1–24.

28. Quoted by Jusserand, *Les Sports et jeux*, p. 141.

29. Illustrated in Raymond Rudorff, *Knights and the Age of Chivalry* (New York: Viking, 1974), p. 104.

30. Felix Niedner, *Das deutsche Tournier im XII und XIII Jahrhundert* (Berlin: Weidmannsche Buchhandlung, 1881), p. 90. A more moderate assessment of the historicity of romance appears in Larry D. Benson's *Malory's Morte d'Arthur* (Cambridge: Harvard University Press, 1976).

31. *The Comedy of Eros*, Norman R. Shapiro, trans. (Urbana: University of Illinois Press, 1971), pp. 19–20.

32. M. A. E. Green, *Lives of the Princesses of England*, 6 vols. (London: Henry Colburn, 1849–1855), 3:176.

33. Keen, *Chivalry*, p. 91; Hahn, *Leibesuebungen*, p. 52.

34. Jean Froissart, *Chronicles*, John Bourchier, trans., 4 vols. (London: J. Davis, 1814–1816) 4:51–60.

35. Anglo, *The Great Tournament Roll*, :28.

36. Cripps-Day, *History of the Tournament*, pp. lxvii–lxxxviii.

37. Jean Verdon, *Les Loisirs au moyen age* (Paris: Jules Tallandier, 1980), p. 179. Roy Strong comments, "the element of actual combat was made subservient to a

carefully rehearsed dramatic plot" (*Splendor at Court: Renaissance Spectacle and the Theater of Power* [Boston: Houghton Mifflin, 1973], p. 38).

38. Anglo, *The Great Tournament Roll*, 1:30.

39. Ibid., p. 29.

40. Ibid., p. 38.

41. John Hutton to Arthur Plantagenet, Viscount Lisle, March 5, 1538, in Muriel St. Clare Byrne, ed., *The Lisle Letters*, 6 vols. (Chicago: University of Chicago Press, 1981), 5:46.

42. Marcia Vale, *The Gentleman's Recreations* (Totowa: Rowman and Littlefield, 1977), p. 11.

43. Volume II of Anglo's *Great Tournament Roll* reproduces the entire roll.

44. Loomis, "Arthurian Influence on Sport and Spectacle," pp. 553–559; Ruth Huff Cline, "The Influence of Romances on Tournaments of the Middle Ages," *Speculum* (1945) 20):204–211; Arno Borst, "Das Rittertum im Hochmittelalter—Idee und Wirklichkeit," *Saeculum* (1959) 10):213–231; Miriam Sambursky, trans., in Frederic L. Cheyette, ed., *Lordship and Community in Medieval Europe* (New York: Holt, Rinehart and Winston, 1968), pp. 180–191.

45. Rosamund Mitchell, *John Tiptoft, 1427–1470* (London: Longmans, Green, 1938), pp. 103–111; in A. R. Myers, ed., *English Historical Documents* (London: Eyre and Spottiswoode, 1969), 1170–1174.

46. Quoted in Anglo, *The Great Tournament Roll*, 1:37.

47. Reproduced in Jusserand, *Les Sports et jeux d'exercice*, p. 155. The same configuration appears in an early 17th-century print of a tournament in the Place des Vosges, reproduced in Franz-Joachim Verspohl, *Stadienbauten von der Antike bis zur Gegenwart* (Giessen: Anabas, 1976), p. 89.

48. Ulrich von Liechtenstein, *Frauendienst*, trans. as *Service of Ladies* by J. W. Thomas (Chapel Hill: University of North Carolina Press, 1969), p. 107.

49. Sir Thomas Malory, *Works*, Eugene Vinaver, ed. 3 vols. (Oxford: Clarendon Press, 1947), 1:13.

50. *The Comedy of Eros*, p. 21.

51. Quoted in Cripps-Day, *History of the Tournament*, p. 45.

52. Barber, *The Knight and Chivalry*, p. 189.

53. Noel Denholm-Young, "The Tournament in the Thirteenth Century," in R. W. Hunt, *Studies in Medieval History* (Oxford: Clarendon Press, 1948), p. 262.

54. Quoted in Cripps-Day, *History of the Tournament*, p. xxv; see also Denholm-Young, "The Tournament," pp. 257–262. The date of the Statute is in dispute.

55. Wildt, *Leibesuebungen*, p. 28; Walter Schaufelberger, *Der Wettkampf in der alten Eidgenossenschaft* (Bern: Paul Haupt, 1972), p. 46.

56. Theo Reintges, *Ursprung und Wesen der spaetmittelalterlichen Schuetzengilden* (Bonn: Ludwig Roehrscheid, 1963).

57. Hermann Goja, *Die oesterreichischen Schuetzengilden und ihre Feste* (Vienna: Verlag Notring der wissenschaftlichen Verbaende Oesterreichs, 1963), pp. 123–124.

58. Roland Renson, "Leibesuebungen der Buerger und Bauern im Mittelalter," in Ueberhorst, *Geschichte der Liebesuebungen*, 3:110.

59. Reintges, *Ursprung und Wesen*, p. 287.

60. Ibid., pp. 297–298.

61. L. A. Delaunay, *Etude sur les anciènnes compagnies d'archers, d'arbalétriers et d'arquebusiers* (Paris: Champion, 1879), p. 247.

62. Klaus Zieschang, *Vom Schuetzenfest zum Turnfest* (Ahrensburg: Czwalina, 1977), p. 47.

63. Hans Germann, *Der Ehrenspiegel deutscher Schuetzen* (Leipzig: Thankmar Rudolph, 1928), pp. 87–101.

64. Goja, *Schuetzengilden*, pp. 45–84.

65. Germann, *Der Ehrenspiegel*, p. 66; Arnold Wehrle, *500 Jahre Spiel und Sport in Zuerich* (Zuerich: Berichthaus, 1960), p. 17.

66. Michel Bouet, *Signification du sport* (Paris: Editions universitaires, 1968), p. 257.

67. Eric Dunning and Kenneth Sheard, *Barbarians, Gentlemen and Players* (Oxford: Martin Robertson, 1979), p. 25.

68. Percy M. Young, *A History of British Football* (London: Arrow Books, 1973), pp. 48, 58.

69. McLean, *English at Play*, p. 8.

70. Dunning and Sheard, *Barbarians, Gentlemen and Players*, p. 29.

71. Quoted in *Ibid.*, p. 28.

72. Quoted in David C. Douglas and George W. Greenaway, eds. *English Historical Documents* (London: Eyre and Spottiswoode, 1953), p. 960.

73. See Francis Peabody Magoun, Jr., *History of Football* (Bochum: Heinrich Poeppinghaus, 1938), pp. 110–111.

74. Quoted in William Heywood, *Palio and Ponte* (New York: Hacker Art Books, 1969), pp. 166–167; see also Theodor Mommsen, "Football in Renaissance Florence," *Yale University Library Gazette* (1941) 16:14–19.

75. Heywood, *Palio and Ponte*, facing p. 170.

76. Young, *British Football*, pp. 68–71.

77. Robert Davidsohn, *Geschichte von Florenz*, 4 vols. (Berlin: E. S. Mittler und Sohn, 1927), 4:284–286; Werner Koerbs, *Vom Sinn der Leibesuebungen zur Zeit der italienischen Renaissance* (Graefenhainichen: Schulze, 1938), pp. 13–15.

3. ENGLISHMEN AND OTHERS

1. See Herbert Schoeffler, *England: Das Land des Sportes* (Leipzig: Tauchnitz, 1935); Christian Graf von Krockow, *Sport und Industriegesellschaft* (Munich: Piper, 1972); Henning Eichberg, *Der Weg des Sports in die industrielle Zivilisation* (Baden-Baden: Nomos, 1973); Richard D. Mandell, *Sport: A Cultural History* (New York: Columbia University Press, 1984), pp. 132–157. Arnd Krueger and John McClelland have recently challenged this view; see *Die Anfaenge des modernen Sports in der Renaissance* (London: Arena Publications, 1984), pp. 9–42, 85–110.

2. See Joachim K. Ruehl, *Die "Olympischen Spiele" Robert Dovers* (Heidelberg: Carl Winter, 1975).

3. See Maria Kloeren, *Sport und Rekord* (Leipzig: Tauchnitz, 1935).

4. Samuel Pepys, *Diary*, Robert Latham and William Matthews, eds. 11 vols. (Berkeley: University of California Press, 1970–1983), 5:4.

5. See my *From Ritual to Record: The Nature of Modern Sports* (New York: Columbia University Press, 1978), pp. 15–55; Eric Dunning, "The Structural-Functional Properties of Folk-Games and Modern Sports . . . ," *Sportwissenschaft* (1973) 3(3):215–232.

6. On the concept of the sports record, see Richard D. Mandell, "The Invention of the Sports Record," *Stadion* (1976) 2(2):250–264; Guttmann, *From Ritual to Record*, pp. 47–54.

7. Quoted in Kloeren, *Sport und Rekord*, p. 196.

8. Quoted in Henry Alken, *The National Sports of Great Britain* (London: Methuen, 1903), no pagination.

9. Christina Hole, *English Sports and Pastimes* (London: Batsford, 1949), p. 104.

10. John Nichols, *The Progresses and Public Processions of Queen Elizabeth*, 3 vols. (London: John Nichols and Sons, 1823), 1:438n2; John Nichols, *The Progresses . . . of King James I*, 4 vols. (London: J. B. Nichols, 1828), 1:36; 2:259, 308; C. L. Kingsford, "Paris Garden and the Bear-baiting," *Archaelogia*, (1920) 70:168.

11. Pepys, *Diary*, 7:246.

12. John Evelyn, *Diary*, E. S. de Beer, ed. 6 vols. (London: Oxford University Press, 1955), 3:549.

13. James Woodforde, *Diary of a Country Parson, 1758–1802*, John Beresford, ed. 5 vols. (London: Oxford University Press, 1924–1931), 1:12.

14. Thomas Platter, *Beschreibung der Reisen durch Frankreich, Spanien, England und die Niederlande, 1595–1600*, Rut Keiser, ed. 2 vols. (Basel: Schwabe, 1968), 793–795.

15. Evelyn, *Diary*, 3:549.

16. Quoted in Keith Thomas, *Man and the Natural World* (New York: Pantheon, 1983), p. 144.

17. Quoted in Kloeren, *Sport und Rekord*, p. 40.

18. Clifford Geertz, *The Interpretation of Cultures* (New York: Basic Books, 1973), pp. 412–453; for a glimpse of cockfight spectators in Heian Japan, see Ivan Morris, *The World of the Shining Prince* (Harmondsworth: Penguin Books, 1979), p. 165.

19. Quoted in David C. Douglas and George M. Greenaway, eds., *English Historical Documents: II, 1042–1189* (London: Eyre and Spottiswoode, 1953), pp. 956–962.

20. René Graziani, "Sir Thomas Wyatt at a Cockfight, 1539," *Review of English Studies* (August 1976) 27:299–303; Joseph Strutt, *Sports and Pastimes of the People of England*, William Hone, ed. (1801; London: Thomas Tegg, 1838), p. 282.

21. Robert Ashton, "Popular Entertainments and Social Control in later Elizabethan and early Stuart England," *London Journal* (Summer 1983) 9(1):9.

22. Quoted in Kloeren, *Sport und Rekord*, p. 36.

23. Pepys, *Diary*, 4:427–428.

24. Robert W. Malcolmson, *Popular Recreations in English Society, 1700–1850* (Cambridge: Cambridge University Press, 1973), p. 49.

25. Zacharias Conrad von Uffenbach, *London in 1710*, W. H. Quarrell and Margaret Mare, trans. (London: Faber and Faber, 1934), pp. 48–49.

26. James Boswell, *London Journal*, Frederick A. Pottle, ed. (New York: Mc-Graw-Hill, 1950), p. 87.

27. Béat Louis de Muralt, *Lettres sur les anglois et les françois*, Charles Gould, ed. (Paris: Honoré Champion, 1933), p. 132.

28. Quoted in Malcolmson, *Popular Recreations*, p. 137.

29. Quoted in John Ford, *This Sporting Land* (London: New English Library, 1977), p. 69.

30. Quoted in Malcolmson, *Popular Recreations*, p. 137.

31. Robert D. Storch, "The Policeman as Domestic Missionary: Urban Discipline and Popular Culture in Northern England, 1850–1880," *Journal of Social History* (June 1976) 9(4):496.

32. Thomas, *Man and the Natural World*, p. 159.

33. James Turner, *Reckoning with the Beast* (Baltimore: Johns Hopkins University Press, 1980), p. 26.

34. Robert D. Storch, "The Problem of Working-Class Leisure . . . ," in A. P. Donajgrodzki, ed. *Social Control in Nineteenth Century Britain* (Totowa: Rowman and Littlefield, 1977), p. 141.

35. Quoted in Malcolmson, *Popular Recreations*, pp. 106, 156.

36. Turner, *Reckoning with the Beast*, p. 15.

37. Alken, *National Sports*, p. ix.

38. Quoted in Malcolmson, *Popular Recreations*, p. 153.

39. On the social aspects of foxhunting, see David C. Itzkowitz, *Peculiar Privilege: A Social History of English Foxhunting, 1753–1885* (Hassocks, Sussex: Harvester Press, 1977).

40. Alan Metcalfe, "Organized Sport in the Mining Communities of South Northumberland," *Victorian Studies* (Summer 1982) 25(4):475.

41. Quoted in Malcolmson, *Popular Recreations*, p. 127.

42. Malcolmson, *Popular Recreations*, p. 132. On the difficulties of the police in this era, see Robert D. Storch, "A Plague of Blue Locusts," *International Review of Social History*, (1975) 20(1):61–90.

43. Alken, *National Sports*, unpaginated text.

44. Henry Mayhew, *London Labour and the London Poor*, 4 vols. (1861–1862; London: Cass, 1967), 3:5, 7–8.

45. Philip Vickers Fithian, *Journal and Letters*, Hunter Dickinson Parish, ed. (Williamsburg: Colonial Williamsburg, 1943), p. 128; see also Jennie Holliman, *American Sports (1785–1835)* (Durham, North Carolina: Seeman Press, 1931), p. 178; Jane Carson, *Colonial Virginians at Play* (Williamsburg: Colonial Williamsburg, 1965).

46. François-Jean de Beauvoir, Marquis de Chastellux, *Travels in North America*, Howard C. Rice Jr., trans. and ed. (Chapel Hill: University of North Carolina Press, 1963), p. 387.

47. Elkanah Watson, *Men and Times of the Revolution*, 2nd ed., Winslow C. Watson, ed. (New York: Appleton, 1861), pp. 300–301.

48. Quoted in John Dizikes, *Sportsmen and Gamesmen* (Boston: Houghton Mifflin, 1981), pp. 8–9, 28.

49. Maxence Van der Meersch, *L'Empreinte du dieu* (Paris: Albin Michel, 1936), p. 118.

50. Kloeren, *Sport und Rekord*, p. 273.

51. Cited in Ibid., p. 237.

52. James Peller Malcolm, *Anecdotes of the Manners and Customs of London during the Eighteenth Century*, 2d ed., 2 vols. (London: Longman, Hurst, Rees, and Orme, 1810), 1:287.

53. Kloeren, *Sport und Rekord*, p. 239.

54. Ibid., p. 240.

55. Pepys, *Diary*, 8:167.

56. Malcolmson, *Popular Recreations*, p. 7.

57. Malcolm, *Anecdotes*, 2:183.

58. Woodforde, *Diary*, 1:90.

59. Kloeren, *Sport und Rekord*, pp. 264–265.

60. Philip Hone, *Diary*, Allan Nevins, ed. (New York: Dodd, Mead, 1936), p. 156; *New York Post*, April 25, 1835.

61. Benjamin Rader, *American Sports* (Englewood Cliffs, New Jersey: Prentice-Hall, 1983), p. 40; a graphic but not always accurate account of this period of American pedestrianism appears in John Cumming, *Runners and Walkers* (Chicago: Henry Regnery, 1981), pp. 5–34.

62. Uffenbach, *London*, p. 107.

63. William Byrd, *Secret Diary*, Louis B. Wright and Marion Tingling, eds. (Richmond: Dietz Press, 1941), p. 75.

64. *Virginia Gazette*, September 30–October 7, 1737; quoted in T. H. Breen, "Horses and Gentlemen: The Cultural Significance of Gambling among the Gentry of Virginia," *William and Mary Quarterly* (April 1977) 34(2):250–251.

65. Fithian, *Journal and Letters*, p. 32. The entry is for November 25, 1773.

66. John Bernard, *Retrospections of America, 1797–1811* (New York: Harper and Bros., 1887), pp. 154–156.

67. Ibid.

68. Thomas Ashe, *Travels in America*, 2 vols. (London: John Abraham, 1808), 1:227, 229; for a general discussion of backwoods violence, see Elliott J. Gorn, " 'Gouge and Bite, Pull Hair and Scratch': The Social Significance of Fighting in the Southern Backcountry," *American Historical Review* (February 1985) (90)1):18–43.

69. Thomas Anburey, *Travels through the Interior Parts of America*, 2 vols. (1789; Boston: Houghton Mifflin, 1923), 2:228.

70. Hugh Cunningham, *Leisure in the Industrial Revolution* (New York: St. Martin's, 1980), p. 19.

71. Ford, *This Sporting Land*, p. 91.

72. Wray Vamplew, *The Turf* (London: Allen Lane, 1976), pp. 18, 38.

73. J. C. Whyte, *History of the British Turf* (1840), quoted by Vamplew, p. 26.

74. William J. Baker, *Sports in the Western World* (Totowa: Rowman and Littlefield, 1982), p. 88.

75. Vamplew, *The Turf*, p. 30.

76. Mary Russell Mitford, *Our Village* (1824–1832; London: J. M. Dent, 1936), p. 283.

77. Charles Dickens, *Uncollected Writings from HOUSEHOLD WORDS*, Harry Stone, ed. 2 vols. (Bloomington: Indiana University Press, 1968), 2:305.

78. Cunningham, *Leisure in the Industrial Revolution*, pp. 19–20.

79. Quoted in Malcolmson, *Popular Recreations*, p. 51.

80. John Ford, *Prizefighting* (Newton Abbot: David and Charles, 1971), p. 85.

81. Ford, *This Sporting Land*, p. 94.

82. Evelyn, *Diary*, 3:476.

83. Ruehl, *Die "olympischen Spiele" Robert Dovers*, p. 193.

84. Malcolmson, *Popular Recreations*, p. 43.

85. Pepys, *Diary*, 4:168.

86. Quoted in Kloeren, *Sport und Rekord*, pp. 42–43.

87. Uffenbach, *London*, pp. 88–89.

88. Quoted in Kloeren, *Sport und Rekord*, pp. 23, 26.

89. William Rufus Chetwood, *A General History of the Stage . . .* (London: W. Owen, 1749), p. 60n.

90. Kloeren, *Sport und Rekord*, p. 56.

91. Ibid., p. 59.

92. Ibid., p. 50.

93. Antoine Prévost, *Mémoires d'un homme de qualité*, 8 vols. (1728–1756; Paris: Champion, 1927), 5:91.

94. Voltaire, *Lettres philosophiques*, Gustave Lanson, ed. 2 vols. (Paris: Edouard Cornély, 1909), 2:110n.

95. Joseph Addison and Richard Steele, *The Spectator* (No. 436, July 21, 1712), Donald F. Bond, ed. (Oxford: Oxford University Press, 1965), p. 34.

96. Uffenbach, *London*, p. 90.

97. Ibid., pp. 90–91.

98. Quoted in Kloeren, *Sport und Rekord*, pp. 45, 56–57.

99. Ibid., pp. 45–46; Malcolm, *Anecdotes*, 2:163.

100. William Hickey, *Memoirs*, Alfred Spencer, ed. 4 vols. (London: Hurst and Blackett, 1913–1925), 1:82–83.

101. Kloeren, *Sport und Rekord*, p. 35.

102. Ibid., pp. 63–64.

103. Pierce Egan, *Boxiana*, 5 vols. (London: Sherwood, Neely and Jones, 1829), 1:58.

104. Ibid., 1:219–220.

105. Ford, *Prizefighting*, p. 149.

106. Quoted from Ford, *Prizefighting*, p. 132. See also Carl Diem, *Lord Byron als Sportsman* (Cologne: Comel, 1950), p. 86.

107. Ford, *This Sporting Land*, 104.

108. Quoted from Ford, *Prizefighting*, p. 148.

109. Ibid., p. 163.

110. Ibid., p. 150.

111. On Egan, see John C. Reid, *Bucks and Bruisers* (London: Routledge and Kegan Paul, 1971).

112. William Hazlitt, "The Fight," *Complete Works*, A. R. Waller and Arnold Glover, eds. 13 vols. (London: J. M. Dent, 1902–1906), 12:1–15.

113. Egan, *Boxiana*, 2:241.

114. Ibid., 4:374.

115. Bernard Darwin, *John Gully and His Times* (New York: Harper and Brothers, 1935), p. 11.

116. Ibid., pp. 11–12.

117. Egan, *Boxiana*, 3:139.

118. Ibid., 5:584.

119. Ibid., 4:287–288.

120. Ibid., 4:308.

121. Ibid., 4:365; 5:164.

122. Carl B. Cone, ed., *Hounds in the Morning* (Lexington: University Press of Kentucky, 1981), pp. 159–160.

123. Quoted in Dennis Brailsford, "Morals and Maulers," *Journal of Sport History* (Summer 1985) 12(2):139.

124. Egan, *Boxiana*, 1:367, 414.

125. H. A. Harris, *Sport in Britain* (London: Stanley Paul, 1975), p. 36.

126. Malcolmson, *Popular Recreations*, p. 79.

127. Mitford, *Our Village*, pp. 63–64, 67–68.

128. Dennis Brailsford, "Sporting Days in Eighteenth Century England," *Journal of Sport History*, (Winter 1982) 9(3):49.

129. Ford, *This Sporting Land*, p. 87; Christopher Brookes, *English Cricket* (London: Weidenfeld and Nicholson, 1978), pp. 71–72.

130. Hole, *English Sports*, p. 62.

131. Quoted in Harris, *Sport in Britain*, p. 41.

132. Hugh de Selincourt, *The Cricket Match* (London: Jonathan Cape, 1924).

133. Quoted in Hans Indorf, *Fair Play und der "Englische Sportgeist"* (Hamburg: Friederchsen, de Gruyter, 1938), p. 67.

134. Siegfried Sassoon, *Memoirs of a Fox-Hunting Man* (New York: Coward, McCann, 1929), pp. 52–81.

135. Richard Cashman, *Patrons, Players and the Crowd: The Phenomenon of Indian Cricket* (New Delhi: Orient Longman, 1980), endpapers. There were also sections where the public mingled.

136. Orlando Patterson, "The Cricket Ritual in the West Indies," *New Society* (June 26, 1969) 13:988; see also C. L. R. James, *Beyond a Boundary* (London: Hutchinson, 1963); Maurice St. Pierre, "West Indian Cricket . . . ," *Caribbean Quarterly* (June and September 1973) 19(2,3):7–27 and 20–35; Frank Manning, "Cel-

ebrating Cricket: The Symbolic Construction of Caribbean Politics," *American Ethnologist* (1981) 8(3):616–632. For an insight into the treatment of colonials at soccer matches in French-ruled Algeria, see Pierre Louis Rey, *Le Football* (Paris: Hachette, 1979), p. 36.

137. Quoted in Kloeren, *Sport und Rekord*, pp. 42–43.

4. MODERN SPECTATORS

1. See my *From Ritual to Record: The Nature of Modern Sports* (New York: Columbia University Press, 1978), pp. 15–55.

2. Carl B. Cone, ed., *Hounds in the Morning* (Lexington: University Press of Kentucky, 1981), pp. 1–26; Siegfried Weischenberg, *Die Aussenseiter der Redaktion* (Bochum: N. Brockmeyer, 1976), pp. 121, 128, 331–332; Harald Binnewies, *Sport und Sportberichterstattung* (Ahrensburg: Czwalina, 1975), p. 18; John C. Reid, *Bucks and Bruisers: Pierce Egan and Regency England* (London: Routledge and Kegan Paul, 1971).

3. Jack W. Berryman, "The Tenuous Attempts of Americans to 'Catch-Up with "John Bull" ': Specialty Magazines and Sporting Journalism, 1800–1835," *Canadian Journal of History of Sport* (May 1979) 10(1)):33–61.

4. Benjamin G. Rader, *In Its Own Image* (New York: Free Press, 1984), pp. 18–19; John Rickards Betts, *America's Sporting Heritage: 1850–1950* (Reading, Mass.: Addison-Wesley, 1974), pp. 53–56, 61.

5. Edouard Seidler, *Le Sport et la presse* (Paris: Armand Colin, 1964), p. 5.

6. Weischenberg, *Aussenseiter*, p. 125.

7. Ibid., p. 158.

8. Seidler, *Le Sport et la presse*, pp. 239–243.

9. Ibid., pp. 48–55.

10. Jean Fayard, *Oxford et Margaret* (Paris: Arthème Fayard, 1924).

11. See J. A. Mangan, *Athleticism in the Victorian and Edwardian Public School* (Cambridge: Cambridge University Press, 1981).

12. Cited in ibid., p. 47.

13. Christopher F. Armstrong, "The Lessons of Sports: Class Socialization in British and American Boarding Schools," *Sociology of Sport Journal* (1984) 1(4):314–331.

14. *Walter Camp's Book of College Sports* (New York: Century Co., 1893), in Steven A. Riess, ed., *The American Sporting Experience* (West Point, N.Y.: Leisure Press, 1984), p. 166.

15. Ira Hollis, "Intercollegiate Athletics," *Atlantic Monthy* (1902) 90:542.

16. Gerald Redmond, *The Caledonian Games in Nineteenth Century America* (Rutherford, New Jersey: Fairleigh Dickinson University Press, 1971), p. 16.

17. Montague Shearman, *Athletics and Football*, 4th ed. (London: Longmans, Green, 1891), p. 55; Jacques Thibault, *Sports et education physique 1870–1970*, 2d ed. (Paris: Vrin, 1979), p. 107.

18. September 20, 1891; see J. Willis and R. Wettan, "Social Stratification in

New York City Athletic Clubs, 1865–1915," *Journal of Sport History* (Spring 1976) 3(1):55–56.

19. *New York Times*, July 6, 1886; see Redmond, *Caledonian Games*, p. 48.

20. R. L. Quercetani, *A World History of Track and Field Athletics* (London: Oxford University Press, 1964), p. xv.

21. Rader, *American Sports* (Englewood Cliffs: Prentice-Hall, 1983), pp. 73–74; John A. Lucas and Ronald A. Smith, *Saga of American Sport* (Philadelphia: Lea and Febiger, 1978), p. 201.

22. Melvin Leonard Adelman, "The Development of Modern Athletics: Sport in New York City, 1820–1870" (Ph.D. diss., University of Illinois, 1980), p. 483.

23. Alan Metcalfe, "Organized Sport in the Mining Communities of South Northumberland," *Victorian Studies* (Summer 1982) 24(4):479.

24. Christopher Dodd, *The Oxford and Cambridge Boat Race* (London: Stanley Paul, 1983), p. 17.

25. Lothrop Withington, "When Harvard Won at Henley," *Outing* (October 1914) 65(1):95–106.

26. Dodd, *Oxford and Cambridge Boat Race*, p. 75.

27. Adelman, "The Development of Modern Athletics," p. 490.

28. Joseph Mathews, "The First Harvard-Oxford Boat Race," *New England Quarterly* (March 1960) 33(1):77.

29. Thomas C. Mendenhall, *A Short History of American Rowing* (Boston: Charles River Books, 1981), p. 27; Guy Lewis, "America's First Intercollegiate Sport: The Regatta from 1852 to 1875," *Research Quarterly* (December 1967) 38(4):637–648.

30. Arthur Ruhl, "Poughkeepsie's Great Day," *Outing* (June 1908) 52(3):316–329.

31. J. R. W. Hitchcock, "The Harvard-Yale Races," *Outing* (July 1885) 6:403.

32. Lewis, "America's First Intercollegiate Sport," 643.

33. Edwin H. Cady, *The Big Game* (Knoxville: University of Tennessee Press, 1978), p. 75.

34. William H. Edwards, *Football Days* (New York: Moffat, Yard, 1916), pp. 2–3.

35. Cited in Cady, *The Big Game*, pp. 11–12.

36. James H. Canfield, *The College Student and His Problems* (New York: Macmillan, 1902), p. 115.

37. Paula D. Welch and Harold A. Lerch, *History of American Physical Education and Sport* (Springfield, Ill.: Charles C. Thomas, 1981), pp. 235–237.

38. Paul Gallico, *Farewell to Sport* (New York: Knopf, 1938), p. 325.

39. Neil D. Isaacs, *All the Moves: A History of College Basketball* (Philadelphia: J. B. Lippincott, 1975), p. 15.

40. Bruce Newman, "Back Home in Indiana," *Sports Illustrated* (February 18, 1985) 62(7):38–61.

41. Benjamin Rader, *American Sports*, p. 65.

42. John A. Lucas and Ronald A. Smith, *Saga of American Sport* (Philadelphia: Lea and Febriger, 1978), p. 160.

43. Donald Mrozek, *Sport and American Mentality* (Knoxville: University of Tennessee Press, 1983), pp. 119–126.

44. Robert Dunn, "Newport, the Blessed of Sport," *Outing* (September 1908) 52(6):697.

45. John Joline Ross, "Some English Lawn-Tennis Players," *Outing* (November 1885) 7(2):132.

46. J. Parmly Paret, "Lawn Tennis on the European Continent," *Outing* (August 1899) 34(5):468.

47. Robert Dunn, "The Country Club: A National Expression: Where Woman Is Really Free," *Outing* (November 1905) 47(2):160–173.

48. The entire account is conveniently reprinted in Riess, *The American Sporting Experience*, pp. 91–103.

49. Gunther Barth, *City People* (New York: Oxford University Press, 1980), p. 155.

50. *New York Clipper*, April 17, 1869; see Adelman, "The Development of Modern Athletics," p. 163.

51. William Croffut, *The Vanderbilts* (Chicago: Bedford, Clarke, 1886), p. 204.

52. Hippolyte Taine, *Notes sur l'Angleterre* (1871; Paris: Hachette, 1923), p. 41.

53. *Monmouth Democrat*, July 20, 1893; see Glenn Uminowicz, "Sport as a Middle-Class Utopia: Asbury Park, New Jersey, 1871–1895," *Journal of Sport History* (Spring 1984) 11(1):51–73.

54. Salomon de Rothschild, *A Casual View of America*, Sigmund Diamond, trans. (Stanford: Stanford University Press, 1961), pp. 114–115.

55. Francis Trevelyan, "Racing at Southern Fairs," *Outing* (September 1888) 12:492, 496.

56. Thomas S. Blackwell, "Reminiscences of Irish Sport," *Outing* (July 1889) 14(4):269.

57. Joanna Richardson, *La Vie Parisienne 1852–1870* (New York: Viking, 1971), pp. 112–114.

58. Vance Thompson, "The Art of Racing in Paris," *Outing* (August 1903) 42(5):561–572.

59. Charles Belmont Davis, "The Americans at Play," *Outing* (December 1903) 43(3):265.

60. Julian K. Quattlebaum, *The Great Savannah Races* (1957; Athens: University of Georgia Press, 1983).

61. Arthur Goodrich, "Racing through France for Automobile Records," *Outing* (October 1905) 47(1):88.

62. See, John Eggleston, "Secondary Schools and Oxbridge Blues," *British Journal of Sociology* (1965) 16:232–243.

63. Keith A. P. Sandiford, "English Cricket Crowds during the Victorian Age," *Journal of Sport History* (Winter 1982) 9(3):6–8. Eric Midwinter thinks crowds of 20,000 were common as early as the 1870s; see W. G. *Grace* (London: George Allen and Unwin, 1981), p. 136.

64. Cited in Christopher Brookes, *English Cricket* (London: Weidenfeld and Nicolson, 1978), p. 91.

65. Sandiford, "English Cricket Crowds," p. 19.

66. Wray Vamplew, "Sports Crowd Disorder in Britain, 1870–1914: Causes and Controls," *Journal of Sport History* (Spring 1980) 7(1):7.

67. George B. Kirsch, "American Cricket," *Journal of Sport History* (Spring 1984) 11(1):36.

68. Sandiford, "English Cricket Crowds," p. 19.

69. Warner, "The End of the Cricket Season," *Badminton Magazine* (1912) 35:396; cited by Wray Vamplew, "Profit or Utility Maximisation?" (unpublished conference paper), p. 49.

70. Richard Cashman, 'Ave A Go, Yer Mug! (Sydney: Collins, 1984), pp. 11–14, 30–31, 48, 89.

71. Ibid., pp. 165–171, 186.

72. Ibid., pp. 121–129, 174–181.

73. Francis Peabody Magoun, *History of Football: From the Beginnings to 1871* (Bochum: Peoppinghaus, 1938), p. 40.

74. Cited by Steven Tischler, *Footballers and Businessmen* (New York: Holmes and Meier, 1981), p. 11.

75. Percy, M. Young, *British Football* (1968; London: Arrow Books, 1973), p. 113.

76. Tischler, *Footballers and Businessmen*, p. 26.

77. Wray Vamplew, "Sport and Industrialization," Flinders University Working Papers in Economic History, no. 9 (July 1985), p. 6. My facts on modern British soccer are drawn from James Walvin, *The People's Game* (London: Allen Lane, 1975); Charles P. Korr, "West Ham United Football Club and the Beginnings of Professional Football in East London, 1895–1914," *Journal of Contemporary History* (April 1978) 13:211–232; William J. Baker, "The Making of a Working-Class Football Culture in Victorian England," *Journal of Social History* (1979) 13(4):241–251; Tony Mason, *Association Football and English Society, 1863–1915* (Sussex: Harvester Press, 1980).

78. Cited by Tischler, *Footballers and Businessmen*, p. 123.

79. Hugh Cunningham, *Leisure in the Industrial Revolution* (New York: St. Martin's, 1980), p. 128; Peter Bailey, *Leisure and Class in Victorian England* (London: Routledge and Kegan Paul, 1978), pp. 136–146.

80. Ibid., pp. 181–182.

81. Cunningham, *Leisure*, p. 78.

82. Walvin, *The People's Game*, p. 77.

83. Wray Vamplew, "Unsporting Behavior: The Control of Football and Horse-Racing Crowds in England, 1875–1914: Causes and Controls," *Sports Violence*, Jeffery H. Goldstein, ed. (New York: Springer, 1983), p. 26.

84. Mason, *Association Football*, p. 150.

85. Wray Vamplew, "Sports Crowd Disorder in Britain," p. 9.

86. Mason, *Association Football*, pp. 163–164.

87. Wray Vamplew, "Sports Crowd Disorder," p. 6; Mason, *Association Football*, p. 166.

88. *Leicester Daily Mercury*, April 19, 1909; quoted in Eric Dunning, et al.,

"Football Hooliganism in Britain before the First World War," *International Review of Sport Sociology* (1984) 19(3–4):231–232.

89. *Birmingham Daily Mail*, February 11, 1902; quoted in Dunning et al., "Football Hooliganism," p. 234.

90. Mason, *Association Football*, p. 242.

91. Charles Edwardes, "The New Football Mania," *Nineteenth Century* (October 1892) 32:627.

92. Vamplew, "Unsporting Behavior," pp. 24–28.

93. Wray Vamplew, "Ungentlemanly Conduct: The Control of Soccer-Crowd Behaviour in England, 1888–1914," in T. C. Smout, ed., *The Search for Wealth and Stability* (London: Macmillan, 1979), p. 151.

94. Dunning at al., "Football Hooliganism," 224, 228.

95. *Birmingham Daily Post*, February 24, 1930; quoted by Eric Dunning et al., "The Social Roots of Football Hooligan Violence," *Leisure Studies* (1982) 1:149.

96. *Leicester Mercury*, March 19, 1934; quoted in Dunning et al., "The Social Roots," 150.

97. Ibid.

98. *Leicester Mercury*, April 23, 1927; quoted by Dunning et al., "The Social Roots," 151.

99. *Leicester Mercury*, April 27, 1929; quoted by Dunning et al., "The Social Roots," 151.

100. Eric Dunning and Kenneth Sheard, *Barbarians, Gentlemen and Players* (Oxford: Martin Robertson, 1979), p. 261.

101. Quoted in David Smith and Gareth Williams, *Fields of Praise* (Cardiff: University of Wales Press, 1980), p. 13.

102. Richard Holt, *Sport and Society in Modern France* (London: Macmillan, 1981), p. 135.

103. Ibid., p. 136.

104. Cited in Holt, *Sport and Society*, p. 137.

105. Ibid., p. 138; on lower-class disorder, see also Mikhail Bakhtin, *Rabelais and His World*, Helene Iswolsky, trans. (1965; Cambridge: MIT, 1968).

106. Alan Roadburg, "Factors Precipitating Fan Violence," *British Journal of Sociology* (June 1980) 31(2):265–276; Janet Lever, *Soccer Madness* (Chicago: University of Chicago Press, 1983), p. 44.

107. On the fabrication of the legend, see Peter Levine, A. G. Spalding and the Rise of Baseball (New York: Oxford University Press, 1985), pp. 112–115.

108. On the origins of the game, see Harold Peterson, *The Man Who Invented Baseball* (New York: Scribner's, 1973).

109. Adelman, "The Development of Modern Athletics," p. 387.

110. William Patten, ed., *The Book of Sport* (New York: J. F. Taylor, 1901).

111. Steven A. Riess argues that photographs of late-nineteenth-century baseball games reveal a "largely . . . middle-class audience," but he admits that working-class fans were also likely to show up in straw hats and derbies; see Riess, *Touching Base* (Westport, Conn.: Greenwood Press, 1980), p. 29.

112. Boston *Globe*, August 19, 1883, cited by Stephen Hardy, *How Boston Played* (Boston: Northeastern University Press, 1982), p. 187.

113. A. G. Spalding to Henry Graham, December 26, 1883; quoted in Levine, *A. G. Spalding*, p. 42.

114. Levine, A. G. *Spalding*, p. 51.

115. Harold Seymour, *Baseball: The Early Years* (New York: Oxford University Press, 1960), pp. 326–327.

116. Quoted in Betts, *America's Sporting Heritage*, p. 165.

117. Rollin Lynde Hartt, *The People at Play* (Boston: Houghton Mifflin, 1909), p. 286.

118. David Q. Voigt, *American Baseball: From Gentleman's Sport to the Commissioner System* (Norman: University of Oklahoma Press, 1966), p. 103.

119. Hardy, *How Boston Played*, pp. 188–191.

120. Gary Ross Mormino, "The Playing Fields of St. Louis: Italian Immigrants and Sports, 1925–1941," *Journal of Sport History* (Summer 1982) (9(2):5–19.

121. See Robert Peterson, *Only the Ball Was White* (Englewood Cliffs, N.J.: Prentice Hall, 1970); Jules Tygiel, *Baseball's Great Experiment* (New York: Oxford University Press, 1983).

122. Seymour, *Baseball*, pp. 18, 40.

123. Walter Camp, "What Are Athletics Good For?" *Outing* (December 1913) 63(3):264–265.

124. Hardy, *How Boston Played*, p. 191.

125. Boston *Herald*, August 18, 1886;; cited in Hardy, *How Boston Played*, p. 8.

126. Seymour, *Baseball*, p. 90.

127. Ibid., p. 328.

128. Riess, *Touching Base*, p. 28.

129. *The Spirit of the Times*, July 24, 1858; cited in Adelman, "The Development of Modern Athletics," p. 343.

130. *The New York Chronicle*, August 22, 1867; cited in Adelman, "The Development of Modern Athletics," p. 406.

131. *Sporting News*, December 11, 1886, cited by Voigt, 1:182; see also New York *Clipper*, April 18, 1885. Male scorn for the motives of female spectators seems to have been almost universal. In the 1870s, Australian newspapers poked fun at women attending a game of cricket of which "few of them understood the simplest rules"; Melbourne *Argus*, March 19, 1877; cited by Cashman, *'Ave a Go*, p. 15.

132. Heywood Broun, *The Sun Field* (New York: Putnam's, 1923), p. 65.

133. Cunningham, *Leisure*, p. 27; Bailey, *Leisure*, p. 13.

134. Cited in Adelman, "The Development of Modern Athletics," p. 566.

135. Rothschild, *A Casual View*, p. 38.

136. Alan Lloyd, *The Great Prize Fight* (New York: Coward-McCann, 1977), pp. 155, 158.

137. Gordon S. Haight, *George Eliot* (Oxford: Oxford University Press, 1968), p. 363.

138. Hardy, *How Boston Played*, p. 169.

139. Boston *Evening Transcript*, August 9, 1887; cited by Hardy, p. 173.

140. Ibid., p. 175.

141. Quoted in Dale A. Somers, *The Rise of Sports in New Orleans, 1850–1900* (Baton Rouge: Louisiana State University Press, 1972), p. 184.

142. Gallico, *Farewell to Sport*, p. 9.

143. Charles Samuels, *The Magnificent Rube* (New York: McGraw-Hill, 1957), pp. 244–248; Randy Roberts, *Jack Dempsey* (Baton Rouge: Louisiana State University Press, 1979), pp. 121, 229.

144. Randy Roberts, *Papa Jack* (New York: Free Press, 1983), pp. 103, 109, 138; see also Al-Tony Gilmore, *Bad Nigger! The National Impact of Jack Johnson* (Port Washington: Kennikat Press, 1975), p. 60.

145. See Pierre Charreton, *Les Fêtes du corps* (Saint-Etienne: Centre Interdisciplinaire d'Etudes et de Recherches sur l'Expression Contemporaine, 1985), pp. 77–78.

146. See Lawrence W. Levine, *Black Culture and Black Consciousness* (New York: Oxford University Press, 1977), pp. 258, 432.

147. Pittsburgh *Courier*, June 29, 1935; quoted by Al-Tony Gilmore, "The Myth, Legend and Folklore of Joe Louis," *South Atlantic Quarterly* (Summer 1983) 82(3):263.

148. Richard Wright, "Joe Louis Uncovers Dynamite," *New Masses*, October 8, 1935; p. 15; cited by Gilmore, "The Myth," p. 263.

149. Dominic Capecci and Martha Wilkerson, "Multifarious Hero: Joe Louis, American Society and Race Relations During World Crisis," *Journal of Sport History* (Winter 1983) 10(3):5–25.

150. Max Schmeling, *Errinerungen* (Berlin: Ullstein, 1977), p. 427.

151. Quoted in Levine, *Black Culture*, p. 229.

152. Eric Dunning, "Social Bonding and the Socio-Genesis of Violence," in Alan Tomlinson, ed., *The Sociological Study of Sport* (Brighton: Brighton Polytechnic, 1981), p. 51.

153. Dunning et al., "Football Hooliganism," 229.

154. Price Collier, "Sport's Place in the Nation's Well-Being," *Outing* (July 1898) 32(4):387.

5. MEDIATED SPECTATORSHIP

1. On the history and demographics of Roller Derby, see Frank Deford, *Five Strides on the Banked Track* (Boston: Little, Brown, 1971).

2. Siegfried Weischenberg, *Due Aussenseiter der Redaktion* (Bochum: N. Brockmeyer, 1976), p. 169.

3. Edouard Seidler, *Le Sport et la presse* (Paris: Armand Colin, 1964), pp. 239–243.

4. "Who Is the American Runner?" *Runner's World* (August 1984) 19(8):46–51, 156–168.

5. These and subsequent data are from subscriber surveys conducted in 1982 (*Boating*), 1983 (*Bowling*), and 1984 (*Golf Digest*).

6. Seidler, *Le Sport et la presse*, p. 260.

7. Weischenberg, *Aussenseiter*, p. 169.

8. Janet Lever, *Soccer Madness* (Chicago: University of Chicago Press, 1983), p. 82.

9. Brigitte Hammer and Mechthild Kock, "Sportzeitschriften," *Sport und Massenmedien*, Josef Hackforth and Siegfried Weischenberg, eds. (Frankfurt: Limpert, 1978), p. 49.

10. Klaus Wehmeier, "Publikum," in Hackforth and Weischenberg, *Sport und Massenmedien*, p. 116.

11. Apropos of editorial reluctance, I must add that in no phase of my research did I receive less cooperation than in my request for data on magazine readership.

12. Erik Barnouw, *A Tower in Babel* (New York: Oxford University Press, 1966), p. 80; Ron Powers, *Supertube: The Rise of Television Sports* (New York: Coward-McCann, 1984), p. 37.

13. Benjamin G. Rader, *In Its Own Image: How Television Has Transformed Sports* (New York: Free Press, 1984), p. 25.

14. Weischenberg, *Aussenseiter*, pp. 141–142; Peter Goedeke, "Sport und Hoerfunk," in Hackforth and Weischenberg, *Sport und Massenmedien*, pp. 20–28.

15. John Ford, *This Sporting Land* (London: New English Library, 1977), p. 223.

16. Weischenberg, *Aussenseiter*, pp. 143–144.

17. Rader, *In Its Own Image*, p. 25; Powers, *Supertube*, pp. 23–30.

18. Clark McPhail and David Miller, "The Assembling Process," *American Sociological Review* (1973) 38:721–735.

19. My statistics on the TV audience, unless otherwise documented, are taken from data generously supplied me by the A. C. Nielsen Co.

20. On McLuhan, see Susan Birrell and John Loy, "Media Sport: Hot and Cool," *International Review of Sport Sociology* (1979) 14(1):5–19.

21. Phil Patton, *Razzle-Dazzle* (Garden City: Dial, 1984), p. 28.

22. Raymond Marcillac and Christian Quidet, *Sport et télévision* (Paris: Albin Michel, 1963), p. 150; Josef Hackforth, *Sport im Fernsehen* (Muenster: Verlag Regensberg, 1975), p. 14.

23. Weischenberg, *Aussenseiter*, p. 145.

24. Ibid.

25. Powers, *Supertube*, p. 33.

26. Patton, *Razzle-Dazzle*, p. 30.

27. Rader, *In Its Own Image*, p. 45.

28. Hackforth, *Sport im Fernsehen*, p. 295.

29. Weischenberg, *Aussenseiter*, p. 152; Knute Hickethier, "Klammergriffe," in Rolf Lindner, ed., *Der Satz "Der Ball Ist Rund" Hat Eine Gewisse Philosophische Tiefe* (Berlin: Transit, 1983), p. 68.

30. Allen Guttmann, *The Games Must Go On: Avery Brundage and the Olympic Movement* (New York: Columbia University Press, 1984), pp. 218–219.

31. Josef Hackforth, "Fernsehen," in Hackforth and Weischenberg, eds., *Sport*

und Massenmedien, pp. 73–86; Powers, *Supertube*, pp. 18–22, 204–220; Horst Seifart, "Sport and Economy: The Commercialization of Olympic Sport by the Media," *International Review of Sport Sociology* (1984) 19(3–4):304–316.

32. Rader, *In Its Own Image*, p. 59; Charles Critcher, "Der Fussballfan," Wilhelm Hopf, ed., *Fussball* (Bensheim: Paedagogischer Extra Buchverlag, 1979), p. 150; Ian Taylor, "Professional Sport and Recession," *International Review of Sport Sociology* (1984) 19(1):15.

33. Rader, *In Its Own Image*, p. 86; Patton, *Razzle-Dazzle*, p. 31.

34. Powers, *Supertube*, p. 173.

35. Rader, *In Its Own Image*, pp. 99, 117–137; Powers, *Supertube*, pp. 172–182.

36. Weischenberg, *Aussenseiter*, p. 177.

37. Powers, *Supertube*, pp. 152–159; Patton, *Razzle-Dazzle*, pp. 86–99; Rader, *In Its Own Image*, p. 91. That such salaries were economically rational, at least in the 1970s, is shown by Roger G. Noll, "Attendance and Price Setting," in Noll, ed., *Government and the Sports Business* (Washington: The Brookings Institute, 1974), pp. 115–158.

38. Rader, *In Its Own Image*, p. 154.

39. Powers, *Supertube*, pp. 107–171, 212; Patton, *Razzle-Dazzle*, pp. 105–112; Don Kowett, "TV Sports," *TV Guide* (August 19, 1978), 2–8.

40. Rader, *In Its Own Image*, pp. 10–113; Patton, *Razzle-Dazzle*, pp. 60–61, 82; Powers, *Supertube*, pp. 18–19, 209–212.

41. New York *Times*, June 28, 1984.

42. On some of the abuses of college sports, see Allen Guttmann, "The Tiger Devours the Literary Magazine, or, Intercollegiate Athletics in America," James H. Frey, ed., *The Governance of Intercollegiate Athletics* (West Point, N.C.: Leisure Press, 1982), pp. 71–79.

43. Patton, *Razzle-Dazzle*, p. 111.

44. Marcillac and Quidet, *Sport et télévision*, p. 26; Weischenberg, *Aussenseiter*, p. 174; Hackforth, *Sport im Fernsehen*, p. 98; Hackforth, "Fernsehen," p. 80; Robert T. Bower, *Television and the Public* (New York: Holt, Rinehart and Winston, 1973), p. 131.

45. Hackforth, *Sport im Fernsehen*, p. 261.

46. Rader, *In Its Own Image*, p. 191; see also Randall Poe, "The Angry Fan," *Harper's* (November 1975) 151:86–95.

47. Edwin H. Cady, *The Big Game* (Knoxville: University of Tennessee Press, 1978), p. 95.

48. William Taafe, "Perspective," *Sports Illustrated* (February 11, 1985) 62(6):170–190; New York *Times*, October 15, 1984.

49. George Comstock et al., *Television and Human Behavior* (New York: Columbia University Press, 1978), p. 143. Similar results appear in Bower, *Television and the Public*, p. 131.

50. Wehmeier, "Publikum," pp. 120–121.

51. Kowett, "TV Sports," 2–8.

52. These may seem like suspiciously low figures, but one must remember that they are averages. In the case of NFL football, there were 94 telecasts.

53. The Winter Olympics peaked on Saturdays with nearly 28% of the audience. It is likely that female spectators were most attracted by figure skating and skiing.

54. New York Times, June 6, 1984.

55. Kari Fasting and Jan Tangen, "Gender and Sport in Norwegian Mass Media," International Review of Sport Sociology (1983) 18(1):66–67.

56. Wehmeier, "Publikum," pp. 115–131.

57. Hans J. Stollenwerk, "Zur Sozialpsychologie des Fussballpublikums," Dirk Albrecht, ed. Fussballsport (Berlin: Bartels and Wernitz, 1979), p. 199.

6. DEHUMANIZED SPECTATORS

1. Ira Horowitz, "Sports Telecasts," Journal of Communication (January 1977) 27:160.

2. Dolf Zillmann, Jennings Bryant, and Barry S. Sapolsky, "The Enjoyment of Watching Sport Contests," in Jeffrey H. Goldstein, ed., Sport, Games, and Play (Hillsdale, N.J.: Lawrence Erlbaum, 1979), p. 302.

3. Bianchi, "Pigskin Piety," Christianity and Crisis (February 21, 1972) 32(2):31.

4. Andrzej Wohl, "The Phenomenon of Soviet Sport and Its New Developmental Stage," International Review of Sport Sociology (1983) 18(3):67; on these claims see Allen Guttmann, From Ritual to Record (New York: Columbia University Press, 1978), pp. 57–64.

5. L. P. Matveyev, O. A. Milstein, and S. W. Moltchanov, "Spectator Activity of Workers in Sports," International Review of Sport Sociology (1980) 15(2):5–26; N. I. Ponomarev, "Sport as a Show," International Review of Sport Sociology (1980) 15(3–4):73–79.

6. D. Findeisen, "Zur Kritik der imperialistischen Deutung des Sports als Ventil fuer Aggressivitaet und Frustration," Theorie und Praxis der Koerperkultur (1973) 22:601–614.

7. Nicholas Petryszak, "Spectator Sports as an Aspect of Popular Culture," Journal of Sport Behavior (February 1978) 1(1):22.

8. Ulrike Prokop, Soziologie der Olympischen Spiele (Munich: Carl Hanser, 1971), p. 21.

9. In addition to Prokop, cited above, see Bero Rigauer, Sport und Arbeit (Frankfurt: Suhrkamp, 1969) [English edition, Allen Guttmann, trans., Sport and Work (New York: Columbia University Press, 1981]; Gerhard Vinnai, Fussballsport als Ideologie (Frankfurt: Europaeische Verlagsanstalt, 1970); Paul Hoch, Rip Off the Big Game (Garden City: Anchor, 1972); Jac-Olaf Boehme, Juergen Gadow, Sven Gueldenpfennig, Jorn Jensen, Renate Pfister, Sport im Spaetkapitalismus (2d ed., Frankfurt: Limpert, 1974); Ginette Berthaud, Jean-Marie Brohm, François Gantheret, Pierre Laguillaumie, Sport, culture et répression (Paris: Maspero, 1972); Brohm, Critiques du sport (Paris: Christian Bourgois, 1976); Brohm, Sociologie politique du

sport (Paris: Jean-Pierre Delarge, 1976); Brohm, *Le Mythe Olympique* (Paris: Christian Bourgeois, 1981); Karin Rittner, *Sport und Arbeitsteilung* (Frankfurt: Limpert, 1976); Sandro Provvisionato, *Lo Sport in Italia* (Rome: Savelli, 1978).

10. Petryszak, "Spectator Sports," 24.

11. Boehme et al., *Sport im Spaetkapitalismus*, p. 37. On sexuality in sports from this perspective, see also Ulrich Dix, *Sport und Sexualitaet* (Frankfurt: Maerz Verlag, 1972).

12. Hans Bloss, "Sport and Vocational School Pupils," *International Review of Sport Sociology* (1970) 5:45.

13. Dieter Hanhart, "Freizeit und Sport in der industriellen Gesellschaft," *Arbeit, Freizeit und Sport* (Bern: Paul Haupt, 1963), p. 42.

14. Angelika Tschap-Bock, *Frauensport und Gesellschaft* (Ahrensburg: Czwalina, 1983), pp. 285–286.

15. Helge Anderson Aage Bo-Jensen, N. Alkaer-Hansen, A. Sonne, "Sports and Games in Denmark . . . ," *Acta Sociologica* (1956) 2:1–28.

16. Leopold Rosenmayr, "Sport as Leisure Activity of Young People," *International Review of Sport Sociology* (1967) 2:23.

17. Hans J. Stollenwerk, "Zur Sozialpsychologie des Fussballpublikums," Dirk Albrecht, ed., *Fussballsport* (Berlin: Bartels and Wernitz, 1979), pp. 203–204.

18. Hans Ulrich Herrmann, *Die Fussballfans* (Schorndorf: Karl Hofmann, 1977), p. 60.

19. Ulrich Pramann, *Das Bisschen Freiheit* (Hamburg: Stern, 1980), p. 65.

20. Felicio Fabrizio, *Storia dello Sport in Italia* (Rimini-Florence: Guaraldi, 1977), pp. 174, 219.

21. Svein Stensaasen, "Active and Passive Sport Interests of Adolescents," *Scandinavian Journal of Educational Research* (1980) 29:49.

22. Garry J. Smith, Brent Patterson, Trevor Williams, and John Hogg, "A Profile of the Deeply Committed Male Sports Fan," *Arena Review* (September 1981) 5(2):26–44.

23. Barry D. McPherson, "Sport Consumption and the Economics of Consumerism," Donald W. Ball and John W. Loy, eds., *Sport and Social Order* (Reading, Mass.: Addison-Wesley, 1975), pp. 252, 257.

24. Asher Mashiach, "A Collective Profile of the American Spectators in the Summer Olympic Games in Montreal 1976," *Journal of Sport and Social Issues* (Fall/Winter 1981) 5(2):25.

25. Data collected by Terry Breen and Peter Roisman, spring 1979.

26. José M. Cagigal, "Social Education through Sport," Gerald S. Kenyon, ed., *Contemporary Psychology of Sport* (Chicago: The Athletic Institute, 1970), p. 343.

27. Geoffrey Godbey and John Robinson, "The American Sports Fan," *Review of Sport and Leisure* (Summer 1979) 4:6.

28. Urs Jaeggi, Robert Brosshart, Jurg Siegenthaler, *Sport und Student* (Bern: Paul Haupt, 1963), pp. 119–122; Anderson et al., "Sports and Games in Denmark," pp. 1–28; Stefan Groessing, *Sport der Jugend* (Vienna: Verlag fuer Jugend und Volk, 1970), p. 26; James E. Curtis and Brian G. Milton, "Social Status and the 'Active

Society,'" Richard S. Gruneau and John G. Albinson, eds., *Canadian Sport* (Don Mills, Ontario: Addison-Wesley, 1976), pp. 302–329; Dieter Voigt, *Soziologie in der D.D.R.* (Cologne: Verlag Wissenschaft und Politik, 1975), p. 55.

29. Hanhart, "Freizeit und Sport," p. 66.

30. Hiram L. Gordon, David Rosenberg, William E. Morris, "Leisure Activities of Schizophrenic Patients After Return to the Community," William P. Morgan, ed., *Contemporary Readings in Sport Psychology* (Springfield, Ill.: Charles C. Thomas, 1970), pp. 118–129.

31. Jeffrey H. Goldstein and Robert L. Arms, "Effects of Observing Athletic Contests on Hostility," *Sociometry* (1971) 34(1):83–90.

32. Robert L. Arms, Gordon W. Russell, and Mark L. Sandilands, "Effects on the Hostility of Spectators of Viewing Aggressive Sports," *Social Psychology Quarterly* (1979) 42:279; see also Joseph X. Lennon and Frederick Q. Hatfield, "The Effect of Crowding and Observation of Athletic Events on Spectator Tendency Toward Aggressive Behavior," *Journal of Sport Behavior* (May 1980) 3(2):61–80; W. Andrew Harrell, "Verbal Aggressiveness in Spectators at Professional Hockey Games," *Human Relations* (1981) 34:643–655.

33. Edward Thomas Turner, "The Effects of Viewing College Football, Basketball, and Wrestling on the Elicited Aggressive Responses of Male Spectators," Ph.D. diss. (University of Maryland, 1968), p. 90; see also John Mark Kingsmore, "The Effect of a Professional Wrestling and Professional Basketball Contest Upon the Aggressive Tendencies of Male Spectators," Ph.D. diss. (University of Maryland, 1968).

34. Unfortunately, the research on this topic has not been gathered into one convenient monograph. See Leonard Berkowitz and Edna Rawlings, "Effects of Film Violence on Inhibitions Against Subsequent Aggression," *Journal of Abnormal and Social Psychology* (1963) 66(5):405–412; Berkowitz, "Aggressive Clues in Aggressive Behavior and Hostility Catharsis," *Psychological Review* (1964) 71(2):104–122; Berkowitz, "Some Aspects of Observed Aggression," *Journal of Personality and Social Psychology* (1965) 2(3):359–369; Berkowitz and Russell G. Geen, "Film Violence and the Cue Properties of Available Targets," *Journal of Personality and Social Psychology* (1966) 3(5):525–530; Geen and Berkowitz, "Name-Mediated Aggression Cue Properties," *Journal of Personality* (1966) 34:456–465; Geen and Berkowitz, "Some Conditions Facilitating the Occurrence of Aggression After the Observation of Violence," *Journal of Personality* (1967) 35:666–676; Donald P. Hartmann, "The Influence of Symbolically Modeled Instrumental Aggression and Pain Cues on Aggressive Behavior," *Journal of Personality and Social Psychology* (1969) 11(3):280–288; Geen and Edgar C. O'Neal, "Activation of Cue-Elicited Aggression by General Arousal," *Journal of Personality and Social Psychology* (1969) 11(3):289–292; Berkowitz and Joseph T. Alioto, "The Meaning of an Observed Event as a Determinant of Its Aggressive Consequences," *Journal of Personality and Social Psychology* (1973) 28:206–217.

35. For the general argument that aggression stimulates aggression, see Albert Bandura, *Aggression: A Social Learning Analysis* (Englewood-Cliffs, N.J.: Prentice-Hall, 1973).

36. Herrmann, *Fussballfans*, p. 37.

37. Dunning and Elias, "The Quest for Excitement in Unexciting Societies," in Guenther Lueschen, ed., *The Cross-Cultural Analysis of Sport and Games* (Champaign, Illinois: Stipes, 1970), p. 31.

7. SPECTATOR HOOLIGANS

1. Sandro Provvisionato, *Lo Sport in Italia* (Rome: Savelli, 1978), pp. 28, 133–134.

2. Jean R. Duperreault, "L'Affaire Richard," *Canadian Journal of History of Sport* (December 1981) 12(2):66–83.

3. Leon Mann, "Sports Crowds Viewed from the Perspective of Collective Behavior," in Jeffrey H. Goldstein, ed., *Sport, Games, and Play* (Hillsdale, N.J.: Lawrence Erlbaum, 1979), p. 349.

4. Cyril White, "An Analysis of Hostile Outbursts in Spectator Sports (Ph.D. diss., University of Illinois, 1970), pp. 91–100.

5. Michael D. Smith, "Sport and Collective Violence," in Donald W. Ball and John W. Loy, eds., *Sport and Social Order* (Reading, Mass.: Addison-Wesley, 1975), p. 305.

6. Mann, "Sports Crowds Viewed from the Perspective of Collective Behavior," p. 351.

7. Desmond Morris, *The Soccer Tribe* (London: Jonathan Cape, 1981), pp. 272–278.

8. Janet Lever, *Soccer Madness* (Chicago: University of Chicago Press, 1983), pp. 68–69.

9. Mann, "Sports Crowds Viewed from the Perspective of Collective Behavior," p. 349.

10. Kurt Weis, Peter Backes, Bernd Gross, and Dirk Jung, "Zuschauerausschreitungen und das Bild vom Fussballfan," in Gunter A. Pilz et al., eds., *Sport und Gewalt* (Schorndorf: Karl Hofmann, 1982), p. 63.

11. *New York Times*, May 30, 1985.

12. Cited by John Williams, Eric Dunning, and Patrick Murphy, *Hooligans Abroad* (London: Routledge and Kegan Paul, 1984), pp. 23, 43.

13. Ian Taylor, "Professional Sport and the Economy," *International Review of Sport Sociology* (1984) 19(1):19.

14. Cited in Williams et al., *Hooligans Abroad*, p. 58.

15. Cited ibid., p. 9.

16. White, "Hostile Outbursts," pp. 100–107.

17. Robert C. Yeager, *Seasons of Shame* (New York: McGraw-Hill, 1979), p. 28.

18. Bil Gilbert and Lisa Twyman, "Violence: Out of Hand in the Stands," *Sports Illustrated* (January 31, 1983) 58:62–74; Yeager, *Seasons of Shame*, pp. 70n, 77.

19. Gisela Helwig, "Die DDR nimmt Fussballfans in die Zange," *Deutschland Archiv* (1985) 18(10):1034; Peter Kuehnst, *Sport und Kunst in der DDR* (Cologne: Verlag Wissenschaft und Politik, 1985), plate 20.

20. Gunter A. Pilz, "Zur gesellschaftlichen Bedingtheit von Sport und Gewalt,"

in Hannelore Kaeber and Bernhard Tripp, eds., *Gesellschaftliche Funtionen des Sports* (Bonn: Bundeszentrale fuer politische Bildung, 1984), p. 169.

21. Dolf Zillmann, Jennings Bryant, and Barry S. Sapolsky, "The Enjoyment of Watching Sports Contests," in Goldstein, *Sport, Games, and Play*, p. 305.

22. Arthur Hopcraft, *The Football Man* (London: Collins, 1968), pp. 180, 192.

23. Ulrich Leinweber and Ebba Geisler, " 'Schalke ist Schalke': Gespraeche mit Schalke-Fans," in Rolf Lindner, ed., *Der Fussballfan* (Frankfurt: Syndikat, 1980), p. 149.

24. Cameron K. Dewar, "Spectator Fights at Professional Baseball Games," *Review of Sport and Leisure* (Summer 1979) 4(1):12–25.

25. Stuart Hall, "The Treatment of 'Football Hooliganism' in the Press," in Ingham, "Football Hooliganism," pp. 15–36.

26. Garry Whannel, "Football, Crowd Behavior and the Press," *Media, Culture and Society* (1979) 1:330.

27. For a good summary of various theories, see Clark McPhail and David Miller, "The Assembling Process," *American Sociological Review* (1973) 38:721–735; regarding the general problem of violence in sports, see also Smith, "Sport and Collective Violence," pp. 281–330; Michael D. Smith, *Violence in Sport* (Toronto: Butterworths, 1983).

28. Gustave Le Bon, *The Crowd* (1895; London: Ernest Benn, 1896).

29. George Elliott Howard, "Social Psychology of the Spectator," *American Journal of Sociology* (1912) 18:36, 44.

30. José Ferrer-Hombravella, "Group Dynamics: Sportsman-Spectator Interactions," in Gerald S. Kenyon, ed., *Contemporary Psychology of Sport* (Chicago: The Athletic Institute, 1970), p. 306.

31. Elias Canetti, *Masse und Macht* (Hamburg: Claassen, 1960).

32. Neil J. Smelser, *Theory of Collective Behavior* (New York: Free Press, 1963), p. 19.

33. White, "Hostile Outbursts," p. 75.

34. Smelser, *Theory of Collective Behavior*, pp. 8, 73.

35. Ralph Turner and Lewis M. Killian, *Collective Behavior*, 2d ed. (Englewood Cliffs, N.J.: Prentice-Hall, 1972), p. 5.

36. Peter Marsh, "Understanding Aggro," *New Society* (1975) 32(652):7–9; Marsh, "Careers for Boys, Nutters, Hooligans and Hardcases," *New Society* (1976) 36(710):346–348; Marsh, Elizabeth Rosser, and Rom Harré, *The Rules of Disorder* (London: Routledge and Kegan Paul, 1978); Marsh, "Life and Careers on the Soccer Terraces," in Roger Ingham, ed., "*Football Hooliganism*": *The Wider Context* (London: Inter-Action, 1978), pp. 68–81.

37. J. A. Harrington et al., *Soccer Hooliganism* (Bristol: John Wright and Sons, 1968), pp. 13–14; see also *Public Disorder and Sporting Events* (London: Sports Council and Social Research Council, 1978).

38. Eugene Trivizas, "Offences and Offenders in Football Crowd Disorders," *British Journal of Criminology* (1980) 20:276–288.

39. Weis et al., "Zuschauerausschreitungen," pp. 61–95.

40. Jerry M. Lewis, "Fan Violence: An American Social Problem," in Michael Lewis, ed., *Research in Social Problems and Public Policy* (Greenwich, Conn.: JAI Press, 1982), pp. 175–206.

41. Peter Marsh et al., *The Rules of Disorder*, pp. 1–2, 107.

42. Hartmut Gabler, Hans-Joachim Schulz, and Robert Weber, "Zuschauer-aggressionen—eine Feldstudie ueber Fusssballfans," in Pilz et al., *Sport und Gewalt*, p. 23.

43. Eric Dunning, "Social Bonding and the Socio-Genesis of Violence," in Alan Tomlinson, ed., *The Sociological Study of Sport* (Brighton: Brighton Polytechnic—Chelsea School of Human Movement, 1981), pp. 1–35; Dunning, Patrick Murphy, and John Williams, "Ordered Segmentation and the Socio-Genesis of Football Hooligan Violence," also in Tomlinson, *The Sociological Study of Sport*, pp. 36–52.

44. Eric Dunning, "Social Bonding and Violence in Sports," in Jeffrey H. Goldstein, *Sports Violence* (New York: Springer, 1983), p. 141.

45. Ibid., p. 145; see also Leon Chorbajian, "The Social Psychology of American Males and Spectator Sports," *International Journal of Sport Psychology* (1978) 9(3):165–175.

46. Dunning, "Social Bonding and the Socio-Genesis of Violence," p. 32.

47. Dunning, Murphy, and Williams, "Ordered Segmentation," p. 51.

48. John Clarke, "Football and Working Class Fans," in Ingham, "*Football Hooliganism*," pp. 37–60.

49. Gabler, Schulz, and Weber, "Zuschaueraggressionen," p. 49.

50. For the progression of Taylor's ideas, see Taylor, "Hooligans: Soccer's Resistance Movement," *New Society* (August 7, 1969) 14(358):204–206; Taylor, "Football Mad," in Eric Dunning, ed., *Sociology of Sport* (London: Cass, 1971), pp. 352–377; Taylor, "Soccer Consciousness and Soccer Hooliganism," in Stanley Cohen, ed., *Images of Deviance* (Harmondsworth: Penguin, 1971), pp. 131–164; Taylor, "On the Sports Violence Question: Soccer Hooliganism Revisited," in Jennifer Hargreaves, ed., *Sport, Culture and Ideology* (London: Routledge and Kegan Paul, 1982), pp. 152–196; Taylor, "Class, Violence and Sport," in Hart Cantelon and Richard Gruneau, eds., *Sport, Culture and the Modern State* (Toronto: University of Toronto Press, 1982), pp. 40–96; "Professional Sport and the Recession," *International Review of Sport Sociology* (1984) 19(1):67–82.

51. Clarke, "Football," pp. 49–50.

52. Whannel, "Football, Crowd Behavior and the Press," 329.

8. MOTIVATIONS

1. For a good survey of sociological and psychological approaches, see John W. Loy, "An Emerging Theory of Sport Spectatorship," in Jeffrey Segrave and Donald Chu, eds., *Olympism* (Champaign: Human Kinetics, 1981), pp. 262–294; Lloyd Reynolds Sloan, "The Function and Impact of Sports for Fans," in Jeffrey H. Goldstein, ed., *Sport, Games, and Play* (Hillsdale, N.J.: Lawrence Erlbaum, 1979), pp. 219–262.

2. Edgar Z. Friedenberg, "The Changing Role of Homoerotic Fantasy in Spec-

tator Sports," in Donald F. Sabo Jr. and Ross Runfola, eds., *Jock* (Englewood Cliffs, N.J.: Prentice-Hall, 1980), pp. 179–180.

3. See Pierre Frayssinet, *Les Sports parmi les beaux-arts* (Paris: Dargaud, 1968); H. T. A. Whiting and D. W. Masterson, eds., *Readings in the Aesthetics of Sport* (London: Lepus Books, 1974); Benjamin Lowe, *The Beauty of Sport* (Englewood Cliffs, N.J.: Prentice-Hall, 1977); Richard D. Mandell, *Sport: A Cultural History* (New York: Columbia University Press, 1984), pp. 282–304.

4. Peter Handke, "Die Welt in Fussball," in Rolf Lindner, ed., *Der Fussballfan* (Frankfurt: Syndikat, 1980), p. 26.

5. See Alyce Taylor Cheska, "Sports Spectacular: The Social Order of Power," *Quest* (Summer 1978) (no. 30):58–71.

6. Michael Roberts, *Fans* (Washington: The New Republic, 1976), p. 16; see also Don Jenkins, *Saturday's America* (Boston: Little, Brown, 1970).

7. *Sueddeutsche Zeitung*, May 30–31, 1984.

8. Ulrich Pramann, *Das Bisschen Freiheit* (Hamburg: Stern Verlag, 1980), p. 147.

9. Michael R. Real, "Super Bowl: Mythic Spectacle," *Journal of Communication* (1975) 25:35.

10. Stanley Cohen, *The Man in the Crowd* (New York: Random House, 1981), p. 8.

11. Wolfgang Decker, "Der unbesiegbare Pharao," *Anno Journal* (1981) (no. 85):44–48.

12. Robert M. Levine, "The Burden of Success: *Futebol* and Brazilian Society," *Journal of Popular Culture* (Winter 1980) 14(3):454.

13. Janet Lever, *Soccer Madness* (Chicago: University of Chicago Press, 1983), p. 64.

14. Ian Taylor, "Professional Sport and the Economy," *International Review of Sport Sociology* (1984) 19(1):25.

15. Garry J. Smith, Brent Patterson, Trevor Williams, John Hogg, "A Profile of the Deeply Committed Sports Fan," *Arena Review* (September 1981) 5(2):26–44; Walter Gantz, "An Exploration of Viewing Motives and Behaviors Associated with Television Sports," *Journal of Broadcasting* (Summer 1981) (15):263–275; Narciss Goebbel, Fedor Jokisch, Peter-Rainer Lange, and Gerd Nitschke, " 'Werder, Werder'—und sonst nichts," in Rolf Lindner, ed., *Der Fussballfan* (Frankfurt: Syndikat, 1980), pp. 52–79.

16. A. A. Brill, "The Why of the Fan," *North American Review* (1929) 228:434.

17. Frederick Exley, *A Fan's Notes* (1968; rpt London: Weidenfeld and Nicolson, 1970), pp. 2, 134.

18. Arnold Beisser, *The Madness in Sports: Psychosocial Observations on Sports* (New York: Appleton-Century-Crofts, 1967), pp. 126–127.

19. Alan D. Ingham and Michael D. Smith, "Social Implications of the Interaction between Spectators and Athletes," *Exercise and Sport Science Review* (1974) 2:194.

20. Cited from Al-Tony Gilmore, "The Myth, Legend and Folklore of Joe Louis," *South Atlantic Quarterly* (Summer 1983) 82(3):265–266.

21. Pekka Kiviaho and Volevi Mustikkamaa, "Intragroup Conflict in Sport Audiences during Intergroup Competition," in Fernand Landry and William R. A. Orban, eds., *Sociology of Sport* (Miami: Symposia Specialists, 1978), pp. 267–282.

22. Clive Gammon, "They're All for One," *Sports Illustrated* (February 18, 1985) 62(7):26–34; Barry Sapolsky, "The Effect of Spectator Disposition and Suspense on the Enjoyment of Sport Contests," *International Journal of Sport Psychology* (1980) 11(1):1–10.

23. Janet Lever, *Soccer Madness* (Chicago: University of Chicago Press, 1983), p. 14.

24. N. I. Ponomariev, "Sport as a Show," *International Review of Sport Sociology* (1980) 15(3–4):73–79).

25. Robert B. Cialdini, Richard J. Borden, Avril Thorne, Marcus Randall Walker, Stephen Freeman, and Lloyd Reynolds Sloan, "Basking in Reflected Glory," *Journal of Personality and Social Psychology* (1976) 34(3):366–375.

26. Klaus V. Meier, "We Don't Want to Set the World on Fire: We Just Want to Finish Ninth," *Journal of Popular Culture* (Fall 1979) 13(2):296.

27. See Roland Barthes, *Mythologies* (1957; Paris: Editions du seuil, 1970), pp. 13–24; Gregory P. Stone and Ramon A. Oldenburg, "Wrestling," in Ralph Slovenko and James A. Knight, eds., *Motivations in Play, Games and Sports* (Springfield, Ill.: Charles C. Thomas, 1967), pp. 503–532; Thomas Henricks, "Professional Wrestling as Moral Order," *Sociological Inquiry* (1974) 44:177–188.

Index